D1523899

ASSESSING
THE NATION'S
REPORT CARD

ASSESSING THE NATION'S REPORT CARD

Challenges and Choices for NAEP

CHESTER E. FINN, JR.

Harvard Education Press
Cambridge, MA

Copyright © 2021 by the President and Fellows of Harvard College

All rights reserved. No part of this publication may be reproduced or transmitted in any form or by any means, electronic or mechanical, including photocopy, recording, or any information storage and retrieval systems, without permission in writing from the publisher.

Paperback ISBN 978-1-68253-725-1

Library of Congress Cataloging-in-Publication Data is on file.

Published by Harvard Education Press,
an imprint of the Harvard Education Publishing Group
Harvard Education Press
8 Story Street
Cambridge, MA 02138

Cover Design: Wilcox Design
Cover Image: denkcreative/DigitalVision Vectors via Getty Images

The typefaces in this book are ITC Legacy Serif and ITC Legacy Sans

CONTENTS

For Emma, Alexandra, and Isabel, with love

INTRODUCTION

I F YOU'RE AN EDUCATION REFORMER or policy wonk, as I like to think of myself today, or a federal or state education official, as I've been from time to time, you probably already know that America's most important testing program is one that most people have never heard of. It's *not* the SAT, the ACT, Advanced Placement, the Armed Forces Qualification Test, the annual state assessments required by federal law, much less the contentious entry tests employed by selective high schools such as Stuyvesant and Boston Latin.

Nope. Those are all widely used, hotly debated, and much in the news of late, but they're far from most important. Topping the list of what really matters is the National Assessment of Educational Progress, aka "the Nation's Report Card" and widely referred to simply as "NAEP."

Most of the time, it doesn't make much news. It's relatively low key—remarkable for any test at a time when testing has grown so contentious—and it rarely elicits strong feelings. Which means it doesn't have many enemies, nor many cheerleaders either. Perhaps because it's been around for more than half a century, those who are even aware of it tend to take it for granted, part of the education furniture that was already in the room long before they entered.

Most people, however, are scarcely conscious of it. In fact, when people asked me in recent months what I was working on and I said "a book about the past, present, and future of NAEP," the response, except among fellow ed-wonks, was often a blank look and polite smile. Educated and worldly though my interlocutor probably was, he or she seldom had any idea what I was talking about.

The main reason, I think, is that NAEP has no immediate impact on most Americans. It tells them nothing about their own child, their own school, or (with a handful of exceptions) their own community. From the standpoint of a parent or grandparent, local taxpayer, teacher, or principal, it's just not very relevant.

Yet the National Assessment of Educational Progress is, and for decades has been, America's premier gauge of whether its children—all our children—are learning anything in school, whether they're learning any more today than years ago, and whether the learning gaps among groups of children are narrowing or widening. Moreover, it supplies that information not just at the end of high school, not just among college-bound students, not just among fifteen-year-olds, and not just for the entire country. Nor does it confine itself to reading and math. Rather, it reports on student achievement in grades 4, 8, and 12. It reports on that achievement in as many as ten different subjects. And it does so (at least some of the time for some of those subjects in some of those grades) not only for the nation as a whole but also for every state and for several dozen big-city school systems, as well as some private schools.

Also important: NAEP is far more than a simple barometer gauging changes in education performance. It also enables users to determine how well what their state expects of its fourth graders, say, in math, or eighth graders in English, stacks up against a widely accepted version of national standards for those subjects. Because it makes accommodations for children with special needs while requiring schools to include most such children in the tested population, it both supplies accurate information on how they're faring academically and sets a good example for states' own assessment regimes. Because it employs a variety of test questions, not just the multiple-choice kind, it provides sophisticated information about how well young Americans can perform important advanced assignments such as writing coherent sentences and paragraphs that explain things and cite evidence.

Besides all that, NAEP subtly causes education in the United States to improve by providing educators with feedback on what groups of their pupils can and cannot do in the subjects that matter most, and it provides this in ways that illustrate how many are good (or not) at various elements of those subjects.

Surprised? You've every right to be. But maybe this is a topic worth knowing a bit more about. Providing readers with some of that added understanding and appreciation is one goal of this book. Another is to lay out the major issues and uncertainties facing NAEP today and examine several scenarios for its future, concluding with one that feels right to me.

NAEP has intersected with my own life since 1969 when, at the unripe age of twenty-five, I found myself behind a desk in the Old Executive Office Building as a very junior participant in President Nixon's White House staff, brought there by my graduate school adviser and mentor, the late Daniel P. Moynihan, who had just become a senior member of a multi-headed domestic policy team back in those heady pre-Watergate days.

NAEP was a toddler then, recently entrusted to the brand-new Education Commission of the States, whose executive director evidently thought he should explain it to this green education staffer at the White House, probably because the federal government was paying for it—and wasn't paying enough. That visit introduced me to the National Assessment, and it's been in and out of my life and work ever since. The busiest phase came in the decade after 1985 when, first as Bill Bennett's assistant secretary for research and then as first chair of the new National Assessment Governing Board, I had a fair amount to do with nudging NAEP onto what might be termed its modern trajectory. In the years since, I've kibitzed, advised, scribbled, and occasionally nudged some more, but from outside. Still, if I were hit by a truck tomorrow and someone grasped for anything worth putting into an obituary, I'd hope that my recurring connection with the Nation's Report Card might make it into the third or fourth paragraph.

So yes, this is a very personal book, and you will encounter in these pages both my satisfaction and admiration for what NAEP has accomplished, my exasperation with its shortcomings, my anguish over its trade-offs and dilemmas, and my hopes for its future. But only occasionally is it about me, and I'm not the reason you should read it. The reason to dig in is that this poorly understood and inadequately appreciated federal program is a precious resource for all who worry about the country's future. No matter whether your foremost concern is international economic competitiveness or domestic equity, the excellence of our workforce or the upward mobility of children born into poverty and discrimination, the performance of our education system or the return on taxpayer dollars, you won't get the information you need without NAEP. Yet NAEP's capacity to deliver that information depends on you and those you place in leadership roles, not only in Washington but also in the statehouse and on the local school board. NAEP is part of a culture and policy regime that value accurate information about educational outcomes. If that culture and policy regime endure, America will continue to need and benefit from a robust national assessment.

I hope the following pages—six chapters of orientation and history, followed by five devoted to today's issues and tomorrow's possibilities—will give you a deeper understanding of how NAEP works, where it came from, why we need it, the challenges that it faces, and the ways it could be even more valuable in years to come.

PART I

What Is NAEP and Where Did It Come From?

CHAPTER 1

NAEP Today

CONSIDERING HOW OFTEN we denizens of the education realm make reference to "NAEP data," it's striking how few people really understand what the National Assessment is and isn't, what it can and cannot do, how it works, why it's important to American education, why it gets so much attention, and yet why, in many ways, it's peripheral and ignorable.

Here's a thumbnail description: the National Assessment of Educational Progress, often referred to as the "Nation's Report Card" or just "NAEP" (rhymes with tape), is a testing program that monitors the achievement of US students attending elementary and secondary schools. Funded by Congress and administered by the federal Department of Education, it periodically tests their knowledge and skills—"what they know and can do"—at three grade levels (4, 8, 12) across as many as ten subjects. Since passage of the No Child Left Behind Act in 2002, NAEP has been required to test reading and math in grades 4 and 8 every two years and to report those results for every state as well as the nation as a whole and many student subpopulations.[1] In those same two key subjects, NAEP also operates a separate "long-term trend" assessment (LTT), which is national only, given to an age-based sample (ages nine, thirteen, and seventeen), and essentially unchanged—with trend lines unbroken—since the early 1970s.

No big surprises there, unless perhaps you didn't know about the LTT sidecar. But that's also just the start. Here are a dozen features of NAEP that are key to understanding it, yet not widely understood. We will revisit most of them in later chapters.

First, NAEP is not a universal assessment such as states administer at year's end to every student in a given grade or course. Rather, its design employs a sophisticated random sample, meaning that it tests only enough

schools and children to yield valid data about the jurisdictions or populations for which results are sought.[2] This typically requires participation of
about a hundred schools in reading and math at fourth and eighth grades
in a given state. About fifty students in each school are actually tested, that
is, about five thousand children per state. (For perspective, Ohio has about
140,000 public school pupils in each grade of its middle schools, while New
Mexico has almost 30,000, though the NAEP sample size is the same in
both.) Federal law requires states and districts that contain schools receiving Title I funding to participate in these assessments, although which
schools get included in the sample in a given year is determined by federal staff and NAEP contractors.[3] Private schools are also invited to take
part and, if enough of them consent, NAEP yields data on their students'
achievement, which can be compared with public school pupils. At all
schools, participating pupils spend no more than ninety minutes, and few
are ever selected more than once.

Subjects beyond math and reading are assessed less often, sometimes
just in one grade, and those results are usually reported only for the entire
country, but—this is crucial to NAEP's role in American education—all
NAEP results are disaggregated by gender and race, as well as children's
poverty, disability, and limited-English-proficiency status.[4] That disaggre-
gation is what's made NAEP our foremost gauge of achievement gaps of
every sort and thus a significant force in monitoring the nation's progress
(or lack thereof) toward more equitable education outcomes. And because
NAEP takes pains to achieve valid samples—including for those disaggregated subgroups—and to note which score changes are statistically significant, it's a much more precise monitoring instrument than tests such as
Advanced Placement, SAT, and ACT, which (in most places) are taken only
by college-bound students who sign up for them—and then usually just at
the high school level.

Second, no child takes an entire NAEP test—another key difference from
most achievement tests. Its assessments are built in a complicated way
known as "balanced incomplete block spiraling," which means, in effect,
that each participating student answers only a portion—typically about
one-quarter—of the test questions for that subject and grade. We can picture the answers given by four kids adding up to a complete eighth grader.
This parceling out of questions enables NAEP to probe a wider expanse of
the subject "domain," and to ask essay-style and open-response questions

in addition to the multiple-choice kind, without making it too long an ordeal for student and school comfort.[5]

Thus NAEP adds no testing burden to most schools or pupils, an important consideration in an era when many Americans—educators, parents, and students alike—have grown test-weary (and wary) and a backlash is visible in many places, including states doing away with some of their own assessments and parents keeping some children home on testing day.

Third, although it was not until the mid-1990s that NAEP began to provide special accommodations for test-takers with disabilities and/or limited English proficiency, such arrangements are now standard practice and make it possible both for more fully representative samples and for accurate data on the performance of more of the diverse pupil groups that fill American classrooms. These accommodations are extensive and varied, the more so now that NAEP has shifted (except for LTT) from paper and pencil to digital test administration.[6]

Fourth, NAEP carries no direct consequences for anybody, not students, teachers, schools, districts, even states. It is intended to function as a low-stakes testing system. Here, again, it differs dramatically from the state assessments that federal law requires to be given in math and reading to *every* public school pupil in grades 3 through 8, the results of which become part of accountability regimes that can have painful (or happy) consequences for schools, districts, and sometimes individual teachers and pupils. NAEP also differs from the end-of-course and graduation exams that some states require their high school pupils to pass. Nobody gets promoted or graduated—or held back or denied a diploma—on the basis of their NAEP score. No school gets a five-star or two-star rating on the basis of its NAEP results. No teacher gets evaluated on the basis of her pupils' NAEP scores.

Low-stakes tests carry the risk that kids won't take them seriously, precisely because their results don't count. That has raised concerns over the years about the validity of twelfth-grade NAEP data—the worry that jaded seventeen- and eighteen-year-olds nearing graduation won't try very hard on yet another test, especially one that doesn't affect them, while fourth and eighth graders (it's assumed) can more easily be convinced by teachers to do their best. But (as discussed in chapter 6), research has shown the twelfth-grade concern to be groundless. Kids at all three grade levels take NAEP seriously enough for their test results to be valid. Yet the absence of consequences means nobody has an incentive to finagle the results, so there's no point in "teaching to the test" and schools and districts have no need to alter their curricula to conform to NAEP—unless of course they find merit in NAEP's framing of a particular subject.

Fifth, though NAEP brings no consequences for students, teachers, principals, or most district leaders, a low-stakes test with as high a profile as this one reverberates up the line. Because NAEP exposes achievement gaps within states and in almost thirty large districts, and because it reports gains, losses, and flat performance at the system level, a NAEP report can lead to embarrassment—or praise—for district, state, and federal officials. It can thus affect reputations and policy choices. It can even figure in political campaigns, and it can certainly rile those—both educators and elected officials—who don't much want their school results (or their claims about those results) to be audited or second-guessed by anyone, especially when the audits reveal large differences between NAEP's definition of student proficiency and the version—almost always easier—that the state is employing.[7]

Thus, the periodic release of NAEP results has become a rather big deal for American K–12 education. Naturally, there's much pressure to get those results out in public as soon as possible after the tests are given, and in years past that has sometimes taken unconscionably long. It's gotten faster lately, at least for reading and math, though still not exactly overnight—fourth- and eighth-grade results from tests given in early spring 2019 were released in late October of that year—but haste can cause glitches.

To forestall screwups, complicated procedures kick in after administration of a full-fledged NAEP assessment. Student responses must be scored and the resulting data analyzed six ways from Sunday, followed by much double-checking and reanalysis, followed by the careful drafting of reports in multiple formats for diverse audiences.[8] The two entities with direct responsibility for NAEP—the National Assessment Governing Board (NAGB) and the National Center for Education Statistics (NCES)—are well aware that their data will be sliced and diced and mixed and remixed over the years by hundreds of analysts and researchers. The numbers need to add up. The multiyear trend lines (usually) need to be unbroken.

As the time for release nears—data have been analyzed, reports carefully written and reviewed—much deliberation and negotiation ensue. The written reports may be phrased in neutral, factual terms, but how will their main findings be depicted—one could say spun—for the media and the public? The drafting of press releases is a delicate task, as is the choreography of release events. Who will speak and what will they say? Will America's achievement glass be described as half full or half empty? As filling or leaking? How about Indiana's? Austin's? It's almost always possible to dig out some good news or promising shifts, but it's also possible to emphasize flat or descending trend lines. (And who was president—or governor—during that period?) Will emphasis be placed on whatever gains can be cited or on the education shortcomings that the data reveal? Since practically every release holds the potential for all of the foregoing, it also matters who will make the presentation? Will the NCES commissioner or a veteran deputy simply report the numbers as drily as possible? Will the secretary of education—a presidential appointee—speak? What about governing board members (and which ones)? Guest speakers from states or districts—or Capitol Hill? Experts on the subjects under scrutiny?

State and local officials face similar choices on release day. Because they get embargoed NAEP data in advance, they have time to decide how they want to brief their publics—and media—on their own results. Usually, and unsurprisingly, these end up being framed in language that they believe will show those results in the most favorable possible light.[9]

Sixth, those results are ordinarily depicted in two ways by NCES and NAGB. In addition to displaying the latest scores on a stable scale using a statistical method called item response theory, they are presented in relation to a trio of achievement levels, which could also be called cut-points, benchmarks, or standards.[10] Labeled basic, proficient, and advanced, these are set by the governing board, which has generally employed a widely used, judgment-based, standards-setting procedure known as the "modified Angoff method."[11] Because NAEP's definition of "proficient"—treated by the board as "a benchmark for solid academic performance," a level to be reached by students who "have demonstrated competency over challenging subject matter"—is quite rigorous, the very large fraction of children who have not been reaching it is thought by some critics to be intended to make American education and its public schools look bad.[12]

For this and a host of other reasons, as we explore in several later chapters, NAEP's achievement levels have been controversial for three decades and in some quarters remain so today. In the final analysis, they're set by human judgments and aspirations, not by an impersonal scientific process.

At the same time, they're the closest thing the US has ever had to stable national standards for student learning in the elementary and secondary years, which in turn gives rise to further controversy in a land where states are responsible for public education, the doctrine of "local control of the schools" remains compelling, and the adjective "national" sometimes serves as a red flag when applied to K–12 schooling.

Seventh, equally sensitive and fraught are decisions about what to put on the test. Thanks to the extraordinary decentralization of American primary-secondary education, especially with respect to curriculum and pedagogy, it's no easy matter to determine what skills and knowledge to incorporate into a nationwide assessment. What is appropriate to probe at which grade levels, mindful that the same test—of, say, eighth-grade US history—will be given in Oregon and Texas, in Boston and Miami? How much emphasis to give to one part of a subject versus another? In math, for example, computation skills must be balanced against problem-solving skills. In writing, how much weight should be placed on correct usage versus reasoning or imagination or style? What fraction of a given assessment should consist of multiple-choice versus constructed response items?

Decisions about the composition of a NAEP assessment are laborious, involving wide input, judgment calls, and compromises. NAGB is responsible for them, but the work is done by a series of committees and contractors before being reviewed by both NCES and the governing board. They are then formalized in elaborate, subject-specific "assessment frameworks" that typically endure over multiple testing cycles—many of the test questions themselves are changed from year to year, of course—but that get revised or replaced from time to time as curricular fashions and pedagogical priorities change. Such changes foment their own controversies within academic disciplines and education groups, controversies that sometimes resemble culture wars.[13] So decisions about how NAEP should accommodate such changes engender vigorous debate, and because any change in a complex nationwide assessment tends to be costly and slow to implement, and because, if the changes are substantial, they can disrupt multiyear NAEP trend lines, the revision process typically lags behind contemporary education fashion—which is further reason that these frameworks get argued over.

The questions that make it into the test itself are the product of another elaborate creation-review-and-approval cycle. They must conform to the governing board's framework in content and format, but the individual items are generated by experts at NAEP's longtime lead contractor, the Educational Testing Service. They then undergo all sorts of field testing and analysis for possible bias and important psychometric properties such as "differential item functioning."[14] (See box 1.1.)

Eighth, substantive questions about reading or math or science aren't the whole story. Participating students are also presented with questionnaires containing a host of background questions about themselves, their own experience with education, and what (and how) they've been taught in school. Twelfth graders taking the NAEP science test in 2019 faced thirty-eight (!) questions on such varied topics as how often they "felt awkward and out of place at school" during the previous year, which adults live in their homes, how many books are in those homes, whether they used a laptop at school, and which science courses they took in which grades.[15] It's easy to see how such questions can trigger controversy and concerns about privacy, but it's also clear why this sort of information about test-takers is valuable to analysts trying to understand and explain their achievement.

Their teachers and principals are also given NAEP questionnaires. These, too, are extensive. The 2019 survey for eighth-grade teachers ran to thirty-eight pages and sought personal data, information about their training and teaching experience, commentary on the resources and functioning of their school, and considerable background on their classroom approach.[16] High school principals that year faced a thirty-six-pager seeking detailed information about their schools, such as "approximately what percentage of twelfth-grade students enroll in more than one mathematics class in a year (including summer school or two-block classes) for remediation or to catch up a grade level?"[17] Here we can begin to sense why school leaders may find participation in NAEP to be a hassle that yields no direct value to them—and why getting enough schools to fill out a proper sample can be a challenge for state leaders.[18]

Ninth, the ways that important NAEP decisions get made are blurry and conflicted. On paper, authority is vested in—and awkwardly divided between—the National Center for Education Statistics and the twenty-six-member National Assessment Governing Board. Neither, however, has clear-cut decision-making power and neither is an entirely free agent. Meant to be a nonpartisan and expert-led federal statistical agency with its own presidentially appointed commissioner, NCES is lodged within the

BOX 1.1   Examples of NAEP questions

Here are three examples of (publicly released) NAEP test items. The first illustrates a multiple-choice question from the 2015 eighth-grade science test.[a] It follows an "investigation" into the life cycle of mosquitos and is classified as a question of medium difficulty. The second is an "open-response" question—the kind that expects an answer of no more than a few sentences—from the eighth-grade history test given in 2006.[b] This one is considered difficult. The third is drawn from the 2013 reading assessment for twelfth graders and expects an "extended response" from test takers, i.e., a brief essay.[c] Its "prompt" follows a lengthy excerpt from Theodore Roosevelt's 1905 inaugural address, and it is also considered to be a hard question.

1. Larvae and pupae normally float. They must use their muscles in order to dive down through water. What type of energy is used by the muscles?
   a. Sound energy from the air
   b. Thermal energy from the water
   c. Chemical potential energy from their cells
   d. Gravitational potential energy from Earth
2. Question refers to the excerpt from the speech below.

   > . . . we here highly resolve that these dead shall not have died in vain; that this nation, under God, shall have a new birth of freedom; and that government of the people, by the people, for the people, shall not perish from the earth.
   > —Abraham Lincoln's Gettysburg Address, 1863

   Why did Lincoln think that the nation was in danger?
3. Roosevelt emphasizes "responsibility" and "duty" throughout his address. According to Roosevelt, why should the nation take responsibility? What are two responsibilities or duties that Roosevelt believed were important?

a. "National Assessment of Educational Progress 2015 Grade 8 Mathematics, Reading, Science: Sample Questions," National Center for Education Statistics, https://nces.ed.gov/nationsreportcard/subject/field_pubs/sqb/pdf/2015_sqb_g8_mrs.pdf.
b. "NAEP Questions Tool (Question ID: 2006-4H8 #8)," National Center for Education Statistics, https://nces.ed.gov/NationsReportCard/nqt/Search.
c. "NAEP Questions Tool (Question ID: 2013-12R11 #6)," National Center for Education Statistics, https://nces.ed.gov/NationsReportCard/nqt/Search.

Institute of Education Sciences, which has its own governance hierarchy and in turn is part of the US Department of Education, which as part of the executive branch is accountable to the president but has its laws made and funds appropriated by Congress. For its part, the governing board, though scrupulously bipartisan, is a Noah's Ark of individuals chosen because of the constituencies that they represent: two governors, two state legislators, two chief state school officers, two local superintendents, an elementary principal, a secondary principal, three classroom teachers, and so forth.

Although admonished by statute to transcend special interest pleading—and NAGB members have generally done well at that over the years—it's impossible for individuals on any such board to shed entirely their own origins, loyalties, and prior experience. This is both asset and liability for NAEP, as the diversity of its governing board lends credibility to its decisions even as that diversity creates the potential for disagreement.

The laws that authorize NAEP are ambiguous on the division of key responsibilities between NCES and NAGB. Moreover, both entities operate within shifting restrictions, constraints, and competing priorities. Most obvious are budget limits and trade-offs. NAEP is relatively expensive. Its fiscal 2021 appropriation of $165 million excludes overheads borne by NCES and participating states and districts as well as a congressional allocation for NAGB of $7.8 million, yet its cost per student test-taker is a whopping $314.[19] While acknowledging that NAEP in some respects is dusty and inefficient, we must also recognize that its budget is insufficient to test everything in all three grades as often as many would like.

Finances, however, are just the beginning of the constraints and pressures on NAEP's decision-makers. Constituency interests are omnipresent, too. In late 2020, for example, as NAGB and NCES struggled to determine whether the congressionally mandated assessment of reading and math could be safely and accurately administered in 2021 amid the many uncertainties of Covid-19, the organization representing the nation's largest urban districts declared that its members were disinclined to participate. They had a point: if not enough kids are in school, the sample cannot be valid and operationalizing a proper sample for NAEP in 2021 would have been a huge challenge in any case, one made far worse by a testing boycott by America's big cities. Yet NAEP could well be the best available gauge of learning damage wrought by the pandemic. The decision was fraught and NAGB was divided. In the event, advised by NCES, it moved to defer the

2021 assessment and Secretary Betsy DeVos successfully urged Congress to accept a one-year delay in the statutory testing mandate.[20] (We revisit NAEP's complicated governance arrangements in chapter 8.)

Tenth, America learns quite a lot from NAEP data, the release of which often leads to revealing analyses by others. Consider, for example, the recent example of civics, which has been much in the spotlight these past few years. The release (two long years after it was administered) of results from the 2018 NAEP civics assessment prompted much attention, even though that test was given only to eighth graders and only at the national level.[21] Average scores had barely budged since four years earlier, yet it remained newsworthy that fewer than one-quarter of test-takers reached NAGB's "proficient" bar—among the worst showings of any subject in the NAEP portfolio.

Sample questions show, for instance, that only half the test-takers seemed to understand that Congress, not the president, decides what's in laws—and just 26 percent could furnish satisfactory answers to a question asking, "In addition to voting and being a candidate, what are two ways that citizens can be involved in presidential campaigns and elections?"[22]

Analysts at the Brookings Institution were encouraged to find in the civics report evidence that the white-Hispanic score gap had narrowed over two decades, although the white-black and rich-poor gaps remained unchanged and alarmingly wide. The NAEP results also prompted them to explore related research on civics, leading to this useful insight:

> The low overall proficiency rate in civics continues to be an area of concern that warrants discussion of what schools can do to more effectively promote civic engagement. Though the causal relationship between classroom practices and democratic participation is not well defined, a growing literature examines the relationship. For example, states that require students to pass a civics exam during high school have higher levels of youth voter registration and turnout. In another study, taking a civics course and participating in extracurriculars shows a positive association with voting as a young adult.[23]

This is but one of hundreds of examples of secondary analyses by outside scholars and organizations that make use of NAEP data, or are catalyzed by NAEP data, but that draw upon other research and sometimes other information sources to develop interesting and potentially actionable findings that NAEP alone cannot supply and that its federal minders are generally wise to steer clear of even as they do their best to provide data products that facilitate analysis by others.

Eleventh, despite the fact that NAEP was originally conceived as a research vehicle, and vast amounts of research are carried out with its data, those data cannot yield definitive answers to a host of important questions about what is and isn't working in American education. NAEP isn't designed to answer "why" questions or to furnish reliable evaluations of specific interventions, innovations, and reforms. This exasperates both analysts and policy makers. NAEP is great at detecting and displaying changes in and differences between learning outcomes, but it cannot explain causation. The most it lends itself to is correlation, as in the Brookings example above.

Another example: we can observe within the 2019 eighth-grade NAEP reading results that both white and Hispanic students were reading worse than in 2017. But NAEP cannot tell us why or explain what changed beyond the outcome itself. Its data may be able to be correlated with other developments in or out of school, but they can go no further. Nor, despite the extensive background questions posed to students, teachers, and administrators, can NAEP tell us much beyond academic achievement, specifically the kinds of academic achievement that tests are able to probe. Is one approach to reading instruction more effective than another—and for which kids? Are students becoming more creative? More adept at working in small groups? Healthier and happier? How about teacher preparation? Technology? School choice? NAEP results can offer clues and help us make educated guesses. Properly analyzed alongside data from other sources, we can often get further. NAEP may also help identify questions for further research, studies that may shed light on causal relationships and potentially worthy interventions. By itself, however, NAEP cannot get us to where we'd like to be in diagnosing and curing the shortcomings of American education.

Twelfth and finally (for a first chapter), we find ourselves facing a paradox. Because NAEP tells US educators and policy makers nothing about individual schools, teachers, or kids, nor even about the great majority of districts, it's peripheral to the immediate needs and interests of parents, the workaday needs of teachers, even the information requirements of most superintendents and school board members. It's tantalizing and in ways

enormously valuable but in other ways hugely exasperating to researchers and reformers alike. Why, then, is it also so important, so respected, so
much the center of attention?

We'll dig deeper in the pages that follow. We'll recount how NAEP
evolved from an obscure and underfunded research activity that few cared
about into a multidimensional monitoring system for American education
that is closely watched, that bears on countless interests, and that generates information with significant implications for many. We'll pay tribute
to NAEP's success in withstanding—and adapting to—the test of time, even
its capacity to become more consequential (and just plain bigger) as concerns about education deepened and appetites for information intensified.
We'll further examine how NAEP originated, how it has changed, how it
operates, how it's governed, and how it is and isn't responding to shifting
priorities, mounting demands, and deteriorating national comity. But we'll
never extricate ourselves entirely from the paradoxes that it embodies.

CHAPTER 2

Origins

FOURTEEN YEARS before the landmark federal report *A Nation At Risk* starkly outlined the need for education reform, the first National Assessment was administered to representative samples of American students ages nine, thirteen, and seventeen, in civics, science, and writing. That same year (1969), a wet-behind-the-ears graduate student and junior White House education-policy staffer found himself being briefed on this new thing by Wendell Pierce, head of a recently formed consortium of state leaders called the Education Commission of the States (ECS). More than five decades later, NAEP remains part of my own life and career.

But where did it come from, and why? NAEP's origin story is definitively recounted by early participant (and Michigan State statistics professor) Irvin J. Lehmann as part of a thick 2004 book edited by Lyle Jones and Ingram Olkin, both distinguished academics who themselves played sizable roles in the story.[1] They were prominent members of a remarkable generation of psychometricians, statisticians, psychologists, educators, and public officials during a can-do period in American life, people who could detect a challenge or problem facing the nation and then set about to devise and execute a solution to it. It was also a time when "public-private collaboration" meant something nimble, creative, and relatively unconfined by red tape, watchdogs, and suspicions on both sides.

The tale begins in the early 1960s when the late Francis W. Keppel, the US commissioner of education (and former Harvard Education School dean), "recognized the need for a national assessment that would provide technically sound and valid data regarding pupils' knowledge, skills and abilities" and asked the celebrated psychologist Ralph W. Tyler (founding director of

Stanford's Center for Advanced Study in the Behavioral Sciences) to suggest how this might be done.[2]

Keppel's request can be seen from several perspectives. On the one hand, it represented an epochal shift by a commissioner of education from decades of tabulating school inputs and processes toward an interest in gauging what was emerging from US classrooms by way of learning. It could even be termed visionary, the more so because it antedated by several years the famous "Coleman Report" of 1966—a 737-page federal study titled *Equality of Educational Opportunity* but commonly nicknamed for its lead author, the distinguished Johns Hopkins mathematical sociologist James S. Coleman—which rocked the education world with the finding that, contrary to what had long been assumed, conventional school inputs had only a hazy relationship to student learning outcomes.[3]

Yet it could also be said that Keppel was harkening back almost a century to Congress's 1867 creation of the first United States Department of Education, a tiny unit that was initially lodged in the Interior Department but given the ambitious assignment to obtain, tabulate, and report information on "the condition and progress of education in the several States and Territories." (See box 2.1.)

Over the years, the federal education agency—in Keppel's time, it was the "U.S. Office of Education," located within the (then) Department of

---

BOX 2.1   Excerpt from 1867 federal statute establishing a "Department of Education"

Chapter 158—*An act to establish a Department of Education.*

Be it enacted by the Senate and House of Representatives of the United States of America, in Congress assembled, That there shall be established, at the city of Washington, a Department of Education, for the purpose of collecting such statistics and facts as shall show the condition and progress of education in the several States and Territories, and of diffusing such information respecting the organization and management of schools and school systems and methods of teaching as shall aid the people of the United States in the establishment and maintenance of efficient school systems, and otherwise promote the cause of education throughout the country.

BOX 2.1   *(Continued)*

Sec. 2. *And be it further enacted*, That there shall be appointed by the President, by, and with the advice and consent of the Senate, a Commissioner of Education, who shall be entrusted with the management of the department herein established, and who shall receive a salary of four thousand dollars per annum, and who shall have authority to appoint one chief clerk of his department, who shall receive a salary of two thousand dollars per annum; one clerk, who shall receive a salary of eighteen hundred dollars per annum; and one clerk who shall receive a salary of sixteen hundred dollars per annum; which said clerks shall be subject to the appointing and removing power of the Commissioner of Education.

Sec. 3. *And be it further enacted*, That it shall be the duty of the Commissioner of Education to present annually to Congress a report embodying the results of his investigations and labors, together with a statement of such facts and recommendations as will in his judgment subserve the purpose for which this department is established. In the first report made by the Commissioner of Education under this act, there shall be presented a statement of the several grants of land made by Congress to promote education, and the manner in which these several trusts have been managed, the amount of funds arising therefrom, and the annual proceeds of the same, as far as the same can be determined.

Sec. 4. *And be it further enacted*, That the Commissioner of Public Buildings is hereby authorized and directed to furnish proper offices for the use of the department herein established.

Approved March 2, 1867

Source: *Thirty-Ninth Congress, Session II, Ch. 158, An Act to establish a Department of Education, March 2, 1867*, 14 STAT 434, cited in Kevin R. Kosar, "Act to Establish a Federal Department of Education, 1867," Federal Education Policy History Blog, https://federaleducationpolicy.wordpress.com/2011/02/19/1867-act-to-establish-a-federal-department-of-education/.

Health, Education, and Welfare (HEW)—had done little by way of monitoring "progress," at least in the realm of student achievement. Still, one could fairly contend that such a mission was buried in its DNA.

Keppel's motives for seeking outcomes data were probably multiple. In a 2001 interview, the late John W. Gardner, himself a former HEW secretary (and close Keppel colleague), recalled that the commissioner's "first con-cern was to find a tool for his own evaluation of how the nation was doing, how states were doing, how school districts are doing . . . Frank had a very keen grasp of his national responsibility, and the absence of metrics and tools to do some of that evaluation—where are we headed, how are we doing."[4]

It appears from congressional testimony submitted by Keppel, even as work was quietly commencing (without congressional knowledge) on what would become NAEP, that the commissioner was frustrated by how little was known about the state of learning in the United States. Americans knew more, he said, about steel production and cattle raising than about the proficiency of their students. He also intimated that there was a need to "work out ways of taking samples of the achievement of students at critical points in their schooling."[5]

But that wasn't necessarily the whole story. In a perceptive account (also within the Jones-Olkin collection) of what he dubbed NAEP's "age of innocence," longtime Carnegie Corporation staffer Frederic C. ("Fritz") Mosher suggests that Keppel "probably also had in mind that if he could show that U.S. students were not doing well in some respects or that there were substantial inequalities . . . , it would strengthen the case for some form of federal assistance for the schools, an issue that was being hotly debated."[6]

Whatever the impulse behind his request, Keppel received a response from Tyler in July 1963 in the form of a five-page memo that criticized the norm-referenced tests then widely used in American K–12 education and suggested "a new type of measurement instrument designed to assess identified objectives whose specifications would be determined by subject-matter [sic] and by lay people working together to reach consensus . . . The instrument would provide information on what groups of people know and can do, rather than on what score an individual receives on a test."[7]

Note that phrase, "what groups of people know and can do," as it has echoed through the history of NAEP for half a century. But it may not have been exactly what the commissioner had in mind, as he was apparently seeking more of an achievement barometer—changes over time—than a gauge of what students are able to do at a point in time. In any case, Keppel then had no spare federal funds with which to pursue such an initiative, so he turned to the Carnegie Corporation of New York, a wealthy private foundation headed at the time by Gardner, whose own three-year term as HEW secretary would commence in 1965. Gardner replied that the foundation would indeed underwrite a meeting of testing experts and educators, thus launching almost six decades of Carnegie involvement with NAEP and related endeavors, including this book. At Keppel's behest, Gardner agreed to chair that meeting himself, a sign that this prominent and influential man glimpsed the potential importance of the conversation.

The nineteen-person conference kicked off in New York in December 1963, followed by a second session the following month. Innumerable questions were raised, and little was settled. Lehmann writes that "conferees left the meeting with various interpretations of the purpose and direction of a national assessment." Yet forward movement continued. By August 1964, Gardner had appointed an "interim committee" to pursue the idea of a national assessment and had enlisted the even-wealthier Ford Foundation to share the cost with Carnegie. Dubbing itself the "Exploratory Committee on Assessing the Progress of Education" (ECAPE), the group was chaired by Tyler and staffed by University of Michigan psychologist Stephen Withey, assisted by Lehmann. As they went about their work, thinking it would take two years (which stretched to four before the first assessment took place), Tyler found himself meeting off-line with many groups of wary educators, notably including local school superintendents who had long been accustomed to running their own shows with no external monitoring.

Plenty of issues had to be worked through—conceptual, political, financial, and technical—and initial discussions needed to be held with potential assessment contractors, whose preliminary proposals were reviewed by yet another group that came to be called the Technical Advisory Committee, comprised of several of the country's foremost psychometricians.

In mid-1965—the year Congress passed the landmark Elementary & Secondary Education Act, inaugurating the modern era of federal aid to public education—ECAPE morphed into a new nonprofit organization that dropped the word "exploratory" and was thereafter known as the Committee on Assessing the Progress of Education (CAPE). Funding was still largely private, but its activities broadened to include several work groups, lay panels, and potential contractors charged with drafting "learning objectives" and developing pilot "instruments" by which children might actually be tested.[8] Much attention also had to be paid to politics and public relations, however, as educator opposition was mounting. Gardner later recalled that the prospect of measuring school performance "almost shot us down when the school administrators heard about the idea."[9] The major organization of local superintendents, the American Association of School Administrators (AASA), went so far as to urge members not to cooperate with the nascent assessment project, and the National Education Association (NEA) also passed a resolution to "withhold cooperation" from it.

Assessment planners understood that elected state and local officials were also apt to be apprehensive about any national encroachment on their customary control, not only of the delivery of public education but also of information that the public received about it. Scarier even than "national" would surely be the fact that Uncle Sam was behind it.

Hence it mattered greatly what sort of organization would take ownership of and actually operate the assessment. If the project remained in the hands of academics, technical experts, and elite private foundations, it would have endless difficulty enlisting the cooperation, much less the goodwill, of the country's sprawling public-education system, which in turn would make it harder to obtain the popular acceptance and federal funding that everyone knew would be required if the enterprise was to endure.

After weighing several very different options, planners found a politically astute home for their infant project. The fledgling ECS—founded in 1967, another product of Carnegie's largesse and active engagement with education—was led by elected state officials.[10] Entrusting the new assessment to ECS, and turning the experts who had been running the show into its advisers, meant it would "belong" to a body of democratically accountable policy makers. Just as important, they weren't *federal* policy makers, thus easing the fear among many educators and organizations that the new assessment was a first move toward some sort of national curriculum or centralization of control over schooling. The first head of ECS, Wendell Pierce, was himself a former local superintendent (Cincinnati) who understood—and likely shared—these anxieties. And ECS was hungry for projects and revenue. In the event, NAEP would come to comprise more than half its budget and engage more than 40 percent of its staff before management of the assessment was moved to the Educational Testing Service (ETS) in 1983.

Working out an arrangement with ECS that was acceptable to the states and to fretful education groups, many of them jittery about their results being displayed in public and comparisons getting made, also meant—as Mosher recaps the sequence—"that the design of NAEP had to be made as unobjectionable as possible. In particular, it meant that results would be reported by regions and demographic groups, rather than by identifiable states or districts."[11] In Gardner's recollection, "We had to make compromises. We had to say that NAEP would not be used for any direct comparison of schools, that it would be used for assessing year-to-year progress, not district versus district."[12]

Thus NAEP planners, almost from the get-go, had to agree that their assessment would yield no information about individual schools, districts, or states. This concession to political reality would limit NAEP's policy utility—and public attention—for two decades, and in many ways still does. At the same time, it meant that NAEP would launch as a low-stakes venture, which both sheltered it from agitated politics and made it less compelling to participate in or pay for. There was little reason to fret about something that "doesn't count" and that wouldn't spotlight the performance of one's own community or state—but also not much reason to bestir oneself to get it funded or help it to succeed.

The handoff from CAPE to ECS was protracted and gnarly, but by mid-1969, as the first assessment round was being given to a sample of seventeen-year-olds, a memorandum of agreement was signed and the transfer of responsibility was complete. A further memorandum, six pages long, signed by the ECS chair (South Carolina governor Robert McNair) and US Education Commissioner James E. Allen Jr., set forth a set of terms and ground rules for federal support of the new venture that recognized the Office of Education's commitment to it over the long haul but also emphasized the grantee's autonomy in conducting the assessment.

Meanwhile, ECAPE and CAPE had labored hard and productively to design, develop, and pilot the assessment itself. As nothing like it had been tried before, countless quandaries had to be debated and resolved. For example, what sorts of test questions would elicit the information the planners wanted, would do so in statistically valid ways, and would attract public attention and ongoing support?

As for the tests themselves, including the questions to be asked and the protocols for administration and analysis, here, too, they were breaking new ground. Lehmann explains that "[i]t was readily apparent to the ECAPE members that the tools and technique available at the time were inadequate for meaningfully reporting education progress at the national level. Accordingly, a new assessment plan was needed."[13] That, however, meant tackling the enormous job of designing a very complicated instrument from the ground up, one that had to be feasible, technically valid, affordable, and politically acceptable. A tall order indeed.

Building the tests required, first, the identification of learning objectives that would determine what sorts of questions—content, format, and so on—to place before students. Test questions, after all, don't appear from thin air. They must be based on a set of assumptions about what those being tested should be expected to know. To take a simple example, consider the written portion of a driver's examination. In Maryland, where I live, new (noncommercial) drivers must pass a fairly straightforward ten-question "knowledge test" before even getting a learner's permit.[14] But behind that short test is a forty-four-page "Driver's Manual" produced by the state that sets forth (along with much else) the "knowledge" that the wannabe driver is supposed to possess. The test is based on the manual, without which those constructing the test would have no idea what questions to ask.[15]

NAEP's planners had to develop something similar. What, exactly, should pupils at various levels of schooling be expected to have learned in a given subject and how would they be expected to demonstrate whether or not they had learned it? But figuring that out for an unprecedented nationwide assessment was a heavy lift. The subject-specific objectives had to connect with what most schools were trying to teach; they had to make sense to practicing educators; they had to satisfy scholars in their respective disciplines that they were integral to the field of study; and it was vital that "thoughtful laymen would consider [them] important for American youth to attain."[16] Although Tyler and many of his colleagues viewed the assessment as first and foremost a research project, education leaders and the wider public also had to find it worth the bother and expense—and not offensive or worrying.

This novel, daunting challenge demanded outside expertise and horsepower, so seven firms were initially engaged to develop objectives and test items. The technical advisers found favor with four of these and then—due to "the unusual nature of the national assessment and the importance of objectives in developing exercises"—asked two or three contractors to work independently on the learning objectives for each subject. A host of others—more than a thousand, including educators, subject experts, and laypeople—was then enlisted to review the draft objectives, complete with four big conferences in 1966 and 1967 and eleven separate panels. Mostly, reports Lehmann, there was "good agreement not only among the lay panels but also between the lay and professional judgments regarding the objectives."[17]

What sort of student sample would be tested? Should it be confined to pupils in school or also attempt to cover young people who had dropped out? (The high school graduation rate in the mid-1960s was about 75 percent.) By age or grade level? Public schools only? How to be sure that individual test items had face validity across a big, diverse country, that they would be fair to different kinds of students, and that their results would lend themselves to analysis and reporting, but without treading on too many sensitive toes? Contractors engaged to develop items—the same for- and nonprofit organizations that had worked on the objectives—were told that, on a given test, one-third of the questions should be readily answered by almost everyone, one-third should be answerable by about half the sample, and the final third should be within the grasp only of advanced students. Constructing a set of valid test questions that met such specifications was both novel and challenging.

As if that weren't enough, assessment planners asked contractors also to be creative in the kinds of test items they developed and not limit themselves to traditional multiple-choice questions of the paper-and-pencil kind. Why not ask a music student to perform? A science pupil to work on an experiment? Sadly, however, recounts Lehmann, "the opportunity to be creative and different resulted in failure . . . It seemed that the professional item writers couldn't extricate themselves from the form and content of the types of items found in conventional achievement tests."[18]

Some ten thousand items were developed, then subjected to innumerable reviews. They must not be offensive or seem like invasions of privacy. Subjects such as civics inevitably get into disputed topics—what constitutes good citizenship, for example—and a number of those items required deliberation, feedback, and revision. Subject-matter specialists had to review them, as did experts in item construction. Were the question prompts unclear? Was there more than one possible right answer? Would students understand what they were being asked?

"Content validity" loomed large in the minds of the technical experts. As Lehmann recalls the challenge, "[E]verything possible should be done to maximize an examinee's understanding of what he is being asked to do in each exercise."[19] This obligation led to a series of feasibility studies during 1967, trying to determine, for instance, "Should classroom teachers be used to administer the exercises? . . . Should the directions be read aloud . . . ?"

Why such punctiliousness? So much research? Ralph Tyler explained that they were creating something new and different, including a quest for accurate information on the achievement of high and low performers: "Tests currently in use," he wrote, "concentrate their exercises on the performance of 'average' students. Very few if any exercises in tests now on the market are directed towards the performance of slow learners or of the more advanced . . . Since test contractors have not heretofore had to meet this specification it is very necessary to find out by try-outs whether the exercises do, in fact, represent this distribution."[20]

Tyler and his associates were indeed breaking new ground in achievement testing. There were plenty of tests of individual aptitude and achievement, mostly used for entry into selective colleges and schools—the SAT, the Secondary School Admissions Test (SSAT)—and for accelerating in school or gaining college credit based on prior learning. Some, such as the decade-old Advanced Placement (AP) program, went beyond multiple-choice items to incorporate extended essays and open-response questions, but participation was limited to students who signed up for them, typically around the end of high school.[21] Though much attention was sometimes paid to ups and downs in the mean scores attained by cohorts of students—this was a big enough deal that for years the College Board concealed the fact that average SAT scores started heading downward in the mid-1960s—no one could claim that such data were representative of the nation's pupil population as a whole.

Nor were the tests then in common use by states and districts helpful as gauges, either of what they "know and can do" or of gains and declines over time. Almost all were "norm referenced," snapshot-style, "standardized" tests that reported the scores of individuals and groups of students in relation to the average score of the "norming" reference group.[22] Thus a parent might learn that her sixth grader was scoring—in reading, say, or math—in the "seventh stanine" or perhaps the "73rd percentile" of the norming group. Alternatively, parents might be told that their son's score was equivalent to that of an average seventh grader during the sixth month of the school year. Sub-scores might also have been provided, indicating how a pupil was doing on various elements of the subject at hand.[23]

That kind of information might help parents wanting to know how their children compare with others and might also be useful for teachers wanting to know how their pupils are faring and what are their present strengths and weaknesses. But the value of that information is powerfully affected by the choice of other students for comparison purposes: other kids in my town? My state? My race, gender, or socioeconomic group? And without item-specific analysis, tests furnish no way to see what exactly a student (or population of students) does or doesn't know. From the perspective of policy makers and political leaders, such tests are unhelpful for tracking the achievement of large populations and its changes over time and, because different tests were in use in various places around the country, there was essentially no information about the nation as a whole or about demographically distinct subpopulations of students.

Tyler and company were bent on filling those gaps—as Commissioner Keppel originally wanted—and addressing other flaws and failings in the extant array of tests. As researchers, however, they also sought a lot of close-up detail about student prowess, which led to NAEP results in the early years being reported by item—how many thirteen-year-olds, say, answered a particular question correctly?—rather than on any kind of uniform scale or in relation to any sort of standard or benchmark. Indeed, the mandate to develop items in such a way that about one-third of test-takers would probably answer correctly—and so forth—precluded aggregate reporting of the sort that Keppel was seeking and that the public would find most informative, although education researchers might learn a lot about what specific skills and knowledge were (and weren't) being acquired by pupils of different age levels.

Tucked into the assessment design from the outset was ambiguity, perhaps intentional, as to its ultimate purpose or purposes. Was the goal to furnish a benchmark for policy makers, a source of useful information for practitioners, a fountain of much-wanted data for researchers, or all of the above? Citing commentators from NAEP's early days, Mosher writes that there may always have existed a "crucial contradiction" between what Tyler and his fellow analysts "thought were the possible uses of the assessment and the expectations of many others, including the staff at the Carnegie Corporation" (where Mosher worked). The latter team, he says, thought the new assessment would

> provide information that would both inform policy and answer research questions. These expectations assumed that the assessment data could be used to establish what is working or failing or to test hypotheses about what might work. [But] the truth is that the kind of sampling involved in NAEP does not allow researchers to establish any causal or evaluative relationships . . . [T]he data cannot be used to explain why anything happens.[24]

Tyler, he says, recognized this limitation but "did not go out of his way to force others" to grasp it, "perhaps because it would have undercut the support for NAEP. But because of these limitations, NAEP has always proved disappointing to those who hoped for answers and puzzling to those who don't understand the intrinsic problem."[25]

That's still true today—and still a problem.

Limited or not, NAEP was a hugely complex and ambitious undertaking that was bound to prove expensive. Where would the money come from? By 1969, Carnegie and Ford had pitched in more than $4 million to offset the costs of planning and development, but once the shift to ECS was complete, it was important finally to secure the federal funding that everyone knew would be essential to operationalize and sustain the venture.

The planners had guesstimated that the NAEP budget would require $3 to $5 million a year, but at the outset the Office of Education was able to commit only $2 million per annum, starting in fiscal 1969. So said Commissioner Harold Howe II, who had succeeded Keppel in that role in 1966. This meant money was very tight, as federal support did not even rise to $3 million until 1973. By then, responsibility for NAEP within the government had shifted to the National Center for Education Statistics (then a subdivision of the Office of Education), and the decision was made (by outgoing commissioner Sidney Marland) to change the funding mechanism from federal grant to contract, which gave executive branch officials added leverage—and came as a big, unwelcome surprise for ECS, which just four years earlier had been promised autonomy by Marland's predecessor.[26]

Lean rations meant that assessment plans had to be curbed. The hoped-for testing cycle of ten subjects every three years was loosened, keeping reading, math, and science on that schedule but moving other subjects to a six-year cycle. Even then, federal funding remained precarious—a "roller coaster" says Lehmann—and "Funding concerns plagued ECS from the time it assumed governance until it lost the contract to ETS" sixteen years later.[27] These fiscal ups and downs led to numerous changes in the assessment design and periodicity, and at times caused ECS to consider jettisoning the whole thing.

Instability also marked the government's management of the project and its funding. Organizational arrangements within HEW kept changing—the National Institute of Education was authorized by Congress in 1972 and lodged in a new "Education Division" that also contained the existing Office of Education and its National Center for Education Statistics. Six years later, responsibility for NAEP and the ECS contract would be moved into the new institute.

During this period, a fluid cast of characters on the federal side led to uncertainties and changing views about the point of this assessment and how—if at all—it furthered the government's own mission. As recalled by Dorothy Gilford, who was then the NCES commissioner, "[I]n 1972, a year following the transfer of NAEP oversight to NCES, John Evans, the assistant commissioner for Planning, Budgeting, and Evaluation, told me that he planned to delete the NAEP project from the next year's budget because the data lacked policy relevance." She convinced him otherwise, but this "first budget crisis" "highlighted the importance of demonstrating the potential policy relevance of NAEP data and of disseminating information about NAEP to as many categories of potential users as possible."[28] This episode also illustrates the fact that NAEP was, for many years, a precarious enterprise whose partisans had to pay as much attention to public affairs and politics as to the assessment activity itself. Besides skepticism within the various units of HEW and antagonism from suspicious education groups, it helped not at all that, for much of this period, Congress and the executive branch were controlled by opposing parties that—to put it gently—did not always see eye to eye. Bear in mind that NAEP, at this stage, was entirely a project of the executive branch with no statutory authorization, which surely contributed to appropriations that were sometimes far below the president's budget request. (In 1974, for example, Nixon sought $7 million for NAEP, but Congress approved just $3 million.)

Shaky as it was in many respects, the infant assessment venture survived and in time would thrive. During just its first half-decade of operation, it accomplished an impressive amount. As summarized by statistics commissioner Dorothy Gilford:

> Between fall 1971 and the end of 1974, NAEP successfully conducted the first round of assessments for five subjects: music and social studies in 1971–72, mathematics in 1972–73, and career and occupational development and writing in 1973–74. They also conducted the second assessment of science . . . and were in the field with first assessments of art . . . and the second assessment of reading . . . In addition, NAEP had published a large number of reports.[29]

It's easy to agree with Gilford's upbeat conclusion that, at the tender age of five, "[t]he NAEP program was indeed meeting its overarching goal 'to provide information useful to educating decision-makers and practitioners in identifying problems, setting priorities, and determining progress.'"[30]

But a long and winding road still lay ahead. In the next chapter, we continue our trek through more of its twists and turns.

CHAPTER 3

Eventful Adolescence

T HOUGH UNDERFUNDED and occasionally under-loved by their federal overseers, as the 1970s unfolded the Education Commission of the States and its NAEP project proved energetic and productive. Assessments continued to be administered in multiple subjects, even one aimed at out-of-school seventeen-year-olds and adults. The reading and math tests given in 1971 and 1973 established baselines for today's Long-Term-Trend NAEP, that is, starting points for a half century of reliable (if much debated) tracking of student prowess and progress in those two indispensable subjects.[1]

Multiple reports were published. The project's headquarters moved from Ann Arbor to Denver, home to ECS, which created a new, six-member "National Assessment Policy Committee," although CAPE continued to operate (in an expert advisory capacity) alongside.

Yet even as much was accomplished, often for the first time, NAEP began to display weaknesses and shortcomings. Its first evaluation was undertaken—again with Carnegie funding—by William Greenbaum and two colleagues at the Harvard Graduate School of Education. They cited various "technical problems" in the way that the assessment's learning objectives and test items were developed and, more broadly, questioned what they termed Ralph Tyler's practice of "defining education as the sum of the objectives of ten subject areas."[2]

In the mid-1970s, the National Center for Education Statistics itself commissioned a pair of reviews of NAEP operations. But far more consequential was a report to Congress in 1976—two years before lawmakers passed NAEP's initial statutory authorization—by the General Accounting Office (GAO), which concluded that "[a]though the National Assessment has contributed to American education, its assessment results have been of limited usefulness." Based largely on surveys of local and state leaders, the GAO's seventy-page report included a host of recommendations for changes large and small in NAEP's design and operation.[3]

The comptroller general's team calculated that the assessment had already cost taxpayers about $35.5 million. They correctly recalled that "[t]he [NAEP] project grew from a realization in the early 1960s, when the Federal Government began investing heavily in formal education, that no comprehensive, dependable information existed on the educational attainments of Americans." Perhaps with the benefit of hindsight—and staking out a role for NAEP that would surprise Tyler and his compatriots—the GAO summarized its purpose as "related to the movement toward accountability in education. This movement emphasizes that the purpose of schools is to provide education and seeks to hold education officials accountable for this. To evaluate education, one needs information about the knowledge and skills of the student population." Yet NAEP's "limited usefulness" thus far "to education decisionmakers, researchers and practitioners" had "prevented the project from achieving its basic goal." Worse still, "it has not demonstrated that the benefits of the project's assessment approach warrant the cost." Perhaps the country would be better served by an "alternative approach."[4]

Unsurprisingly, the GAO survey showed that few local leaders were even aware of NAEP's existence—unsurprising because district superintendents had blocked project planners from generating any local data! Their complaints about its meager value to them recalls the fellow who, having slain his parents, sought mercy from the court on grounds that he was now an orphan. Yet criticisms from state and federal policy makers and researchers, suggesting that assessment data weren't supplying them with much of value, either, deserved to be taken seriously, even though some were attributable to NAEP's tight budget and some to its initial design, which owed much to the states' own wariness of this new national venture.

The GAO report did offer a bit of positive reinforcement for NAEP, attesting to the planners' pioneering work in creating a new approach to achievement testing that, by the mid-seventies, was proving helpful in other ways: "The National Assessment has made a valuable contribution to educational assessment technology by developing and implementing a model for objective-referenced assessment . . . In addition to developing objective-referenced tests, . . . the major aspects of the model include (1) the sampling plan, (2) test administration, (3) scoring and analysis of test data, and (4) reporting results."[5]

These innovations had real-world implications, as many states were beginning to develop new tests of their own and starting to seek assessment formats that might be used for accountability purposes: "Thirty-six of the 47 states responding to our questionnaire that have or are planning statewide assessment programs indicated that they used tests based on educational objectives in their programs. Although it is difficult to verify that States' increased use of these tests relates directly to the [NAEP] project, some educators believe that such a direct relationship exists." Thus we see a glimmer of what time has shown to be one of NAEP's subtler but more pervasive contributions to education across the US and beyond: serving as a laboratory or test kitchen for the invention, design, and continuing evolution of large-scale assessments of student learning and school performance.[6]

Another GAO conclusion proved prophetic—but also way ahead of its time: NAEP would be much more valuable if it incorporated standards or expectations into its analyses. Foreshadowing the rationale for adding the achievement levels that would appear years later, the GAO had this to say:

> A factor contributing to the lack of interpretation of National Assessment data is the lack of standards against which test data can be compared to judge performance. An example of a performance standard might be: "80 percent of the 9-year-olds should meet this objective 90 percent of the time." The National Assessment contends that no one knows for sure what a reasonable percentage of success should be, partly because concrete achievement data has never been available. Because the project has not attempted to define them, establishing performance levels is left to the reader or interpreter of National Assessment results . . . In our opinion, unless meaningful performance comparisons can be made, States, localities, and other data users are not as likely to find the National Assessment data useful.[7]

Yet this, too, would come as a surprise to Ralph Tyler and his colleagues, for they had never sought to build standards into their new assessment. Rather, they set out to determine what American school kids "know and can do," not to say how many of them *should* know something. For them, NAEP was a research investigation, not a normative or prescriptive undertaking, although item writers *had* been instructed to come up with test questions that one-third of the test-takers should be expected to answer correctly, and so forth. But early NAEP was item-centric, and early NAEP reports contained statements like this:

> About 60% of the teenagers knew that the sides of a square are of equal length, and about half the 13-year-olds and nearly three-fourths of the 17-year-olds could calculate the area of a rectangle given its length and width. Yet only 12% of the 13-year-olds and 42% of the 17-year-olds successfully figured the area of a square when the length of only one side was shown.[8]

Such close-to-the-curriculum revelations may have value for educators, curriculum designers, and some analysts, but they're not very informative for mayors, governors, federal officials, or anyone else who is primarily focused on policies, structures, resources, and the requisites of an educated workforce. They certainly held scant value for parents. That such potential consumers—and cheerleaders—were getting little of value from early NAEP reports illustrated both the political and interest-group constraints that project designers had to work under—the obligation to avoid judgments and potentially awkward comparisons—and the fact that those designers were nearly all academics ill-attuned (or downright allergic) to the information needs of policy makers and school-level practitioners.

What's called "item-level" reporting was clearly their intention. "[T]he whole point," recalled Lee J. Cronbach, a highly regarded, Stanford-based psychologist and psychometrician who served for many years on NAEP's Technical Advisory Committee, "was to get away from reports about 'people are proficient,' 'people are meeting the national objectives,' or whatever . . . If the exercises did not strike the public as being educationally useful, OK, that was a reasonable matter for public discussion, for a school board to consider. But we were just giving the facts on things that somebody had thought was a reasonable part of educational growth."[9]

That such information would not aggregate into generalizations about student performance was fine with them, even though, as Cronbach acknowledged, "The issue with reporting at the item level is that you don't have any teachers or other readers in your report to want to sit in front of the screen and go through 100 items at a clip . . . The issue of the width of the audience attention span is how much information the audience wants

. . . So we have problems in communication here as distinct from just getting the information right."[10]

"Problems in communication" indeed. In hindsight, it's as if NAEP's
architects had set out to generate information about student learning that
wouldn't be easily comprehended or helpful to many people, that is, as if
they had intentionally chosen a path to even greater obscurity than just
avoiding the comparisons the school superintendents opposed.

Indeed, obscurity may well have been what they intended, or perceived they must do, as anxiety and mistrust about what this mysterious
project might lead to was more widespread than the education interest
groups that had noisily made their worries known at the outset. Members
of Congress were also wary of moves by the executive branch that could
be seen as intruding on local control of schools or fostering thorny comparisons among them. Education commissioners Keppel and Howe were
themselves somewhat evasive about the mission of this new assessment
project even as they encouraged and supported it, surely because they
deemed vagueness a strategic necessity. In budget hearings for the Office
of Education in 1967, for example, Illinois Republican congressman Bob
Michel—whose thirty-eight years in Congress would include a lengthy stint
as House minority leader—stated that he was fearful "of having everything
nationally standardized." He and several colleagues were also concerned
that federal outlays for education statistics gathering and analysis were
wasteful and they routinely demanded explanations of $2 and $3 million
line items in the education budget that, even then, might have been viewed
as "rounding errors."

Whatever the reasons—scholarly precision, political nervousness, interest-
group resistance—NAEP's initial design left it vulnerable to the charge that
it wasn't doing anyone much good, and by the late 1970s this had become
a real problem, such that the project's very existence was in jeopardy. As
NAEP's later major domo (at ETS), Archie LaPointe, recalled it:

> In 1978, when the National Institute of Education [NIE] requested
> proposals for the National Assessment of Educational Progress, they
> received a single submission. The Education Commission of the States
> (ECS) had been managing NAEP for almost ten years and submitted
> the sole proposal.

The NIE engaged a panel of reviewers to evaluate the ECS proposal. After an initial review process, the four members who were present agreed that the proposal was inadequate and that NIE reject it
[*sic*].[11]

That could have been the death knell for national assessment, until
a fifth reviewer arrived in the form of Gregory Anrig, then Massachusetts
commissioner of education and later head of the Educational Testing Service. Anrig, says LaPointe, "felt strongly that NAEP was an important asset,
and he was unwilling to risk its sudden demise." So he "pleaded with his
four colleagues to alter their recommendation." Which they did, leading
the NIE to send the proposal back to ECS with criticisms and invite the
organization to resubmit. It made revisions, resubmitted, and received
another five-year contract.

Also in 1978, after fifteen years of obliviousness-cum-skittishness about
NAEP, Congress moved for the first time to construct a statutory foundation for it, more or less along the lines that NIE and ECS were already
following but specifying that reading, writing, and math be assessed on a
five-year cycle. To encourage states with districts and schools chosen for the
NAEP sample to participate—they were under no obligation to do so—the
new law authorized NAEP to provide "technical assistance" and to furnish
them with a (vaguely phrased) "statement of information collected by the
National Assessment."

Half of the skimpy two-page authorization consisted of specifications
for a mandatory "assessment policy committee," which was to be appointed
by the lead NAEP contractor but which had obligatory categories for membership (e.g., two state legislators, four teachers, one local school board
chair) and was to have delegated authority "to design and supervise the
conduct" of the assessment. Thus Congress added itself formally to the federal bodies setting ground rules for NAEP while introducing the requirement that a quasi-independent board consisting of key constituencies and
audiences was to make major decisions about its design and content, right
down to the "selection of goal statements and assessment items."

Congress was then also struggling with President Carter's proposal to
carve a cabinet-level Department of Education out of HEW—that measure
became law in late 1979—and controversy was intense about the proper
federal role in education. Considering the added sensitivity of a national

assessment project, we can readily understand lawmakers' impulse to superimpose an additional layer of governance—a Noah's Ark of constituency representatives—atop it.

Statutory backing plus a new five-year contract meant that NAEP would continue under ECS auspices, but it had been a close call. NAEP's seeming inutility, its irrelevance to—perhaps avoidance of—real-world policy concerns, would continue to raise basic questions about its worth and thus continue to menace its existence. So Carnegie's Frederic Mosher proposed yet another external review—an "assessment of the assessment"—this one underwritten by Carnegie (and two other foundations) and conducted by former labor secretary Willard Wirtz and Archie LaPointe himself. Mosher's concern, recalled LaPointe, was that NAEP's "funding from Congress was in decline, its data were not being widely used, and the project management seemed to be growing weary."[12]

Not coincidentally, those were among the criticisms that LaPointe and Wirtz rendered in an eighty-four-page report published in 1982: NAEP's data had drawn little public notice or interest; states were independently devising their own "minimum competency tests" and "[s]tudents are already spending a disturbing amount of time being tested to find out how the educational system is working"; and funding was declining such that "the NAEP program has already been cut in half," both because its costs were rising and because the (Reagan) administration was trimming the education budget, resulting in a program that "is presently operating at below marginal utility."[13]

Instead of calling it quits, however, they recommended an overhaul, which arose from their "central conclusion that the essential elements of the Assessment are critically important to the effective implementation of the new educational standards policy," which they associated with the push for minimal competency on the part of high school graduates. They listed a host of reasons for persevering with NAEP, including advantages that it already possessed, notably "its capacity—however incompletely it has been developed—to provide reliable and dependable information on what is happening to educational achievement throughout the country as a whole."

Inadvertently, they also illustrated—as the 1976 GAO report had done—a kind of adaptability or malleability in the various rationales and justifications for NAEP over the years: the assessment's capacity to be seen as a tool that might be deployed for various education-related jobs. These missions, assignments, and emphases would change over the years, changes that could be read into or superimposed on the national assessment and that in turn would lead to changes in how it functions.

The two-year study by Wirtz and LaPointe (much of it conducted by Paul E. Barton, then with the National Institute on Work and Learning) drew in a host of high-status advisers and suggestions from some 150 commenters. It yielded a baker's dozen of weighty recommendations, several of which were worthwhile tweaks, but most of which would require a radical overhaul of NAEP's design and operations. Wirtz and LaPointe stopped short, however, of recommending either state-level reporting of results or the setting of performance levels. Those would both come later, but in 1982 the authors termed them desirable yet politically unattainable.

Still, the changes they urged were fundamental, including a shift to assessing students in grades 4, 8, and 12 rather than ages nine, thirteen, and seventeen, and reporting results in an "aggregated" fashion rather than item by item. With an eye to making NAEP better known and more useful to more constituencies, they recommended that it provide "services to state and local assessments, testing, and standard-setting agencies." Also urged was creation of an "Educational Assessment Council," akin to the version Congress called for in 1978 but constituted separately from the NAEP contractor and charged with, among other things, interpreting the assessment results and communicating them to the many constituencies that should welcome such information.[14]

In short order, there followed what turned out to be the first of two NAEP overhauls during the 1980s. The action-forcing event was another new federal competition for the NAEP contract, the 1978 award to ECS having run its course. This time, however, ECS was not the only bidder: the Princeton-based Educational Testing Service, joined by Westat, proposed to take NAEP forward more or less according to the Wirtz-LaPointe redesign—and theirs turned out to be the winning bid.

The combination of the Wirtz-LaPointe report and NAEP's subsequent contract award to ETS could be seen as foreordained because, by the time the NIE issued its 1983 request for proposals, Anrig was leading ETS and LaPointe was working there.[15] Unsurprisingly, their proposal contained—in

LaPointe's recounting—twelve of the thirteen recommendations that had been made a year earlier by none other than LaPointe and Wirtz! Be that as it may, the accumulation of discontent over NAEP's first decade plus the shifting demands of—and on—American K–12 education argued for a makeover, and the Wirtz-LaPointe recommendations, bold as they were in some ways and limited in others, made sense at the time. They also led to ETS's (so far) almost-four-decade management of most NAEP operations, a high-visibility feather in that organization's enormous cap, and for many years a fine public platform for the able, affable, articulate LaPointe and the excellent team he put onto the project.

The alterations wrought by ETS were profound.[16] Included therein were important technical changes in the assessment itself. As recalled by Ina Mullis, who helped lead NAEP for more than two decades under the flags of both ECS and ETS, the winning proposal "described innovative methods and procedures for NAEP, such as balanced incomplete block designs for matrix sampling, item response theory (IRT) scaling, and extensive use of student- and school-level background data to frame the achievement results for policy analysis." Wonky as those may seem, they constituted a sea change in testing methods, analysis, and reporting. In Mullis's words, under the new design:

> The results were analyzed using the new IRT scaling technology, which provided the basis for a new reporting approach. Results for the nation and population subgroups, as well as trends over time, were summarized on numerical achievement scales (from 0 to 500). The transition to IRT scaling methods from Tyler's reliance on percentage correct on individual items was fundamental in enabling trend measurement from assessment to assessment.[17]

The year 1983 would be a watershed for American K–12 education without reference to NAEP, as it brought *A Nation At Risk*, the federal commission report that famously declared the United States to be in peril due to the poor performance of its schools. By then, and especially thereafter, many governors craved comparative data on their states' education performance, recognizing that their stunted economies were being held back in part by the weak education of their citizens. Yet all they could get by way of achievement data was Education Secretary Terrel Bell's infamous "wall chart," which depended largely on SAT and ACT scores that weren't representative of the entire student population and that said nothing about the performance of elementary and middle schools.[18]

By now, however, several states had experimented with the use of NAEP data to obtain information about their own students. The most consequential of these experiments began in 1984, when the Southern Regional Education Board (SREB), prodded by its chair, Tennessee governor Lamar Alexander, invited member states to join a pilot project that would use NAEP to supply data—and comparisons—for participating states. Three of them (Tennessee, Florida, and Virginia) opted in and, during spring 1985, a sample of their eleventh graders was given items from the 1984 national reading assessment, leading to a report on the "average scale score" of each state's students. Comparisons were then supplied, such that leaders of those three jurisdictions could see how their pupils were faring in comparison with each other and with the national and southeastern populations of seventeen-year-olds. The SREB also published the results in 1985, marking, to my knowledge, the first time that NAEP was publicly employed, even if somewhat indirectly, to show states how their students were doing. As the SREB proudly stated:

> These states have demonstrated that student achievement can be assessed in ways that make state, regional, and national comparisons possible. Prior to these results it had not been shown that the testing technology could be used in a plan that states would find feasible, nor had any states ever agreed to cooperate in a student testing program which would produce results that were comparable among states.[19]

In 1986, the SREB did it again, this time with eight participating states and using NAEP test items for both reading and writing.[20]

With more governors seeking reliable data on their schools' performance and their states' standing, and with SREB showing that this could be done via NAEP data, attitudes toward the regular deployment of NAEP in this way gradually shifted, although state school chiefs generally lagged behind their governors in making that shift. In 1984, a year after A Nation At Risk, even as the SREB was mounting its initial experiment, the Council of Chief State School Officers (CCSSO) held a vote on whether NAEP should contain a state-by-state element, and nineteen chiefs voted nay. (Twenty said aye, so the proposal squeaked through.)

The governors persisted. Meeting in Idaho in August 1985, the National

Governors Association (NGA) did something unprecedented. Prompted by then NGA chair Lamar Alexander—who turns up time and again in NAEP's history—it committed to a full year's focus on education, to be undertaken through seven task forces, each led by a governor and charged with answering one of the big questions that Alexander posed to his colleagues. This gave rise a year later to a set of sweeping reform recommendations that the governors, in effect, made to themselves and each other, as well as a five-year implementation-and-monitoring project that would endure into 1991.

Although none of the NGA task forces was charged with assessment per se, their reports were pervaded by an appetite for more and better outcomes data. And when Alexander was asked in 1986 whether there was a common thread among the task force findings, his response hinted at the extent to which the measurement of learning results would become essential. "The governors," he said,

> are ready for some old-fashioned horse-trading. We'll regulate less, if schools and school districts will produce better results. The kind of horse-trading we're talking about will change dramatically the way most American schools work. First, the governors want to help establish clear goals and better report cards, *ways to measure what students know and can do.* Then, we're ready to give up a lot of state regulatory control-even to fight for changes in the law to make that happen—*if* schools and school districts will be accountable for the results.[21] [emphasis added]

But how would anyone be able to ascertain their results without better assessments?

Soon after he became education secretary in early 1985, William J. Bennett directed his team to focus on the need to revamp NAEP yet again, this time in response to the nation's mounting appetite for achievement data more robust than anything the Excellence Commission had access to and more precise than anything the hungry governors could obtain. By September, he was able to outline seven principles for such an overhaul, principles that were discussed by ETS's assessment policy committee at a meeting in Dallas, after which Statistics Commissioner Emerson Elliott and I, then serving as assistant secretary for research and improvement, brainstormed possible mechanisms for moving from principles to action.

In January 1986, we proposed to Bennett that he name a blue-ribbon "study group" to tackle the matter, essentially a commission by another name (to be operated with private funding and to sidestep innumerable rules for government commissions). A few months later, that's exactly what we did. Lamar Alexander—then in his final year as Tennessee governor—agreed to chair it so long as we found someone else to do the heavy lifting. Fortuitously, former Stanford education dean H. Thomas James had just stepped down as founding president of the Spencer Foundation and was game to serve as vice chair and study director, bringing with him considerable credibility in the education and research communities. Several private foundations agreed to underwrite the project via grants to the National Academy of Education, which undertook to supply its own expert review of the study group's report and recommendations.

Besides Alexander and James, the group named by Bennett was a diverse and distinguished bunch of educators, public servants (including Hillary Rodham Clinton, then first lady of Arkansas), business leaders, and academics. The latter included Stanford professor Michael Kirst, who played a key role (along with Emerson Elliott and, if I may, myself) in developing analyses and recommendations that would bring NAEP up to date, would likely command reasonable consensus, and would pass muster with the National Academy.

Here's how *Education Week* reported those recommendations in March 1987 (while Alexander was enjoying a post-gubernatorial sabbatical with his family in Australia):

> Plans for a radically more ambitious and expensive version of the nation's "report card'" on student achievement were unveiled last week by a blue-ribbon panel convened by Secretary of Education William J. Bennett.
>
> In its report, the 22-member study group advocates redesigning the National Assessment of Educational Progress to provide state-by-state data, measure learning in more core subjects, include out-of-school 17-year-olds, and provide a larger sampling of private-school students.
>
> The panel also recommended a new governance structure for NAEP that would place its future direction in the hands of an independent

council "buffered from manipulation by any individual, level of government, or special-interest group in the field of education."

Such changes would "vastly improve our ability to keep track of what our children know and can do,'" the study group argues in "The Nation's Report Card: Improving the Assessment of Student Achievement."

Current assessments, it states, "are not producing answers to the questions most often asked at this moment in history by parents, by concerned citizens, and by educators."

At a press conference held here to release the report, Mr. Bennett warmly endorsed the panel's work. Few reform proposals of the 1980's, he said, would have a "more significant long-term impact" on education in the United States.[22]

The National Academy of Education largely concurred. Its fourteen-page commentary raised a number of technical and philosophical questions and caveats, including the funding challenge—a more-than-quadrupling of NAEP's budget would be required—but registered overall support for the study group's key recommendations.

This would turn out to be a watershed moment. As Kirst said at the press conference, "What is being discussed today wouldn't even have been considered 20 years ago. Anyone who had proposed it would have been laughed out of the room." American Federation of Teachers President Albert Shanker, who was part of the academy's review group, declared that strengthening NAEP was "one of the most important things we can accomplish in this round" of education reform.

The stickiest wicket, of course, was the study group's recommendation that NAEP undertake to report "achievement in each of the fifty states and the District of Columbia," which it termed "the single most important change" urged in its report. But the glacier of resistance to such reporting (and the comparisons that would inevitably follow) was already melting. The governors wanted it. The SREB had demonstrated its feasibility. And the "chiefs" were gradually coming around.

Because nobody was suggesting that NAEP also report at the district level, the local superintendents who had raised such a ruckus in the 1960s had little to fight about—and by now they had other challenges to worry about. For 1987 brought another disruptive development on the testing front when a West Virginia physician named John J. Cannell jolted the education community with word that he "had surveyed all 50 states and discovered that no state is below average at the elementary level on any of the six major nationally normed, commercially available tests," which were what nearly every school system in the land was using to gauge its students' learning and then report back to parents, voters, and taxpayers.[23]

Cannell also declared that 90 percent of local school districts were claiming average student scores that exceeded the national average and "more than 70 percent of the students tested nationwide are told they are performing above the national average." His out-of-the-blue study was swiftly dubbed the "Lake Wobegon Report" after the mythical town popularized by Garrison Keillor in which "all the women are strong, all the men are good-looking, and all the children are above average."

Cannell was no social scientist, yet his riveting allegations turned out to be essentially correct. The US Education Department invited several of the nation's foremost psychometricians to see if they could replicate his findings. Which in essence they did.[24] It turned out that most states and localities, in tacit or overt collusion with test publishers, were availing themselves of the misleading and manipulable elements of norm-referenced tests and, in many cases, were also "teaching to the test."

Cannell's report and its subsequent validation had repercussions. They helped to discredit norm-based "standardized" testing. They also prompted a number of states to develop new schemes for measuring and reporting student progress, now more often the criterion-referenced variety that incorporate learning expectations rather than simply report average performance. They may have fed public mistrust of the "education establishment." They certainly helped catalyze the "national education goals" process that would shortly get underway. And they obviously underscored the need, expressed in the Alexander-James report and the National Academy of Education's commentary thereon, to expand and improve NAEP, which was the closest thing we then had—and have today—to a trustworthy report card on educational achievement in the United States.

Even as it was being tasked with weightier responsibilities, NAEP was showing itself to be a delicate instrument, a complex apparatus with many moving parts, such that a few grains of sand in one gear can throw the whole thing out of kilter. A vivid example had appeared in 1986 in what became known—infamous, really—as the "NAEP reading anomaly." Abruptly, the reading scores of nine- and seventeen-year-olds—but not thirteen-year-olds—on that year's assessment were markedly lower than just two years earlier. Was this evidence of truly diminished reading prowess or possibly an artifact of various changes that NCES and ETS were making in the NAEP machinery?

ETS undertook an elaborate postmortem that yielded nothing definitive, declaring that "[w]hile some hypotheses, such as inaccuracies in sampling, scaling, and quality control, were ruled out beyond any reasonable doubt, results of the studies are inconclusive."[25]

This wishy-washy review didn't satisfy NCES leaders, who empaneled their own fifteen-member expert group to examine the "anomaly." It concluded (in 1988) that technical changes in test design probably accounted for a decline in the scores of relatively weak readers—and also that (for whatever reason) the 1984 scores might have been abnormally high. Importantly, the group (led by Stanford psychometrician Edward Haertel) also recommended a series of measures that NCES and NAEP contractors should put in place—audits, technical reviews, and such—to minimize the recurrence of such glitches and to be ready to explain any that may occur in the future. "Nobody can guarantee something like this won't happen again," Haertel said, "But there should be procedures in place so that if a drop like this did occur, we would have enough confidence in the results we can believe even a surprising change. If the confidence in the assessment is such that when something surprising shows up, people look for other explanations, it's not doing us much good."[26]

Two months earlier, in a rare example of cooperation between the Reagan administration and a Democratic Congress, lawmakers had reauthorized NAEP along the lines recommended by the Alexander-James study group and ratified by the National Academy. Henceforth, it would be more directly and explicitly an undertaking of the Department of Education, with the NCES commissioner made responsible for its operation, but with an independent governing board—no longer a creature of the contractor— charged with setting its policies and determining its content. Moreover, NAEP was given authority to generate state-level data on a "trial" basis and also to set what were called "achievement levels" against which to report student results.

In September 1988, as Reagan's second term neared an end and Secretary Bennett and his team began to pack for our departure from the Education Department, he named the first twenty-three members to the new National Assessment Governing Board. He also asked me to serve as its first chair.[27]

The next few years, as we shall see, turned out to be exceptionally eventful.

CHAPTER 4

Creating "The Nation's Report Card"

T WENTY-FIVE YEARS after Frank Keppel's initial query to Ralph Tyler about the possibility of creating some sort of achievement barometer for the United States, the sickly child and gawky adolescent that NAEP resembled when young was turning into a fairly sturdy adult. The test design itself had been reshaped and rendered far more informative, which boosted its value in an era with a keener appetite for such information. The project enjoyed backing in Congress (mainly in the Senate), protectors in the executive branch, and support from many state leaders. Its lead contractor was widely respected—and large enough that the NAEP contract was not a matter of life and death for it. The assessment's new look was endorsed by a wide spectrum of experts. And it had acquired a new governance arrangement meant to enhance its legitimacy, independence, and stability.

That was 1988. Yet the very next year brought another seismic shift in the ground under NAEP. In this chapter, we first explain how that jolt created an unprecedented challenge-cum-opportunity for the assessment that would eventually transform its role in American education. Then we turn to NAEP's new governing board and its dual response to the new demands. Finally, we look at the launch of state-by-state assessments and begin to plumb the issues associated with benchmarking student achievement.

With the election of George H. W. Bush, the White House was home to its first-ever self-styled "education president," and eight months after his inauguration he convened forty-nine of the governors in Charlottesville,

Virginia, for a bipartisan education "summit."[1] Those two days—with a key role played by Arkansas's Bill Clinton—led to agreement on a wildly ambitious set of "national education goals" for the US to achieve by century's end. Among them, Goal 3 turned out to hold big implications for NAEP: "By the year 2000, American students will leave grades four, eight, and twelve having demonstrated competency in challenging subject matter including English, mathematics, science, history, and geography."[2]

It was a grand aspiration, never mind the unlikelihood that it could be achieved in a decade—but how would anybody know whether progress toward it was being made? Who would define "competency" in those five core subjects and what measures would track how many students were getting there? Just as perplexing: who would define "challenging subject matter" and create some sort of link between a subject's degree of challenge and students' levels of competency? Was it just coincidence that the summiteers fixed on the same three grade levels that NAEP now tested?

As of the summit's conclusion, in fact, the United States had *no* mechanism by which to monitor progress toward that optimistic target, no agreed-upon way of specifying it, nor yet any reliable gauge for reporting achievement state by state. But such tools were obviously necessary for tracking the fate of education goals established by state governors and the president.

They wanted benchmarks, too, and wanted them attached to NAEP. In March 1990, just six months after the summit, the National Governors Association encouraged NAGB to develop "performance standards," explaining that the "National Education Goals will be meaningless unless progress toward meeting them is measured accurately and adequately, and reported to the American people." This, declared the NGA, meant that three things had to happen:

> First, what students need to know must be defined . . . Second, when it is clear what students need to know, it must be determined whether they know it . . . The governors urge the National Assessment Governing Board to begin work to set national performance goals in the subject areas in which NAEP will be administered. This does not mean establishing standards for individual competence; rather, it requires setting targets for increases in the percentage of students performing

at the higher levels of the NAEP scale. Third, measurements must be accurate, comparable, appropriate, and constructive.[3]

A few months later, the White House and NGA established—by executive action that Congress would modify and adopt several years later—a National Education Goals Panel (NEGP) to monitor progress toward the end-of-century targets. It consisted of senior administration officials (including Lamar Alexander, now secretary of education) and half a dozen governors, as well as (ex officio) the bipartisan congressional leadership. The new panel then swiftly named a half dozen expert "resource groups" to advise it on how best to track movement toward the six goals.

The resource group assigned to focus on student achievement (Goal 3) met early in 1991 and emerged with recommendations that included a major role for NAEP:

> The Resource Group recommends that data from NAEP be used to report trends over time in national student achievement. The report should include data on the performance levels of the lowest achievers, racial and ethnic minorities, male and female achievement, and the achievement of students attending public and private schools . . . [Going forward], an expanded NAEP can serve as the program monitoring component of this system. The group recommends that it be maintained in its current matrix sampling form. States and localities should be authorized to use NAEP results and the frequency of assessment in all major subject areas should be increased.[4]

The resource group (of which I was a member) actually went considerably further, also recommending creation of a national examination system akin to those in many other advanced countries, to be erected atop a "carefully developed national educational standards framework." Such a system would serve, said the group, "to motivate student and teacher effort to high levels of academic achievement."

That was too great a leap for its time—and arguably still is—but the NAEP portions of the group's plan dovetailed nicely with weighty moves already underway on two fronts within the new NAGB: the launch of state-by-state reporting and the creation of student performance benchmarks, to become known as "achievement levels."

The 1988 legislation had dealt with the issue of state-by-state reporting via a classic congressional compromise, in this case between a House that wanted no part of state-level NAEP and a Senate (mostly Edward M. Kennedy and his staff) that strongly agreed with the Alexander-James panel (and the Reagan administration) that such data had become essential. What emerged was authorization for a two-stage "trial" assessment in willing states, to consist of eighth graders in math in 1990 and, two years later, eighth graders (again) in math plus fourth graders in both math and reading, after which there was to be an evaluation of how well this had worked.

Although the governors' appetite for comparable achievement data, combined with the Alexander-James emphasis on it, led to the congressional action that legitimized this pilot version of state-by-state NAEP, the burden of making it happen would fall on the chief state school officers as well as NAGB and NCES—and the "chiefs'" cooperation was essential for getting enough states to participate in what would remain a voluntary activity until 2002. That meant enlisting their national organization, the Council of Chief State School Officers (CCSSO), as a working partner not only in recruiting states to volunteer but also in the design of the assessments in which they would be participating.

In a 2004 essay, the late Ramsay Selden, who had served as CCSSO's lead staffer on assessment, focused on the big initial challenge of agreeing on "what to test" in those trial assessments. "Because states set their own priorities for education," he recalled, "it was conceivable that large differences in what was taught might exist among the states. In that case, consensus would be difficult if not impossible."[5]

It stood to reason that state education leaders would resist comparisons based on assessments of things their schools weren't even teaching. The absence of any sort of national curriculum—or, at the time, even statewide academic standards—could turn this into a very sticky wicket. It certainly made NAEP's job more complicated, for its assessment frameworks and test items had not previously needed to embody this sort of agreement.

CCSSO threw itself into the quest, teaming up with NCES and NAGB to "develop consensus frameworks for the state-by-state assessments." The first of these—for math—was ready in time for the 1990 assessment and was followed by kindred frameworks for six more subjects. "This process," wrote Selden, "resulted in a statement of the subject matter and related cognitive skills to be assessed in each subject." That "process," however, was elaborate and protracted, consisting of multiple large committees and several stages of review, including scrutiny by interested states. Through it, Selden explained, "attempts were made to identify current directions of instruction in the country, major approaches in the field, and the extent of diversity among state curricula, local curricula, and teacher practice. This was seen as an essential base on which to make decisions concerning subject matter." But they didn't try to dumb it down: in Selden's recollection, "A gratifying quality of this effort was that, in every subject, the opportunity was taken to set an ambitious standard."[6]

This was a big shift in several ways. In its earlier manifestations, NAEP content was shaped chiefly by scholars and subject specialists who focused on the elements of their respective disciplines that they deemed most important for children to learn. Now, however, what NAEP tested had to harmonize to a considerable extent with what was actually being taught—and how and when it was taught—in American public schools. It also had to balance the whats and hows of schools located in very different states and circumstances. With practicing educators and education leaders now much involved in the decision process, as well as a governing board comprised largely of practicing educators, NAEP was also pushed to try to keep up with pedagogical trends. "For example," Selden recalled, "many participants [in the consensus process] wanted the assessments to include open-ended items or other activities beyond multiple-choice tests."

Such initiatives pointed toward more modern and thorough testing of student achievement, but they placed pressure on item writers more familiar with the "bubble tests" that ETS typically devised and that NAEP had theretofore relied on. Incorporating more complex questions also added to assessment costs and complexity and took longer to score, adding to the challenge of speedy reporting. Moreover, the inclusion of such items gave—and today still gives—conniptions to those who fret that NAEP tests should not be altered in ways that "break the trend line." But NAGB and NCES bent over backward to accommodate the CCSSO-led consensus process, which in time would enhance NAEP's value to the nation as well as its legitimacy in the eyes of educators, while furthering a gradual shift toward greater state "ownership" of what also remained a national assessment.

Meanwhile, NCES and its NAEP contractors were struggling with the many technical issues that came with states' inclusion in the assessment. For example, the federal contractors were expected to administer the tests to students in the national sample while local staffers managed the state samples. But what if they administered the tests differently? How then to control for such variability and equate the resulting data? How to avoid a new "Lake Wobegon" effect? "The technical solution," wrote NCES leaders Emerson Elliott and Gary Phillips, "was to augment the state sample of schools in order to embed a small, nationally representative sample of schools within the state sample."[7] Yet not every state was participating. (The 1990 math trial ultimately engaged thirty-seven of them, plus the District of Columbia and two territories. Two years later, forty-one states took part in the reading assessment.) And those that did volunteer, per the 1988 legislation, were supposed to share in the cost of doing so.

How big would those state samples need to be? Would they be the same for Delaware and California? How to ensure that "the precision of the estimates for each state" would be "about the same as for the four regions [of the country] that had long been reported for NAEP in the national samples"? Would private schools be included in the state samples, as NCES was striving to do for the country as a whole? (Some states have many private schools, while others have almost none.) And what if states wanted larger samples so they could do more refined analyses of their own data?

It's little wonder that, when the time came for the congressionally mandated evaluation of the first two "trial" state assessments, multiple issues would arise and many changes would be urged. We'll return to these in the next chapter.

As we've seen, the education goals agreed upon in Charlottesville lent urgency to the quest for gauges of "competency" and "challenging subject matter." Yet this wasn't entirely unprecedented. Although building such benchmarks into an overhauled NAEP had not been hugely important to the Alexander-James panel, it had loomed large in the National Academy of Education review: "For each content area," the academy declared in words reminiscent of the GAO's 1976 evaluation, "NAEP should articulate clear descriptions of performance levels, descriptions that might be analogous to such craft rankings as novice, journeyman, highly competent, and expert . . . Much more important than scale scores is the reporting of the proportions of individuals in various categories of mastery at specific ages."[8]

In crafting the 1988 legislation, the initiative came from the Senate, with modifications and compromises subsequently negotiated with the House of Representatives. The final act made the new governing board responsible for "[i]dentifying appropriate achievement goals for each age and grade in each subject area to be tested under the National Assessment." This wording, a Kennedy staffer later explained, was "deliberately ambiguous" because nobody in Congress was sure how best to express this novel, somewhat nebulous, and potentially tempestuous assignment.

This amorphous provision of the law drew little attention at the outset, but after Charlottesville it became important. The NGA wanted such "achievement goals" and NAGB was already working on them and indeed had been since its second meeting in January 1989. At that session, South Carolina governor Richard Riley, newly appointed to the board (and later to serve as Bill Clinton's secretary of education), asked whether NAGB was "just . . . involved in . . . deciding what the child does know; . . . or should we be into what the child should know?"[9]

As board chair, I replied that "[w]e have a statutory responsibility that is the biggest thing ahead of us to—it says here: 'identify appropriate achievement goals for each age and grade in each subject area to be tested.' . . . It is in our assignment."

Yes, I pushed. I felt the board had to try to do this. But, as education historian Maris Vinovskis recorded, "[M]embers responded positively to these remarks" and "NAGB moved quickly to create appropriate standards for the forthcoming 1990 NAEP mathematics assessment."

By early 1990, reported Vinovskis, the board "listened to seven hours of testimony on the proposal to create grade-level achievement goals." Education Secretary Lauro Cavazos sent a letter encouraging us to move forward with this work, and AFT President Albert Shanker also endorsed the creation of performance standards, while cautioning against setting just one. In my memory, Shanker warned that, if we had only one, we would set it too low. Vinovskis's chronicle has it slightly different. Shanker, he wrote, worried that "having a single standard . . . might cause schools to focus only on helping those near the cutoff point, while ignoring those well above or below that mark."[10]

The board's staff proceeded to recommend three achievement levels, and in May 1990 NAGB voted to move forward and begin reporting the proportion of students at each level. Built into its definition of the middle level, dubbed "proficient," was the actual language of Goal 3: "This central level represents solid academic performance for each grade tested—4, 8 and 12. It will reflect a consensus that students reaching this level have demonstrated *competency over challenging subject matter*." [emphasis added] Lower and higher levels, termed "basic" and "advanced," were also specified.[11]

Thus, just months after Charlottesville, three months before the Goals Panel was even established, and a year before its expert resource group recommended a heightened role for NAEP vis-à-vis the national goals, a standard-setting and performance-monitoring process for Goal 3 was already in the works. I will cheerfully accept responsibility, as chair, for nudging my NAGB colleagues to take an early lead on this—but in the event they needed minimal encouragement!

It can be argued that NAEP's inexperienced governing board was jumping the gun, beguiled by its crafty leader into treating something permitted under the new law as if it were an urgent requirement, and reaching deep into risky territory before even solidifying its own legitimacy. Yet ETS had already been deploying benchmarks of its own for NAEP. Its innovative use of item response theory and creation of a stable 500-point scale, common across subjects as well as over time, and vertically aligned across NAEP's three grade levels, had opened the door to performance monitoring and created the possibility of superimposing some kind of standards—cutpoints, one might say—on those scales so as to be able to report how many test-takers were reaching what levels.

Within two years of winning the NAEP contract, ETS had done precisely that. The "Reading Report Card" it issued in 1985 reviewed thirteen years of reading achievement over four NAEP cycles and did so by "anchoring" five "levels of proficiency" to intervals on the 500-point scale. Achievement at the 150 level was dubbed "rudimentary," for example; at the 250 level it was "intermediate," and at 350 it was "advanced."

Anchoring made it possible for analysts, to report, for instance, that 60 percent of thirteen-year-olds were "intermediate" readers in 1984, while just 18 percent of nine-year-olds were. (No nine-year-olds were "advanced," but 5 percent of 17-year-olds were.) They could also show change over time, observing, for example, that "[b]etween 1971 and 1984, at both the basic and intermediate levels, the proportion of 13-year-old Black students increased some 15 percentage points." They could illustrate with examples of test questions representative of pupil achievement at each level and could make perceptive observations about which kinds of skills which kids were getting better at—or not.

It was an impressive achievement, devised after careful analysis by ETS's Ina Mullis, Al Beaton, and their colleagues. The report card's technical appendix explained, for instance, that "[i]n the scale anchoring process, NAEP selected sets of items that were good discriminators between proficiency levels. The criterion used to identify such items was that students at any given level would have at least an 80 percent probability of success with these reading tasks, while the students at the next lower level would have less than a 50 percent probability of success."[12]

This mode of reporting had made NAEP much more informative, especially regarding changes over time, yet it wasn't quite what the third national goal required or what the new governing board was hastening to create. Although the ETS version described how many students could do what, it was not prescriptive. It did not say how many *should* be able to do what. Once the national goals were set, some form of prescription would be necessary to monitor progress toward "competency in challenging subject matter." It was now important to define both "competency" and "challenging" in normative terms, not simply to pin the term "adept," say, to level 300 on a 500-point scale. NAGB believed its job was to frame proficiency as a "should" that was connected to mastery of "challenging" subject matter; then to determine what point on the scale denoted proficiency for each of the three grades being assessed; and then to calculate and report how many young Americans were getting there—and how many were not.

This would prove to be a heavy lift for a new board whose members were still getting to know each other, form committees, ponder their multifaceted duties, navigate ties with NCES, the secretary's office, and other elements of the Education Department, peer over their shoulders at Congress, establish diplomatic relations with America's innumerable education groups, and engage competent staff. Why rush to take on this demanding project, too? Surely it would prove contentious. Which indeed it did. In fact, NAGB staff testing specialist Mary Lyn Bourque later wrote that "developing student performance standards" was "undoubtedly the board's most controversial responsibility."[13]

To carry out its May 1990 resolution to proceed with that development and hastening in hopes that their new achievement levels would be ready in time to report that year's math results, NAGB and its staff and contractors had to tackle myriad issues. The foremost challenge at the outset was how—and who—to set these levels.

As Bourque wrote, the first big decision was to use "a modified Angoff method" with "a panel of judges who would develop descriptions of the levels and the cut scores on the NAEP score scale." But "[w]hile the policy was simple and straightforward," she added, "its implementation was complex and very contentious."

The term "modified Angoff method" has now reverberated for three decades in connection with NAEP and its achievement levels. Named for ETS-based testing psychologist William H. Angoff, this procedure is widely used to set standards on various tests. At its heart is a panel of subject-matter experts who examine every question and estimate how many test-takers might answer it correctly. The Angoff score is commonly defined as the lowest cutoff score that a "minimally qualified candidate" is likely to achieve on a test. The "modified" Angoff method uses the actual test performance of a valid student sample to adjust those predicted cutoffs in case reality doesn't accord with expert judgments.

There is no perfect way to go about standard-setting in any endeavor that involves human performance—think about judges at the Olympics striving to score athletes' prowess at diving or figure skating—and any method that's chosen will generate controversy. Such controversy will be especially intense when the chosen method is then used to report on—and judge and compare—the performance of America's 55 million strong and extremely diverse K–12 student population, divided across 50 states, 14,000 districts and almost 35,000 private schools. It's one thing for referees of high school students' performance on Advanced Placement exams to decide whether an individual test paper warrants a score of 1, 2, 3, 4, or 5. That's a private testing program, participation in it is voluntary, and scores apply to individual test-takers. It's quite another thing to judge the performance of groups of students and units of government in a universal, Washington-run program.

At the heart of most of the recurrent fracases over NAEP's reporting standards—that is, NAGB's achievement levels—is the plain fact that, in the end, they do rely on human judgment rather than science. It's not quite the same as Olympic diving scores or AP exam scores, because the board's role is to set the rules, parameters, and expectations, not to engage in actual scoring. Still, we're dealing with human judgments, not scientific certainties. Moreover, the board was striving for its "proficient" level to function as the equivalent of "competency in challenging subject matter" as decreed in Charlottesville. This meant the judgments it was applying and reporting would also reverberate through the realms of national and state policy and politics.

As the process got underway, there were stumbles, missteps, and miscalculations. Bourque terms the maiden voyage of standard-setting a "learning experience for both the board and the consultants it engaged." She observes that

> NAGB did not realize the resources it would take to carry out a project of this magnitude, nor had NAGB members thought through many of the specific details of the process. Such questions as who should be impaneled as judges, how long would setting standards take, what kind of training should the judges have, how much information about NAEP do the judges need in order to complete their task, and many other questions went unanswered until it became clear that decisions were required. Consequently, the inaugural effort was carried out on an ad hoc basis.[14]

The first round of standard-setting took three days, which proved insufficient, leading to follow-up meetings and a dry run in four states. It was still shaky, however, leading the board to dub the 1990 cycle a trial and start afresh for 1992. It also engaged an outside team to evaluate its handiwork.

Those reviewers didn't think much of it, reaching some conclusions that in hindsight had merit as well as a number that did not.[15] But they also fouled their nest—and their relationship with NAGB—by distributing their draft critique without the board's assent to almost forty other individuals, "many of whom," writes Bourque, "were well connected with congressional leaders, their staffs, and other influential policy leaders in Washington, DC." This episode led board members to conclude that their consultants were keener to kill off the entire level-setting effort than to perfect its methodology, resulting in an abrupt termination of their contract. This also qualified as the first big public dustup over the creation and application of achievement levels.

But that was just the beginning. "During the entire last decade," Bourque wrote in 2004, "a continuous barrage of evaluation reports provided extensive qualitative and quantitative analyses of the NAEP achievement levels. One researcher has said that NAEP has the most evaluated student performance standards in the world."[16]

We shall return more than once to the ups and downs of achievement levels.

As if launching a new governance structure, mounting state assessments for the first time, and devising inherently contentious performance standards weren't enough burden for NAEP, as the 1990s unfolded, some wanted to pile even more onto the national assessment.

If it was expandable, and would now be employed to yield reliable and comparable data on states, then why not districts, too? Individual schools? Maybe even individual students? Why not go whole hog and build a national examination system, whether constructed as part of NAEP or associated in some way with it, along the lines that the Goals Panel's resource group envisioned?

That's more or less what President Bush himself proposed in 1991 as part of his "America 2000" plan, an ambitious, multifaceted strategy for moving the country toward those lofty national goals. On the testing front, it had two parts: first, the creation of an entire new set of "American Achievement Tests," described by the White House as "a system of voluntary examinations" to be made available "for all fourth, eighth and twelfth grade students in the five core subjects." And second, the expansion of NAEP into an instrument that could—at states' option—be deployed "at district and school levels."[17]

Congress wanted in on the national goals venture, too. In 1994, at President Clinton's behest, it would pass the "Goals 2000" Act—thus catching up with and adding cars to the train that had been moving since Charlottesville—as well as a reauthorization of the Elementary and Secondary Education Act that pressed states to develop their own academic standards and assessments: a precursor to No Child Left Behind and a move that would drag NAEP in as independent auditor of state standards and achievement claims. But it also called for appointment of a "National Council on Education Standards and Testing" (with the unfortunate acronym of NCEST). This unwieldy thirty-two-member body (myself included), cochaired by two governors, recommended an extremely ambitious effort to develop national academic standards, an intricate plan to construct new assessments that would be linked to those standards and reported at the individual pupil level, and a permanent twenty-one-member "National Education Standards and Assessment Council" to manage the whole thing. Within that structure, NAEP—and NAGB's new achievement levels—would "function as the program/system monitor."[18]

Some of that actually started to happen, as the Education Department and National Endowment for the Humanities made grants to half a dozen groups to develop academic standards for their respective subjects—standards that proved voluminous, volatile, and sometimes ideological, and that, save for math, got little or no traction in the K–12 world.[19] But the rest of NCEST's recommendations fell victim to fears of governmental overreach, of inappropriate centralization of K–12 education—Secretary Alexander began to refer with trepidation to a "national school board"—and of the council's heavy emphasis on school inputs, resources, and services (known as "opportunity to learn" standards) in addition to achievement standards and actual school results.

Half a decade later, President Clinton tried again, using his 1997 State of the Union address to propose the creation of "voluntary national tests"—soon dubbed VNT—in fourth-grade reading and eighth-grade math. These were intended to be "based" on NAEP and employ NAGB's achievement levels. Eager to get the new tests operational before Clinton's second term ended, the Department of Education hastily engaged contractors to develop the new tests. Although NAEP and its governing board were not directly involved with the original plan, opposition to that plan soon arose on both left and right, particularly from GOP congressman Bill Goodling, the powerful chair of the House education committee. After much to-ing and fro-ing, Clinton and Education Secretary Dick Riley moved to relocate their VNT plan within the NAEP structure. In a radio address in late August, Clinton declared that in response to the "worry that the federal government would play too large a role in developing the test . . . I have instructed my staff to rewrite our proposal to make sure that these tests are developed not by the Department of Education but by an independent, bipartisan Board created by Congress many years ago." By which, of course, he meant NAGB.[20]

The Senate endorsed that move, but in mid-September the Goodling-influenced House voted overwhelmingly to ban all funds for the VNT project. A shaky compromise was eventually reached, and the governing board took over the test-development project—eventually creating thousands of new test items—but political opposition continued to mount, and Congress effectively wound down the entire venture by forbidding actual deployment of the resulting tests.

Through all the *Sturm und Drang* of the period, the national assessment endured, and its governing board forged ahead. Though often embattled, especially on the matter of achievement levels, its work was contributing to NAEP's emergence as the central barometer of pupil achievement and school performance across the US. By mid-decade, the board had separated what became known as "main NAEP" from long-term monitoring with trend lines dating back to the early 1970s. This Solomon-like decision sought to balance two incompatible goals: on the one hand, securing unbroken trend data that would document ups and downs in student achievement over the decades by—in effect—giving the same test over and over to changing pupil populations; and, on the other hand, periodically updating its assessment frameworks and test items to keep pace with evolving academic standards, curricula, pedagogy, and testing practices in the core subjects taught in American schools. Updating what's assessed and how that's done risks "breaking the trend line." Yet preserving a static test over long periods results in data that get further and further out of sync with what's actually happening in US classrooms. Feeling responsible for both missions and with no obvious amalgam in reach, NAGB opted to have it both ways. This important decision resulted in NAEP's ability to carry out the twin mandates but also led to confusion as to "which NAEP to believe." And it put pressure on the budget, pressure that the board eased by moving to confine the long-term trend assessment to reading and math and to administer it less often.[21]

From beyond American borders came a kindred impulse to compare and benchmark student achievement and educational accomplishment among and between nations. A little-known Amsterdam-based group of academics called the International Association for the Evaluation of Educational Achievement (IEA) had been piloting multinational studies of student achievement since 1960, and its work began to attract wide visibility in the 1980s with its comparative studies of math and science in grades 4 and 8. Post-Charlottesville—where another lofty national goal called for the US to become "first in the world" in math and science—Education Department leaders played a key role in reshaping those IEA studies from intermittent, research-centered tests into more regular comparisons of country performance. This evolved into the "Trends in International Math and Science" program that we know today as TIMSS, which the US has regularly taken part in since 1995. Because TIMSS matches the end-of-elementary and end-of-middle-school grade levels that NAEP assesses and is designed to test what's taught and learned in schools, it's relatively straightforward to construct "linking studies" that not only compare the US with other countries but also compare individual states with other countries. That's how we learned, for example, that Massachusetts eighth graders performed almost as well as their counterparts in Japan in math in 2011, while Texas was tied with Israel. Perhaps more important, we learned from the same study that the US overall (as well as the state of Arkansas) was tied with Slovenia, well behind Canada, Russia, and the "Asian tigers."[22]

In a move that would eventually lead to international comparisons with a much higher profile than TIMSS, the Paris-based Organisation for Economic Co-operation and Development (OECD), a multinational body that enrolls most of the planet's advanced countries, began during the 1990s to develop what became the Programme for International Student Assessment (PISA). Though modeled in many respects on NAEP—a sample-based, large-scale assessment with a stable vertical scoring scale—it also differs in key ways. PISA tests fifteen-year-olds, which in the United States generally means ninth graders, but it's age- rather than grade-based. More fundamentally, PISA does not claim to be school-centric or curriculum-related. Rather, it's an assessment of the overall prowess of a country's young people at age fifteen. As a briefing paper by the Congressional Research Service explains, PISA "aims to measure the achievement of students at the end of their compulsory education. The PISA is not designed to measure 'school-based learning' and is not designed to be aligned with academic content standards. Instead, PISA intends to measure students' preparation for life and focuses on science, reading, and mathematics problems within a real-life context."[23] This, however, can prove extremely revealing and sometimes quite alarming. Germany, for example, famously suffered from "PISA-shock" after its leaders saw their first results (in 2001) and thereupon embarked on an ambitious set of education reforms.[24]

PISA's construction makes it more difficult than TIMSS to align with NAEP, so to coax any valid comparative results from it, an individual state must opt to participate directly in the testing as if it were a country—and must pay for it. Four states (plus Puerto Rico) have done that at least once, and although no US state took part in the most recent (2018) round of PISA, the results of such participation can be quite revealing.[25]

Though NAEP itself has never reached beyond US borders, its design, test specifications, item types, and forms of reporting have had considerable influence on the emergence of credible international testing programs as well as the development of other large-scale assessments. Most prominent were those that states were developing—and in a few years would find themselves required by law to administer. As that happened, NAEP's role in American education would continue to grow, this time as auditor, arbiter, and truth squad. We resume this saga in the next chapter.

CHAPTER 5

Auditor, Judge, and Unwitting Political Player

AS THE TWENTIETH CENTURY wheezed toward a close, much had changed in US education, including a higher-profile role for NAEP. As Ina Mullis, who helped lead it for many years (and is now at Boston College and a leader of the multinational TIMSS program), writes, "Compared with the little-known NAEP that existed prior to the 1990s, the state-by-state assessments had led to increased attention on NAEP by a 'host of interested parties, from the nation's capital to state assemblies and local school districts.'"[1]

In this chapter, we see the attention level rise even higher as changing federal policy recasts NAEP's role, bringing greater scrutiny by critics and heightened political risks, the mandating and regularizing of state participation, the introduction of district-level reporting, and nearly nonstop controversy over how to report assessment results.

As we have seen, getting state-level NAEP right was no walk in the park, both because of myriad technical issues and because it began to turn the national assessment, conceived as a low-stakes barometer of student achievement, into a more politically sensitive enterprise, both for state leaders and—as we shall see—potentially for national figures.

On the technical side, the congressionally mandated evaluation of the first two rounds of the "trial state assessment" in 1990 and 1992 gave rise to three volumes of analysis, criticism, and recommendations from the National Academy of Education, which had contracted to carry out the evaluation and then named a fourteen-member panel (and thirteen-member staff!) to do the heavy lifting.[2]

The academy ultimately concluded that state-level NAEP was technically feasible and should continue but said it should remain labeled a "trial" and—of course—should remain subject to ongoing (and seemingly constant) evaluations. Many of the recommended changes were ambitious, complicated, and costly—leading to a final recommendation that Congress appropriate more money for NAEP, including enough to subsidize "an annual state NAEP in at least one subject at three grade levels."

Before getting to those recommendations, however, the academy panel flagged numerous issues concerning the methodology of state NAEP and the challenges of generating and reporting state-level results that could be legitimately, fairly, and validly compared with each other and with the country as a whole. Many involved consistency of sampling and test administration, and some dealt with issues that would dog NAEP for years to come. Most prominent was the variability from state to state in test participation by students with disabilities and/or limited English proficiency. For example, the exclusion of pupils (in 1992) owing to language issues ranged "from less than one percent in Alabama to . . . 10–11 percent of the fourth graders in California."[3] So long as states were voluntarily participating in NAEP—and sharing in the cost of doing so, as well as managing their own test administration—NCES and its contractors could set participation norms but obviously had no sway over states' differing demographics and not much ability to enforce uniform criteria for exclusion of students from the test population. That can make a big difference, as score comparisons are shaky if one jurisdiction tests a sample of 99 percent of all its pupils while another samples just 90 percent.

The panel's report also devoted twenty-four pages to the "content validity of the assessment," that is, how well did NAEP's multifaceted "consensus projects" yield frameworks for testing reading and math that created "an appropriate balance between established practice [in those subjects] and cutting-edge advances in education."

This balancing act has challenged NAEP from the outset but grew trickier when state assessments commenced, due to the difficult judgments needed in responding to what many different jurisdictions were actually teaching their students in addition to what experts in these disciplines believed they should be teaching. Nor is that the end of it, for once the subject frameworks are constructed, test items must be developed that reasonably reflect what's in the frameworks as well as meeting sundry psychometric standards.

In the end, while the academy's review surfaced a number of issues and recommendations for the future of state participation in NAEP, it was bullish about continuing this practice. That—as we shall see—was in vivid contrast to its view of NAGB's fledgling achievement levels.

State participation would remain optional until passage of No Child Left Behind in 2002, but most jurisdictions wanted in. In the 1996 math assessment, for example, all but seven states took part (along with the District of Columbia, Guam, and the Defense Department schools).[4] That same year, state level reporting of NAEP data having proven itself, Congress dropped the word "trial" from the state assessment program.

This was two years after Congress passed the "Goals 2000" and "Improving America's Schools" acts, which accelerated the development of state-specific academic standards, the adoption of new state testing regimes, and the gradual construction of results-based school accountability systems. As tabulated by analyst Chad Aldeman, "States began implementing school accountability systems in the early 1990s, but by the time of NCLB's enactment in 2002 just 29 states had adopted some form of consequential accountability system. Another 14 relied on [test-based] transparency alone, and the remaining 7 states did nothing."[5]

Did those accountability systems—and the standards and tests they rested on—have integrity? Were they designed to reveal problems and motivate achievement gains or to whitewash the status quo? With Cannell's "Lake Wobegon" report lingering in people's memory, with the national goals' aggressive target date just a few years in the future, and with greater political and reputational stakes attached to the academic achievement of a state's schools and children, it was reasonable to wonder whether those developing the state's standards and tests, reporting their results, then employing those results as part of "consequential accountability" for schools, were shooting straight with the public or spinning the outcomes to suit themselves. As with corporate directors and shareholders wanting assurance that the company treasurer isn't cooking the books, there was clear need for some sort of external auditor. And there, in plain view, was NAEP, now accessible to every state and equipped with achievement levels that could be used to show whether the percentage of students that the state termed "proficient" on its tests was in the same ballpark as the percentage earning that designation on a well-regarded national test.

Deploying NAEP as auditor of state performance was never in the minds of its architects, but thirty years later it seemed to make sense. Yet NAEP wasn't—and isn't—a flawless instrument for this purpose. Its achievement levels were controversial, even embattled. It's not given every year, and back then its results emerged slowly. Some states didn't participate at all, and some that took part failed to get enough schools to administer the tests or were otherwise unable to satisfy all of Westat's and NCES's persnickety sampling rules. More importantly, NAEP did not necessarily probe the same skills and knowledge as a state's own assessments or probe them in the same ways. A state's tests should be (but were not always) aligned with its academic standards, while NAEP's tests were based on painstakingly constructed, consensus-driven frameworks for the country as a whole. Those could differ in simple ways—NAEP might assume that fractions would be covered by fourth grade, say, but state X might not expect them to be taught until fifth grade—or in subtler ways such as incompatible strategies for analyzing English texts. A state might encourage curricular acceleration, such that many eighth graders took algebra that was absent from the NAEP eighth-grade math assessment. The state's rules for test participation by children with disabilities might differ from NAEP's. And demographics matter hugely. Even if NAEP's and a state's reports on individual subgroups should turn out to be compatible—which would be affected by the nature and extent of bias in the different tests—that state's overall scores would be affected by the overall racial, ethnic, socioeconomic, and immigrant composition of its population, which in turn would affect how its achievement compared with national averages and those of other states.[6]

Even when NAEP's results for a state closely track that state's standards and test scores, NAEP's design leads to no trustworthy explanation of *why* the results are what they are—why they are higher or lower than before, why they are higher or lower than those of the country or another state, why they show widening or narrowing subgroup differences, and so on. One can, of course, cite circumstantial evidence and coincidental goings-on, can control for various factors, and can offer informed conjectures about causation, but—just as a company's auditor cannot explain to shareholders *why* the firm made or lost money last year—NAEP cannot yield any solid conclusions about why a state's (or nation's) scores are the way they are. In truth, no test can do that unless it's incorporated into a proper experiment.

Within those limits, however, NAEP data can legitimately be deployed to validate state leaders' claims of progress, as well as to shine a spotlight on state standards set so low or state tests made so easy that the appearance of success may be labeled fake news. NAEP data can also help identify some content or skill areas where student performance is weak (or exceptionally strong). That meant, for better and worse, that as NAEP was pulled into the role of outside auditor or truth squad for states as well as the nation, it was also drifting into political crosscurrents.

In 1997, that reality was firmly embraced by NAGB chair Mark Musick, who also headed the Southern Regional Education Board. In a paper presented to the annual assessment conference of the Council of Chief State School Officers, he challenged his audience to recognize how discrepant were the academic standards that their states were setting, and he used NAEP data to illustrate the problem. The "dramatic differences," he reported "are not so much in what states believe should be taught but in how much they expect students to learn." He framed the problem in this striking way:

> Delaware has the lowest percentage of students meeting its eighth-grade mathematics standard (13 percent). Georgia [Musick's home state] has one of the highest percentages of students meeting its eighth-grade standard (83 percent). Recently both states had their students take the same eighth grade mathematics test, the National Assessment of Educational Progress. The eighth graders in Delaware, where 13 percent of its students met the state's low standard, scored *higher* than students in Georgia where 83 percent of its eighth graders met its own standard.[7]

Besides noting inconsistent expectations from one state to the next, Musick made a general point that should worry state leaders seeking to use academic standards as the basis for education-reform efforts: "A few states are setting standards as high as the National Assessment 'proficient' (good enough) standard, but most states have standards that appear to be lower." He cautioned that states would mislead their own citizens—and fail to strengthen the achievement of their young people—if their reform strategies hinge on high-stakes tests that employ low standards.[8]

As the cautionary quip has it, be careful what you wish for. As Musick's 1997 presentation indicated, NAGB members and other NAEP partisans very much wanted their assessment to get noticed, used, and valued in the real world of education policy and practice. Otherwise, what good was it— and why should anyone work hard and expend resources to keep it going? Yet the more visible and impactful NAEP became, the more it risked becoming embroiled in political controversy that could undermine its Olympian objectivity and credibility. As the contested 2000 election grew near, this risk materialized in two high-profile episodes.

In February 1999, results were available from the 1998 NAEP cycle and Vice President Al Gore, by then the leading candidate for the Democratic presidential nomination the following year, was keen to participate in their release. NCES and NAGB couldn't easily refuse him. So joined by Education Secretary Dick Riley, the vice president appeared at the press conference and cited the (mixed) NAEP results as evidence of his and President Clinton's successes on the education front. As CNN reported:

> Gore called the gains "not huge, but statistically important" and said the "largest gains are still ahead." He said that he and President Clinton feel America does not "have a moment or child to waste" . . . The study found young people are beginning to read more and watch television less, which Gore said is a "move in the right direction." He said such improvement is evidence the Clinton administration's agenda to put "education first" is working and should be continued.[9]

Education Week described NAEP's press event as a "campaign-style rally" at which "education lobbyists and political appointees at the Education Department received the best seats" and Gore "was greeted with and departed to standing ovations."[10] The *New York Times* reported that "[t]oday's event, with Mr. Gore in attendance, was more political than usual. Dozens of education lobbyists attended the event in an auditorium at the Education Department. The difference in tone was noted by the collectors of education statistics, who pride themselves on being nonpolitical."[11] And, in fact, Education Commissioner Pascal Forgione's review of the NAEP results, delivered shortly after Gore's remarks, was notably less upbeat than the vice president's.

NAGB chair Mark Musick and his colleagues were not happy—to put it mildly—with this event's visible appropriation of statistical data for political purposes. They were extremely uncomfortable with the potential precedent, too, namely exploiting the release of NAEP results for partisan or personal advantage. Though NAGB had—and has—no ability to control the uses made of NAEP data once released, Musick knew that, in addition to issuing accurate data and neutrally worded reports on those data, NAEP's custodians must strive to keep the release itself free from politics. Which led to a carefully worded yet unmistakable complaint meant to deter such things from happening again.

Musick's letter to Commissioner Forgione—almost surely copied to Secretary Riley, who had made him NAGB chair—stated that "[t]he format, tone, and substance of that event was not consistent with the principle of an independent, nonpartisan release of . . . data."[12] He gently suggested that the event was "more political than usual" for NAEP releases and that if this sort of thing were to happen on a regular basis, "it eventually won't matter how much attention is paid to the results; people won't believe them."

Education Week asked Forgione for comment and reported that he "appeared to agree" that the February 10 incident was "anomalous" and that that sort of thing shouldn't happen in the future. To my knowledge, it has not, at least not so baldly. But Forgione himself may have suffered the consequence of (very mildly) disputing the vice president's data spin, for a few months later the Clinton administration declined to renominate him as commissioner of education statistics—and more than a few observers viewed this decision as political payback.[13]

As the 2000 election itself heated up, NAEP data reappeared in the campaign, this time on the Republican side, as they were deployed to suggest that Texas governor George W. Bush, now the GOP nominee for the White House, had done an exceptional job of boosting educational achievement and narrowing gaps in the Lone Star State, a success that was cited as burnishing his qualifications to lead the nation. Whether that claim affected the election outcome is unknowable, but it's pretty clear that once Bush became president, they lent credibility and momentum, as well as some architecture, to what would emerge from Congress as No Child Left Behind.

This saga unfolded from a trio of (somewhat contradictory) reports from the RAND Corporation. The central document was a 312-page monograph published in 2000 that sought to use state-level NAEP math results, plus subgroup results and a lot of collateral data, to understand the extent to which education-reform efforts were succeeding around the country.[14] This was a vivid example of NAEP as auditor and a source for analysts, in this case employed on a multistate comparative basis. Its central conclusion was upbeat: "[S]ignificant math gains are occurring across most states that cannot be traced to resource changes, that the rate of gain varies significantly by state, and that reform efforts are the likely cause of these gains. The results certainly challenge the traditional view of public education as unreformable."

It's unlikely that either RAND or its able analysts intended this scholarly analysis to enter the political arena. But it did, mostly because on page 59, it invoked an earlier (1998) RAND paper and said this:

> Texas and North Carolina—the states showing the highest rate of improvement—were the subject of a case study to determine whether their state-administered test scores showed similar gains and to try to identify plausible reasons for such large gains (Grissmer and Flanagan, 1998). The state-administered tests given to all students statewide showed similarly large gains in math scores in both states, providing an independent verification of the NAEP trends. The case study concluded that the small changes in key resource variables and teacher characteristics could not explain any significant part of the gains. The study identified a set of similar systemic reform policies implemented in both states in the late 1980s and early 1990s as being the *most plausible reason* for the gains. These policies included developing state standards by grade, assessment tests linked to these standards, good systems for providing feedback to teachers and principals, some accountability measures, and deregulation of the teaching environment. [emphasis theirs]

The RAND analysts added several qualifications and took pains to make clear that—assuming the data showing gains and gap reductions were valid—they still couldn't be certain what led to those encouraging results. They also urged that additional states get similar scrutiny. Yet in the heat of a national election, campaign teams grab at every headline, report, or finding that they can celebrate. Texas had indeed made substantial gains over the previous decade, both overall and in narrowing achievement gaps between white and minority pupils. North Carolina had done the same, and governors Bush and (Democrat) Jim Hunt understandably took pride in those accomplishments. Both were certain that their school-reform initiatives were responsible, especially the standards-testing-accountability triad. RAND seemed to concur.

The Bush campaign team was already making a big deal of his education record in the Lone Star State and his plans for nationwide education reform. The RAND study armed them with additional "evidence" that their candidate was an effective education change agent. (They weren't about to add—as *Education Week* later did—that the policy changes given plausible credit by RAND for achievement gains and gap narrowing in Texas had mostly been instituted before he even became governor![15])

Whether studies like these, and campaign boasts based on them, make any difference in election outcomes is unknowable. Even in 2000, there was also evidence—from another RAND study released just months later and touted by the Gore campaign—that, when data are analyzed differently or other years chosen for comparison, different conclusions can be reached.[16] Such divergent interpretations, and the seeming malleability of data, at least the lessons to be drawn from them, may cast a shadow over the entire enterprise. NAEP's reputation for unimpeachable, apolitical objectivity and certainty can easily erode as the information it promulgates seems to get twisted, exploited, and debated. Such visibility is double-edged for a data enterprise such as NAEP that depends for so many of its elements on consensus and nonpartisanship and that depends for its credibility on a general understanding that it's incorruptible.

What remains indisputable from this particular episode is that the positive reinforcement George W. Bush brought from Austin to Washington, derived in part from NAEP's apparent validation of his actions as governor to boost educational achievement and narrow gaps, fed directly into the testing-transparency-and-accountability thrust of No Child Left Behind, with all of its consequences, some good, some not, for American education. Among those legacies would be the institutionalization of semi-annual NAEP tests of reading and math for *every* state as part of a *national* school-accountability strategy, as well as opportunities for large districts to join the NAEP action themselves.

Some districts already wanted in during the 1990s—a far cry from the local superintendents' hostility to the entire assessment project a few decades earlier.

The Improving America's Schools Act of 1994, which reauthorized NAEP, removed the prohibition on "below-state" reporting of results, a change supported by NAGB in hopes that some districts would choose to use NAEP data to inform their own education-reform efforts. During the 1996 and 1998 assessment rounds, different pathways were experimented with. In September 1995, the board announced that several districts had applied to participate: "The Philadelphia, Atlanta, and Milwaukee school districts intend to pay to augment NAEP state samples for math and science assessments in grades 4 and 8. Fairfax County, Va., wants to do the same for the math test for those grades. New York City school officials have said they intend to participate but have not made a formal application."[17]

Participation wasn't simple, however, as sampling requirements were demanding, and the price tag eventually dissuaded all but Milwaukee, which obtained funds from the National Science Foundation to subsidize its participation in the 1996 cycle. Even then, sampling was a challenge, and Milwaukee was finally able to obtain valid data only for eighth grade.[18]

Before the 1998 round, NCES and Westat determined that there were six "naturally occurring" districts, that is, places that comprised at least 20 percent of their state's sample and thus met the minimum sampling requirements as determined at the time. There was outreach to several of them, but for various reasons none signed up. Meanwhile, however, the Council of the Great City Schools (CGCS), a membership organization of dozens of the country's largest urban districts—seventy-six of them today—was getting interested in working out a more systematic (and cost-free!) way for interested school systems to take part in NAEP.

In 2001, after discussions among the council, NCES, and NAGB, and effective Capitol Hill lobbying by the council, Congress appropriated funds for a district-level NAEP assessment on a provisional basis. It was dubbed—and two decades later is still called—the Trial Urban District Assessment or TUDA. It would focus on urban education, not on districts as such—and would therefore exclude large suburban systems such as Fairfax County. In collaboration with NCES and CGCS, NAGB invites districts that meet certain selection criteria to volunteer to participate. Those criteria are based on district size and percentages of African American and Hispanic students or low-income pupils. At the outset, in 2002, six qualifying districts took part in NAEP's reading and writing assessments, a number that would slowly rise to twenty-seven by 2017.[19]

Adding districts lent further complexity to an endeavor that was already plenty complicated and fraught with controversy. This was clearest in the realm of NAGB's trinity of achievement levels, which drew crossfire throughout the 1990s and into the twenty-first century, both in their own right and in relation to state-by-state NAEP. The basic issue, as noted in the previous chapter, is that they're judgmental and aspirational, not an analysis of what is but, rather, a declaration of what should be, coupled with a comparison of present performance to that aspiration.

Hence this kind of standard-setting is not something that statisticians and social scientists are comfortable with. They want to work with data, not hopes or assertions, with what is, not what should be, and they want their analyses and comparisons to be driven by scientific norms such as validity, reliability, and statistical significance.

NAEP's contractors and NCES overseers do all of those things with NAEP data, and do them pretty well, taking pains to ensure that the results they present, the comparisons they make, and the changes they describe have rigorous scientific integrity—or carry cautionary notes when that's not possible.[20] Those data are typically what other researchers and analysts work from when employing NAEP results for their own studies. They're valuable in their own right and much used. But they're free from expectations, standards, and judgments, while judgments are precisely what NAGB had set out to furnish, confident that this was permitted by the assessment's authorizing statute, was wanted by governors, was a vital element of the "goals process" and a necessary tool for education reformers, and was the best way for Americans to see to what extent their nation was or was not still at risk.

NCES's statisticians resisted the board's standard-setting initiative for years. At times, it felt like guerrilla warfare as each side enlisted external experts and allies to support its position and find fault with the other.

As longtime NCES commissioner Emerson Elliott reminisces on those tussles, he explains that his colleagues' focus, reminiscent of Ralph Tyler's original vision for NAEP, was "reporting what students know and can do." Sober-sided statisticians don't get involved with "defining what students *should* do," as that "requires setting values that are not within their purview. NCES folks were not just uncomfortable with the idea of setting achievement levels, they believed them totally inappropriate *for a statistical agency*."[21] He recalled that one of his senior colleagues at NCES was "appalled" when he learned what NAGB had in mind.

At the same time, Elliott continued, he and his colleagues knew that something more than plain data was needed, indeed were "troubled about how to make the data meaningful. They were well aware that the simple item response reports that NAEP initially provided not only could not be compared with anything, but also were impossible to interpret in terms that either educators or the public understood."[22]

Before NAGB's achievement levels came along, NCES and ETS had labored with some success to crack this conundrum. For example, their epic 1990 report on math achievement nationally—and, for the first time, in participating states—ran to 525 pages (the "executive summary" alone required 42) and sought to present the math results in multiple revealing modes and formats, along with auxiliary information about students' school experiences with math and about their teachers.[23] It offered examples of math problems of varying levels of difficulty and how students did on them, it offered sub-scores for different parts of math, it gauged achievement gaps between different pupil groups, and it retained the 50-point intervals on the 500-point vertical scale that ETS analysts had pioneered (as outlined in the previous chapter). In so doing, it came close to depicting "challenging subject matter" in this subject, as sought by the governors and president at their summit the previous year. All this was informative and enlightening in various ways for various audiences. It's hard to imagine a more comprehensive or earnest—or lengthy—effort to render NAEP data "meaningful" to audiences that might benefit from it.

Yet even that massive volume lacked any sense of academic "standards" as we now conceive of them, and that's what the summiteers were working toward when they specified that young Americans should be "proficient" in "challenging subject matter." The 1990 math report admirably displayed what statisticians are capable of, but it didn't—it's fair to say, couldn't—spell out how well students *should* do in math.

That same shortcoming applied to every NAEP subject and report until NAGB resolved to analyze results and craft reports in ways that would answer the question "How good is good enough?" Yet that straightforward impulse gave rise to round after round of argument and controversy, arguments that really proceeded on two paths at once: (1) *should* the board be setting normative benchmarks for student achievement, and (2) if yes, then *how* should it go about this?

After fumbling in its hasty attempt to get all this done in time for the 1990 assessment, by 1992 NAGB had, in veteran staffer Mary Lyn Bourque's recollection, "arrived at a three-prong solution: (1) the Board would develop policy definitions (PDs) that articulate the *expectations* for each level in general terms, (2) the PDs would be operationalized into grade- and subject-specific statements of performance levels for use in the standard-setting process (achievement-level descriptions, or ALDs), and (3) the Board would be the final arbiter of the recommendations provided on all aspects of the levels, including the ALDs, the cut scores and the exemplar items."[24]

Working out how best to do those things took time, because the methods NAGB used, though widespread today, were all but unprecedented at the time. In Bourque's words, looking back from 2007, "The use of ALDs . . . in standard setting has become de rigueur for most agencies today; it was almost unheard of before the National Assessment."[25]

In addition to pushback from NCES, criticism of the achievement-level venture came fast and furious from multiple outside sources, including such eminent bodies as the National Academy of Education, National Academy of Sciences, and General Accounting Office. Phrases like "fundamentally flawed" were hurled at NAGB's level-setting efforts.

But the board stuck to its guns, engaged experts of its own to rebut unjust elements of the criticism while working for the better part of two decades—and, arguably, still today—to refine and augment its standard-setting work. Some criticism was constructive, however, and the board and its staff and contractors—principally the American College Testing organization (ACT)—took it seriously and adjusted the process, including a significant overhaul in 2005.

By 2009, after NAEP's achievement levels had come into widespread use and a facsimile of them had been incorporated into Congress's own accountability requirements for states receiving Title I funding, the methodological furor was largely over.[26] A congressionally mandated evaluation of NAEP that year by the universities of Nebraska and Massachusetts finally recognized the "inherently judgmental" nature of such standards, noted the "residual tension between NAGB and NCES concerning their establishment," then went on to acknowledge that "[m]any of the procedures for setting achievement levels for NAEP are consistent with professional testing standards."[27]

That generally approving review's one big caveat faulted NAGB's level-setting process for not using enough "external evidence" to gauge and calibrate the validity of its standards. It was entirely reasonable to ask whether a target such as "proficient" on NAEP correlates with other expectations of proficiency in the world around us, and social scientists routinely inquire into the "validity" of their instruments and findings, that is, whether they accurately measure that which they're supposed to be measuring. But it's challenging with an aspirational standard such as "NAEP proficient" because it was never meant to match what existing schools and school systems may regard as "grade level" work, and it doesn't necessarily correlate with "college readiness"—not, that is, if readiness means being able to be admitted to college.[28] We know that many young people enroll in colleges and universities who are ill-prepared to succeed with the academic challenges they find there and are routed into remedial (or "developmental") courses. Many end up quitting.

Continually prodded by such concerns, seeking to address the validity uncertainty surrounding its achievement levels, and troubled by recurrent concerns that it had set "proficient" at too high a level, NAGB commissioned additional research that eventually bore fruit, as we will see in the next chapter. The achievement levels turn out to be more solidly anchored to reality, at least for college-bound students, than most of their critics have supposed.[29]

As the years passed, NAGB and NCES reached a modus vivendi for analyzing and presenting NAEP results. Simply stated, NCES "owns" the vertical scales and is responsible for ensuring that the data are accurate, while

NAGB "owns" the achievement levels and interpretation of results in relation to those levels. The former may be said to depict "what is," while the latter is based on judgments as to how students are faring in relation to "how good is good enough?" Today's NAEP report cards incorporate both components, and the reader sees them as a seamless sequence. Yet the tension has not entirely vanished. The portions of NAEP reports based on achievement levels continue to carry this note: "NAEP achievement levels are to be used on a trial basis and should be interpreted and used with caution." And the NCES website continues to carry this wary explanation:

> The authorizing legislation for the National Assessment of Educational Progress (NAEP) requires that the NAEP achievement levels be used on a trial basis until the Commissioner of the National Center for Education Statistics (NCES) determines that the achievement levels are reasonable, valid, and informative to the public (20 USC § 9622(e)(2)(C)). The NCES Commissioner's determination is to be based on a congressionally mandated, rigorous, and independent evaluation. The latest evaluation of the NAEP achievement levels was conducted by a committee convened by the National Academies of Sciences, Engineering, and Medicine in 2016. The evaluation concluded that further evidence should be gathered to determine whether the NAEP achievement levels are reasonable, valid, and informative. Accordingly, the NCES commissioner determined that the trial status of the NAEP achievement levels should be maintained at this time.[30]

That tautness and unease—between what one may term statistical integrity and ambitious aspiration—will probably never disappear. Yet with all the caveats, NAEP has come to accommodate both. So has veteran participant/observer Emerson Elliott. Reflecting from the perspective of 2020 on years of tussles between expertise and judgment, he offered this thoughtful resolution:

> I think, generally, that non-statisticians should be coming up with benchmark performances—not just in what students should be doing, but for the economy, health care, housing and every other area of public activity. They should be able to defend their choices. Statisticians, then, should report in relation to those benchmarks. They should be familiar with multiple ways of making data interpretable, even if they

have their own preferred or standard presentations. However, their role should be to devise statistics so that analysts and the public can make calculations for different interpretations.[31]

As we'll see in the next chapter, the gradual acceptance of NAGB's achievement levels paled in significance when compared with Congress's move at the dawn of the twenty-first century to mandate NAEP in every state.

CHAPTER 6

Modern Times

THE TWENTY FIRST CENTURY has elevated NAEP's stature, even as it has revealed the assessment's limitations and heightened the risk of collision between this apolitical measurement project and the mounting sensitivities and divisions that have characterized this stressful period in our national life. In this chapter, we examine a half dozen of the most consequential changes and challenges that have emerged and how they have—or haven't—reshaped today's National Assessment.

When President George W. Bush affixed his signature to the No Child Left Behind Act (NCLB) on January 8, 2002, it propelled NAEP into an even higher-visibility role as monitor of the nation's ongoing quest for better schools, stronger student achievement, and closer attention to gaps in that achievement.

For the first time, NCLB required states (in order to keep receiving Title I funding, which of course all wanted) to take part in an assessment that theretofore had been optional, and it directed NAEP to report every two years on reading and math achievement, nationally and by state (and TUDA districts) in grades 4 and 8. Those were the new law's two key subjects for school and district accountability as well as NAEP's new mandate, aligned with NCLB's requirement that every student in grades 3 through 8 be tested annually. This promoted NAEP to chief monitor of the country's progress (or not) toward universal proficiency as well as its foremost gauge of whether learning gaps between different pupil populations were widening or shrinking, and the de facto scrutinizer of every state's progress as well as the rigor of its standards and tests.

This enhanced mission for NAEP, accompanied by a sizable budget boost, was part of a grand if awkward political compromise, whereby each state would determine its own academic standards and choose its own tests, which could (and turned out to) be all over the place in quality and rigor. But the country—and Uncle Sam—would henceforth be watching over their shoulders. To be sure, NAEP was not the sole oversight mechanism, as states also had to get their voluminous NCLB compliance plans okayed up front by the US Department of Education and its multistage peer review process. But once a state's plan was approved, NAEP would serve as the primary external watchdog on how well it was succeeding with pupil achievement and gap reduction. Recall that NCLB's overriding target—as extravagantly naive in its way as the goals set in Charlottesville thirteen years earlier—was to get every US child to be "proficient" in reading and math by 2014, while also closing gaps among designated pupil groups. States would define "proficiency" themselves, but NAEP had its definition, too, and every two years a state's results would be displayed on that metric for all to see.

NCLB had flaws, including its clumsy blend of federal overreach and standoffishness, and its rigidities eventually caused a backlash, leading the Department of Education to issue waivers to many states and eventually leading Congress to overhaul the statute. But it had virtues, too, especially the light it shed—bright and relentless, year after year—on achievement and achievement gaps at every level of the K–12 system from the entire nation down to tens of thousands of individual schools, plus information for practitioners and parents about the reading and math achievement of every public school pupil in the designated grades. Almost two decades later, former president George W. Bush and his second-term education secretary, Margaret Spellings, were still citing NAEP's crucial role in making every state's educational performance transparent and its "truth squad" function in showing which states' proficiency standards were as rigorous as NCLB's authors hoped they would be and which fell short.[1]

Due to continuing wide discrepancies in their academic standards, discrepancies made visible primarily via NAEP, state governors and education leaders came together to develop what emerged in 2010 as the Common Core State Standards for English Language Arts and Math. These were privately funded and voluntary, yet (combined with Washington's big-spending response to the Great Recession) soon became entangled in a big new federal initiative named Race to the Top. Under that program, the

Department of Education created strong financial incentives for states to opt into the Common Core and simultaneously funded development of a pair of multistate assessments. The hope was that most states would sign up for those new tests, initially leading some seriously to ponder NAEP's future role, even the need for it in years to come, if states were going to harmonize their standards and adopt common measures that would make achievement comparisons easy.[2]

What transpired, however, was different and sobering. The education and political worlds found themselves enmeshed in a rollicking controversy over perceived "federalization" of standards—the slippery slope toward a dreaded "national curriculum," all aggravated by widening political schisms and intense partisanship that went far beyond the realm of education. In consequence, many states eventually backed away from the Common Core (or modified or relabeled it), and the multistate assessment consortia also encountered rough sledding and many dropouts. It gradually became clear that the new tests would not be able to do what NAEP does.

By the end of the Obama administration, NCLB was itself replaced by the Every Student Succeeds Act (ESSA), which freed state accountability systems from most federal shackles while retaining mandatory (even enhanced) transparency. But it did not spare NAEP from anything; rather, it reinforced the National Assessment's role as America's lead mechanism for audits and comparisons of standards, expectations, and outcomes.

As NAEP gained visibility and influence, it was inevitably asked to do more. Trying to be responsive and strategic, its governing board and NCES took on (or were assigned) more missions, almost all of which added to its complexity and cost and some of which brought fresh controversy.

Outside groups pressed to have their favorite subjects included, if only to enhance their legitimacy and importance. There were also pushes to test more often, to include more students, and to supply data for more jurisdictions and populations. Assessment frameworks needed updating and methodologies needed adapting. Everyone wanted the data to come out faster, and researchers wanted those data made more accessible for analysis. With added demands, however, came heightened risk of glitches arising as well as fresh budgetary challenges and the threat of mission creep.

That peril was most obvious in decisions about what subjects to include. Between 1990 and 2000, along with periodic long-term trend assessments,

NAEP tested eight subjects: reading, writing, science, math, US history, geography, civics, and the arts. The next fifteen years would add economics and "technology and engineering literacy," bringing the total to ten. With reading and math having to be tested every two years per NCLB and ESSA, the logistic and fiscal burdens were heavy, and questions legitimately arose as to how much NAEP could handle. In 2004, for example, a pilot foreign language assessment (to be conducted in Spanish) failed to generate a sufficient sample to yield valid data.[3] This setback, plus the budget crunch, led NAGB to put off the language assessment until some future date—which still has not arrived, almost two decades after board members agreed to include the subject.[4]

The heavy lift that's needed just to assess reading and math every two years has also crowded other important subjects, causing them to be tested infrequently or only at a single grade level or maybe two—and only for the country as a whole. Eight- and nine-year testing gaps grew more common, particularly for civics, history, and geography—and when those three subjects were assessed in 2014, the tests were just given to eighth graders. NAEP's arts assessment has never been taken by fourth or twelfth graders.[5]

The more attention a test receives and the more impact follows from its scores, the more doubts get raised as to its reliability and validity. For NAEP during this period, such concerns took two forms: do its results, particularly when reported according to the board's achievement levels, have any relationship to real-world demands and expectations? For example, does being "proficient" on the NAEP scale relate to anything that actually matters? And can the twelfth-grade results be trusted in the first place, considering how casually many high school seniors view these low-stakes, no-fault tests?

Most assessment regimes strive to align their scores with something tangible. Passing a state's end-of-course exam in a subject is often a prerequisite for getting a high school diploma. The Advanced Placement program asserts that scoring 3 or higher on its 5-point scale should qualify for college credit (or at least skipping an introductory course), and in most universities something like that actually happens. The ACT program declares that students meeting "college readiness benchmarks" on its exams will "have approximately a 50% chance of earning a B or better and a 75% chance of earning a C or better in the corresponding college course or courses." The College Board does much the same thing for its SAT tests.[6]

Although NAEP scores don't matter for individual students, they can matter quite a lot for state policy makers and district leaders. And when NAEP's definition of "proficiency," for example, is used to benchmark states' own standards and test results, which then count for individual schools and students, one sees why the score associated with that definition should mean something real, not just an arbitrary point on a 500-point scale above which students are said to be proficient and those below are not. In psychometric terms, we're talking about a test's "validity," and when it comes to cut scores we're talking about "criterion validity."[7]

Because NAGB's achievement levels are judgmental and aspirational, they've been set with reference to the questions asked on the NAEP test, which in turn is based on the content of a school subject at various grade levels, as gauged by expert panels. Both the assessment content and the level-setting are done with considerable sophistication and wide-ranging understanding of what schools teach and what kids should be expected to know and do. But in response to endless controversy over its achievement levels, especially concerns about their validity, NAGB undertook a series of studies designed to gauge whether in fact those levels match anything beyond the K–12 system.

The most important linkages would be found at the end of high school, when young people emerge into the real world. That's also a point of mounting policy interest, generally framed as "college and career readiness." What sort of NAEP score in the foundational subjects of reading and math might signify a young person's (or group of young persons') readiness to succeed without needing remediation or otherwise stumbling as they commence the next stage of their lives?

That's where NAGB focused its research efforts, which were bound to be complicated, as colleges in the United States come in so many flavors and with such differing levels of academic rigor, while post–high school jobs are even more varied in their cognitive demands. Multiple studies were undertaken, culminating in 2014 with a persuasive validity finding: in reading, a NAEP score of 301 translated to college readiness, and this was almost identical to the 302 score that denoted twelfth-grade "proficiency" on the 2013 assessment cycle. (The bad news was that just 38 percent of twelfth graders reached that level, though many more were headed to college.) The counterpart score for college readiness in math was somewhat lower than "NAEP proficient"—163 on the NAEP scale, versus a "proficient" cut score that year of 176, although later analysis by the American Institutes of Research placed the math-readiness score closer to "proficient" as defined by the board.[8]

NAGB split down the middle over whether to declare that twelfth-grade NAEP proficient signifies college readiness. (Chair David Driscoll's motion to tout that connection lost by a single vote.) NCES statisticians were reluctant, too. Yet this research has made it possible for NAEP in subsequent years to estimate and report the percentage of twelfth graders who are academically prepared to succeed in college, much as ACT and the College Board do.[9] ("Preparedness" rather than "readiness" is now NAEP's term of art.) But it's still not a pretty picture; indeed it is essentially unchanged since the research was done. In the most recent assessment cycle (2019), NAEP reported that, while more than 60 percent of twelfth graders were applying to college, just 37 percent were prepared in math, and the same modest fraction—not necessarily the same students—was prepared in reading.[10]

Efforts to link NAEP scores to *career* readiness have proven less successful, doubtless because post–high school jobs range from fast-food slinger to wind turbine technician and practical nurse. So far, to my knowledge, there's no obvious cut-point on the NAEP scale (or achievement levels) that correlates with generalized career readiness for twelfth graders.

But can these kids' NAEP scores even be trusted? They're seniors, after all, in their late teens. Many are test-jaded and school-weary. Why take seriously another test that doesn't count for themselves or even for their school? And if the kids just fool around with their test papers, why should anyone care about their scores?

NCES dug into the matter, beginning with school and student participation rates. After all, if young people won't even take the test or their high schools can't be bothered, there's obvious reason to question the reliability of the resulting data.

High schools chosen for the NAEP sample are typically less willing to take part than elementary and middle schools. In 2015, for example, 88 percent of them did so, compared with 97 percent at grade 4 and 96 percent at grade 8. Still, that was up from 70 percent in 1998.

At the student level, 78 percent of sampled twelfth graders took part in the assessment in 2015, falling below the NCES statistical standard of 85 percent participation. Indeed, twelfth-grade participation stayed below that threshold every year from 1998 through 2015. This automatically triggers what NCES calls a "nonresponse bias analysis," designed to determine "if the responding sample accurately reflects the population."[11]

As in other assessment cycles, the extra analysis showed that the 2015 data could be trusted: "no differences found in the distributions when the adjusted weights were applied. Thus, there is no evidence that the sample failed to accurately represent the population."[12]

Yet it's definitely preferable to start with school and student participation rates that clear the thresholds, so NCES has made several efforts to boost those rates. These include earlier notification of the schools and various incentives for kids, ranging "from recognition of participation to free food."

Participation isn't the whole story, however. There's also the matter of what NCES calls student "engagement," that is, the seriousness with which participating young people approach the test instrument itself. Are they playing tic-tac-toe with the questions, rolling dice on the multiple-choice items, or doing their best to answer correctly? Ten- and fourteen-year-olds may be sweet-talked by their teachers or nudged by their peers into taking the tests seriously but what about those burned-out seniors?

On that front, the news was unexpectedly good. NCES looked at response rates—"the extent to which students respond to all of the questions with which they are presented"—and in 2015 the twelfth-grade rate was equal or superior to the response rates of fourth and eighth graders: in the high 90 percents for all. Close inspection of the 2015 responses themselves—this is important on open-ended and free-response items where a student might jot down something frivolous—also found that "off-task" responses were fewer than 1 percent in every grade, including twelfth.

Combining NCES's own analyses and external studies led to this encouraging 2017 conclusion: "[M]ost 12th grade students participate in and are engaged when taking NAEP assessments. Student response rate percentages are in the mid-90's, off-task and nonresponse rates are low, and most schools have found that simple techniques (such as a thank-you or certificate of participation) are enough to encourage students to participate."[13]

A different challenge for NAEP has been erratic participation by private schools chosen for the sample. Although Catholic parochial schools have regularly taken part in large enough numbers to generate valid data on their students' achievement—which has consistently been higher than that of public school pupils—other private schools haven't participated on a regular basis in recent years.[14] Thus, for example, 2013 was the last NAEP administration for which valid data for the private sector as a whole are available for eighth-grade reading, and 2003 was the last year for which eighth-grade math data are available for non-Catholic private schools. In other subjects, however, private school participation has been more robust, including eighth-grade history, civics and geography in 2014, and the arts in 2016. With private-sector participation optional, it's likely affected by the many subsets of such schools in the US—for example, Baptist, Lutheran, Jewish, independent, Catholic—and the lack of any central authority. One may also wonder, however, whether perhaps some private schools prefer not to have comparisons made, perhaps especially in the core subjects of reading and math.

An escalating challenge for NAEP, its governing board, and NCES during this period was how to deal with youngsters who find it difficult even to take tests, notably children with disabilities and those (often recent immigrants) with limited English prowess. Equity demands that we know how they're doing academically, and federal law places them among the distinctive subpopulations of students whose achievement—and gaps—must be reported. So NAEP (and state assessments) must not ignore them. But what if they're unable to take or understand—or even see—what's on the test? And how to deal with big differences among states in how many students—and proportions of students—fall into these categories? Such discrepancies arise both because state demographics vary and because their special education and bilingual education practices do, too.[15]

This situation poses countless problems for accurate reporting and comparison of achievement data, including the risk of ill-serving students in those subpopulations by underreporting or misreporting, even failing altogether to report, how much and how well they're learning.[16]

In the NAEP world, such issues have typically arisen and been addressed under two headings: to what extent can "accommodations" be provided to these kids to facilitate their access to NAEP and its assessments, as well as their opportunity to truly demonstrate what they know and can do? And who decides—and by what criteria—which children should be accommodated, how that should be done, and which should be excused altogether from test participation?

As in other important tests, "inclusion" in NAEP can be a challenge, and accommodations can take many forms.[17] The simpler forms include extra testing time, directions and test questions read aloud, and large-print test items. More ambitious accommodations include providing questions (and allowing responses) via Braille, sign language, and in bilingual form. As with much else in special education and the education of non-English speakers, these extras take time, care, and budget to supply. Those are not trivial considerations, but students who can satisfactorily be accommodated are at least able to take part in the assessment and—it's certainly hoped—generate accurate results.

Yet some children—typically those with multiple or severe disabilities—simply cannot take part in NAEP assessments, so it's always been permissible to withhold some students from these tests as well as from state assessments. But how many? Who decides? And on what grounds?

NAEP's inclusiveness or lack thereof first boiled up as an issue in the mid-1990s. Until then, NAGB, NCES, and the NAEP contractors had done little to accommodate children with special needs and worried that trying to do that would so alter the sample of test-takers as to disrupt NAEP's trend lines. Budgetary concerns also loomed. But Education Secretary Richard Riley pushed NAGB to change its rules and provide more accommodations, and with some misgivings, in September 1995 the board revised its policies to include more special-needs students. That was surely the right decision on grounds of equity and accuracy, but it did cause wobbles in trend lines, such that every subsequent NAEP reading and math report that shows changes since the 1990s has displayed dotted lines or footnotes indicating "before and after accommodations."

Budget trade-offs also had to be made, and the same 1995 meeting that led to the inclusion of more special-ed students shelved several add-on studies and test-item modifications that had previously been planned for the following year's cycle. (In the next chapter, we dig deeper into budgetary challenges and trade-offs.)

That, however, was far from the end of it, for states retained much discretion as to which youngsters to include in or withhold from their own NAEP samples, and they exercised that discretion in very different ways. As a Department of Education study drily reported in 2009, "Since the late 1990s, participation rates of students with disabilities (SDs) in the National Assessment . . . from different states have fluctuated."[18]

This variability had consequences for state NAEP scores and for many additional studies, scores, and rankings—such as *Education Week*'s influential annual *Quality Counts* analysis—that make use of those scores. There's reason to believe that some state leaders manipulated pupil participation in order to boost those scores and thereby boost their states' rankings. As recently as 2013, reported the *Washington Post*,

> When Maryland officials recently trumpeted the performance of their students on national reading tests, they failed to mention one thing: The state blocked more than half its English language learners and students with learning disabilities from taking the test, students whose scores would have dragged down the results . . . The state led the nation in excluding students on the 2013 National Assessment of Educational Progress, posting rates that were five times the national average and more than double the rate of any other states.[19]

Post reporter Lyndsey Layton went on to observe that the percentage of students excluded from NAEP testing had been rising for years in Maryland even as other states were including more and more of their pupils.

The Old Line State was probably the worst offender, but it wasn't alone—and such variations weren't always intentional. States' widely differing practices regarding the classification and schooling of children with disabilities and those with limited English proficiency also built variability into their NAEP samples. Though federal laws such as No Child Left Behind put guardrails around how many students may be excluded from *state* assessments, the only constraints on NAEP participation were NAGB's policies and NCES's reporting standards.

As those have evolved with the years, they've taken two forms. The first is guidance from the board saying that no more than 5 percent of students should be excluded from NAEP assessments for any reason and the goal should be inclusion of 85 percent of ELL students and those with disabilities. To put some teeth into this—the second constraint—NAEP reports now flag the data of any state that doesn't hit those targets, and if participation is too low to yield a representative sample, NCES won't report the results at all.[20]

As national concern about the lagging achievement of poor and minority students—and the widening gaps between their academic performance and that of well-off, white, and Asian pupils—intensified in recent decades, particularly since NCLB's passage in 2002, anxiety also rose about the many young Americans whose NAEP scores are "below basic."[21]

NAGB's achievement levels are all ambitious, keyed to what kids *should* know and be able to do rather than where they are today. That's true even at the "basic" level, which means that "below basic" spans an enormous range and sweeps in a great many kids while delivering scant information about them. In 2009, for example, the "basic" level for eighth-grade reading was set at 243 on NAEP's 500-point scale, placing it close to the halfway point. And 25 percent—a full quarter—of that year's eighth-grade test-takers wound up in the "below basic" range. More troubling still, 43 percent of black students and 39 percent of Hispanic pupils had scores in that range.

Those big fractions signal a huge literacy problem for the country, one that recurs with similar magnitude in other subjects tested by NAEP. Yet because "below basic" spans nearly half the scale, it runs from "completely unable to read" all the way to "on the cusp of basic." This poses a problem for interpretation and intervention. After all, eighth-grade reading entails an array of skills and competencies from simple decoding of letter sounds to distilling core concepts from what one is reading. How is a state leader, for example, to know whether schools seeking to propel more kids to and beyond basic should focus intensively on phonics, background knowledge, coaching students in phonemic awareness, or purchasing a wider range of materials for middle school libraries? And when—as happened in 2009—more students clear the basic bar than in earlier years, how to interpret what may have contributed to that gain?

Politics enters, too, especially during the modern education-reform era when states and districts and schools are held to account for how many of their pupils make progress toward "proficiency" and when elected officials are judged by such progress.

As a result, along with repeatedly being accused of setting all three of its achievement-level bars too high, NAGB has been faulted by some for supplying no guideposts below the basic level—and for not trying to anchor the "basic" level to anything real, as it has striven to do with "proficient." Thus, for example, a 2007 "validity study" of the NAEP math assessment came to this conclusion:

> [B]ecause NAEP does not have simple arithmetic calculations on the assessment (as one would find on assessments for second- and third-grade students), it is not valid to infer that low-achieving students who score in the below basic range *cannot* perform simple arithmetic calculations. NAEP provides no direct information on this question. If some students can perform arithmetic, but cannot manage word problems very well, NAEP may be underestimating their achievement. Equally important, users of NAEP results cannot draw valid conclusions about what it means to be "Basic" or "Below Basic" with respect to basic arithmetic.[22]

Although some board documents in recent years have optimistically declared that future NAEP reports will unpack and illumine the wide swath of "below basic" students and scores, there have been just a few systematic efforts to distinguish among the skills (and skill gaps) at various tiers of student achievement within that swath. Probably the most impressive emerged from NCES in early 2021: a special analysis (done under contract with the American Institutes of Research) of the oral reading fluency of a sample of fourth graders who scored below basic on the NAEP scale in 2018. The analysts were able to sort the sample into three subgroups according to their scores and then to identify "variations in performance among the below NAEP Basic subgroups for every dimension of reading fluency . . . and for each of two 'foundational skills.'"[23]

Some of those variations were sobering indeed, such as the overrepresentation of black youngsters in the lowest of those subgroups, a population that encountered exceptional difficulty with "fluent reading of connected text."

Recent NAEP report cards have also done more to identify trends in student populations at the tenth as well as the ninetieth percentile of the assessed samples, that is, very low and high scorers, and more of that kind of analysis lies ahead. Decrying "how little information current NAEP technologies generate about students at the bottom of the NAEP scoring distribution," in early 2021 IES director Mark Schneider engaged the National Academies of Science, Engineering, and Medicine to undertake a close study of the assessment and make recommendations regarding its modernization and transparency.[24] Part of that assignment is to offer suggestions for unpacking and illuminating the "below basic" category and the many youngsters whose scores fall into that wide range.

What is legitimate to include in the background questions that NAEP poses to participating students without violating their privacy or trying their endurance?[25] Are those questionnaires too nosy? Do they invade students' privacy and poke into personal and family matters that are none of the government's business?

In fact, there are two concerns, governmental overreach being just one of them. The other is actual data privacy: is there a risk that the identity of individual students may be revealed? That's an issue with every government statistical program, and doubly so with children and students, who have had their own privacy protections fixed in statutes dating back to the Ford administration.[26] Those protections have mostly to do with school records, but they apply to government data, too. That's why researchers seeking access to NAEP's "raw" data (or other NCES data at the individual level) must undergo an elaborate application process to obtain a "restricted-use" license that includes numerous safeguards against revelation of personal information.[27]

That system has worked well, but it wasn't designed to deal with the nosiness issue. Students answering NAEP background questions and—especially—parents seeing what's being asked of their kids, may judge some queries to be too personal. As recently as 2019, for example, the student questionnaire asked twelfth graders participating in NAEP's reading assessment how often they "felt awkward and out of place at school." In earlier years, youngsters were asked many more questions, some of which poked into matters that hold keen interest for researchers but may upset privacy-minded parents and watchdog groups. In 2003, for instance, fourth graders taking the reading assessment were asked thirty-nine background questions, many dealing with school but some ranging far afield, from the existence (or not) of an encyclopedia in the child's home and the extent of her mother's education to how often she "writes in a private diary or journal outside of school" and "How often do you talk about things you have studied in school with someone in your family?"

Sprawling arrays of questions like those started to worry some NAGB members and were brought to congressional attention by concerned parents and advocacy groups. As NAEP assessments grew more frequent and universal under NCLB, Congress moved to bar it from asking questions that delve into "personal or family beliefs and attitudes," limits reinforced in that same year's Education Sciences Reform Act (ESRA), which reorganized the Education Department's research and statistics operations, and which remains the principal authorizing statute for NAEP. Assessment designers would henceforth have to confine themselves to issues "directly related to the appraisal of academic achievement."

This prompted the governing board in 2003 to overhaul its guidelines for background questions—and to reissue the new guidelines, with modest revisions, a decade later. Its goal was to limit the "noncognitive" questions routinely asked of test-takers to a core of items required by law or necessary for depicting achievement clearly. The board rejected the view—strongly held by many researchers who always want much more background information on students and their homes, their attitudes, and their school experiences—that NAEP was responsible for explaining *why* achievement was rising, falling, or static. NAGB's policy statement notes that data from other sources—surveys, research studies, census reports, and more—can be combined with NAEP data to facilitate more sophisticated analyses. NAEP itself ought not be expected to supply all of that, although the board did agree to rotate some of the nosier background questions over the years, sometimes to administer them to a small subset of the NAEP sample, and periodically to add temporary items of compelling interest.[28]

These are fraught decisions, because researchers seeking more data about students and teachers, though naturally keen to advance and enhance their own work, are generally also eager to deploy that information in ways that lead to improvements in a K–12 system that plainly needs them. They tend to view background questions as a treasure trove of data that can be factored into analyses, controlled for, compared, and so on. In 2012, as the governing board was revising its guidelines for such questions, an "expert panel" complained to it that "[c]urrently, the NAEP background questions are a potentially important but largely underused national resource. The background questionnaires have been cut back over the past decade. They now cover only a small fraction of important student, teacher, and school issues and have been little used in recent NAEP reports, in contrast to the first state-level NAEP Report Cards in the early 1990s."[29]

Those responsible for NAEP, on the other hand—both board members and Education Department officials with Congress looking over their shoulders—must take heed of political and parental concerns about privacy, about testing burdens (and test participation, which can erode if filling out questionnaires is too much hassle), and about costs, which involve participants' time and congressional sensibilities as well as appropriation levels.[30]

As we conclude this review of NAEP's history, we've seen how America's foremost barometer of educational achievement has faced challenges, generated complications, and invited controversy. At the same time, we've seen it notch impressive accomplishments, most recently including moves to modernize its own tests. As recounted by veteran participant-observer Ina Mullis:

> NAEP had been exploring new testing methods and question types that capitalized on the growing use of technology in education since 2001 . . . [I]n 2015, NAEP piloted mathematics and reading assessments on tablets with an attached keyboard, a stylus, and earbuds. Some test questions included multimedia, such as audio and video. Among other benefits . . . these new technologies are improving NAEP's ability to offer accommodations to students with diverse backgrounds, including students with disabilities and ELs. In 2016, NAEP piloted mathematics and reading assessments that included online tools (such as calculators) . . . In 2017, NAEP completed a major step into the future, using its experience with the 2015 pilot to fully transition to digital-based assessments for reading and mathematics, assessing over half a million fourth- and eighth-graders across the country . . . Moving forward, NAEP will use a digital format for all subjects it assesses.[31]

NAEP still has quite a distance to go on the technology front—we'll get into that later—but its minders deserve credit for bringing it this far along. Though less intentional, they and their predecessors also get points for the ways that NAEP has served as a model for assessments across the United

States and around the world. That's a secondary role, to be sure, but one that has enhanced the influence and respect, even deference, that NAEP has accumulated over the decades.

NAEP's original design, plus many of the enhancements and innovations that have followed, have shaped criterion-based, large-scale assessment domestically and internationally. This begins with the use of careful sampling rather than universal testing, thus easing testing burdens, reducing costs, and improving accuracy by eliminating the temptation to force-feed students in preparation for it.

NAEP (and assessments resembling it) tests populations and education-delivery units, not individuals, and tracks their performance over multiple years. Its vertical scaling enables changes over time to be calibrated and sometimes to align performance at key grade levels within the same subject.[32] Its "bib-spiraling" method makes possible a substantial probe into the content of each subject and grade level without children having to endure lengthy testing sessions.

In those ways and more, NAEP has helped to shape modern educational assessment. Perhaps even more consequentially, at least domestically, NAEP has also worked its way into education policy at the state, national, and sometimes local levels. Writing in 2019, Mullis identified eight "policy-relevant uses" of NAEP that ranged from promoting equity to advancing educational excellence to national and state-by-state monitoring of actual changes in school performance.

NAEP's standards—that is, NAGB's aspirational achievement levels— have played a constructive role in raising the academic expectations of many states, beginning in the mid-1990s when North Carolina legislators instructed their State Board of Education to "develop a plan to create rigorous student academic performance standards for kindergarten through eighth grade and student academic performance standards for courses in grades 9–12. The performance standards shall align, whenever possible, with the student academic performance standards developed by the National Assessment of Educational Progress." Much the same thing has happened in other jurisdictions from Tennessee to Massachusetts.

None of this, however, is reason to relax or rest on laurels, for multiple challenges still confront NAEP and its handlers in the second quarter of the twenty-first century. And that's where we turn next.

PART II

Issues, Challenges, and the Path Ahead

PART

Issues, Challenges,
and the Road Ahead

CHAPTER 7

Tough Choices

N AEP'S PRESENT-DAY MASTERS and influencers confront a host of trade-offs and dilemmas. Indeed, the number of live issues and level of contention around some of them are remarkable for a half-century-old governmental venture that one might expect to be stable if not stodgy. On the other hand, some of today's choices arise from efforts to modernize this aging assessment vehicle, even as others emerge from changes in the world around it.

In this chapter, we examine several such quandaries, beginning with some driven mainly by fiscal constraints.

As shown in table 7.1, NAEP's budget rose almost ninefold between 1990 and 2020, from nearly $18 million to more than $160 million, a greater rate of increase than appropriations for the entire Education Department, greater even than the budget of so high profile an agency as the National Institutes of Health.[1] Unsurprisingly, the biggest jumps occurred in the late 1980s when NAEP was essentially relaunched with a larger mission, and again in the early 2000s, coincident with NCLB's further expansion of the assessment's mandate. Yet it's risen—and occasionally fallen—in fits and starts, often with a sizable mismatch between what the executive branch proposes in its budget and what Congress agrees to by way of appropriations. From the perspective of the governing board and NCES, of course, there's never enough to do all that they want NAEP to do, but the erratic course of presidential budgets and their congressional alterations has forced a number of changes, false starts, and compromises.

There have also been fiscal false alarms from time to time and a few instances of crying wolf, as well as times when broadcasting the tough

TABLE 7.1:   NAEP Budget History: 1970–2020

	Requested by President (millions)	Congressional Appropriation (millions)	Disparity: Appropriation minus Request (millions)
2020	156.7	160.7	4.0
2015	132.3	137.2	4.9
2010	138.8	138.8	0.0
2005	94.8	94.1	–0.8
2000	44.5	40.0	–4.5
1995	38.7	32.8	–5.9
1990	12.1	17.7	5.6
1985	4.6	5.7	1.1
1980	4.0	3.9	–0.1
1975	7.0	4.6	–2.4
1970	4.0	2.4	–1.6

Sources: Congressional allocation data from 1995–2020 is from "Education Department Budget History Tables: FY 1980–FY 2021 Congressional Appropriations," U.S. Department of Education, https://www2.ed.gov/about/overview /budget/history/index.html. These data include the allocations to cover the expenses of the National Assessment Governing Board that may not be strictly NAEP related. Data for congressional appropriations from 1970–1985 come from the U.S. Government Accounting Office, *Changes in Funds and Priorities Have Affected Production and Quality*, PEMD-88-4 (Washington DC, 1987), 99. Data for the 1990 appropriation come from Maris A. Vinovskis, *Overseeing the Nation's Report Card: The Creation and Evolution* (NAGB, 1998), 17. Data for the president›s budget from 1970–1990 come from James A. Hazlett, *A history of the National Assessment of Educational Progress, 1963-1973,* (University of Kentucky, 1973) diss., 255; Mary L. Bourque, *A History of NAEP Achievement Levels: Issues, Implementation, and Impact 1989–2009,* (Washington, DC: National Assessment Governing Board, 2009) 1; U.S. Congress, House of Representatives, *Committee on Appropriations, Departments of Labor and Health, Education, and Welfare Appropriations for 1980: Hearings Before a Subcommittee of the Committee on Appropriations*, 96th Cong., 1st Sess., Part 10, (1979), 794; U.S. Congress, House of Representatives, *Departments of Labor, Health and Human Services, Education, and related agencies appropriations for 1985 hearings before a subcommittee of the Committee on Appropriations*, 98th Cong., 2nd Sess., Part 6, (1984), 1236 and 1289; and the Consortium of Social Science Association, "COSSA Washington Update," (1989) 8(2), 12.

choices that an overly tight budget would force helped to forestall that situation.

In January 1989, for instance, as chair of NAGB, I advised executive branch budgeteers in writing that NAEP would need "at least" $15 million in fiscal 1990 or "radical reductions must be made, probably the elimination of part or all of the state-by-state trial assessment, one or more entire grade levels, one or more subjects, or some combination of such reductions." Yet that year's presidential budget sought just $12 million, and the department's cognizant assistant secretary at the time assured Congress that this sum would suffice.[2] In the end, however, more sympathetic lawmakers appropriated the amount that NAGB said was needed, which amounted to a whopping 50 percent increase over the 1989 figure.

On a few other occasions, congressional appropriators have channeled more funds into NAEP than the White House sought. More often, though, the president's budget request was trimmed on Capitol Hill—and sometimes whacked hard. In preparing the White House request for fiscal 1992, GOP education secretary Lamar Alexander succeeded in doubling his predecessor's 1991 figure—and asking for $37 million. But the Democratic Congress cut it back to $30 million, followed by a much greater reduction in 1993, when less than half of President Bush's budget for NAEP was ultimately appropriated. At least eighteen more times between 1994 and 2020, the appropriation lagged the budget request, whether by small sums or large whacks, compared with just five years when lawmakers furnished more than the White House sought.

Another example occurred during the administration of the second President Bush. Late in 2007, NAGB chair Darvin Winnick—a longtime colleague and friend of the chief executive—warned his board colleagues that the pending appropriation for fiscal 2008 would force a number of cutbacks.[3] In the end, Congress earmarked almost $13 million less for NAEP than the White House sought—and cuts were indeed made.

In addition to the miseries that such fiscal ups and downs have caused those in charge of the assessment, we see a vivid illustration of the fact that NAEP has generally held higher priority for the executive branch than for Congress. We also observe the consequence of NAEP having had few true champions on Capitol Hill.

There's no doubt that the assessment—and education statistics more generally—had to subsist on extremely lean rations in the early days. In recent years, as more mandates have hit NAEP even as some obsolete practices have boosted costs, it's harder to say just how much funding NAEP really needs. This naturally depends on how much it's trying to do and the true costs of doing that well. Those contingencies, however, don't make the choices and trade-offs any easier in the near term.

The most obvious impact of tight money is that NAEP cannot assess every subject that people want data on; cannot assess anything as often as some would like; cannot always muster the wherewithal to test all three of its designated grade levels; and most of the time cannot supply state-level data. Because present law requires that reading and math be tested in every state every two years, that assignment commands top priority and consumes lots of resources, though a reasonable (and to me compelling) case can be made that student achievement changes so slowly that this cycle is needlessly compressed.

Costs are rising, too, partly (and perhaps temporarily) due to NAEP's big shift to digital-based assessments, partly due to archaic practices still used during test administration and inefficiencies built into the aging assessment system, but also resulting from the quasi monopoly that a group of long-term contractors, now dubbed the "NAEP Alliance," has come to enjoy whenever the government calls for bids to conduct future rounds of the assessment. As drily noted in the Education Department's justification documents for its fiscal 2021 budget request, "The recent effort to renew the NAEP Alliance Contracts that support NAEP administration has shown that NAEP costs are rising . . . Initial bids for activities on the original NAEP schedule were far higher than expected, necessitating significant modifications to the assessment schedule."[4]

Lengthening the NCLB/ESSA cycle of mandatory assessments from two to three or four years would require congressional assent, but I'm not alone in favoring such a change. In her November 2020 letter to Congress, triggered by the Covid-induced need to defer the 2021 testing round, then-education secretary Betsy DeVos also urged that the biennial cycle be stretched, both to conserve scarce resources amid rising costs and because shifts in large-scale test scores are nearly always very gradual.

On NAEP's 500-point scale, for example, the average eighth-grade reading score of 263 in 2019 was exactly the same as in 1998. Over the course of those two decades, the most it fluctuated was down to 262 and up to 268. The most it ever changed between two years was 4 points. In eighth-grade math, too, the largest shift in average scores between two years (since 2003) was 3 points.

As DeVos wrote,

It seems clear that the costs of conducting the core NAEP tests every two years far outweigh the benefits of marginally enhancing well-established achievement trend lines. This is why our FY 2021 budget request proposed exploring the option of administering reading and math assessments on a staggered, four-year schedule . . . This would save as much as $20 million per administration—money that could be redeployed for the needed modernization of NAEP or used to expand other important tests, including civics.[5]

Of course, there's another side to this argument. In a private communication, a veteran NAGB member offers this view of testing frequency:

> You are correct that reading scores don't change much in 2 years. They haven't changed much in 20 years. So what about an every-other-decade NAEP? . . . Measuring reading achievement less often isn't going to increase reading performance. If anything, more frequent assessment is one of the only things that keeps us focused on the stagnation and makes it annoyingly uncomfortable for education leaders and reading experts to avoid really addressing it. It seems to me to be somewhat of a *non sequitur* to suggest that stagnation is a reason to measure less frequently. I also have a concern about the long-term viability of the only thing left in American education that has a prayer of providing stable information over time. If people think NAEP is disconnected from classrooms and largely irrelevant now, at least it pokes its head up every couple of years and reminds folks about what is (or isn't) happening.[6]

In other words, this individual contends, frequent documentation of weak achievement helps maintain pressure to do something about it—and NAEP's very existence hinges in part on its regular visibility.

DeVos would direct any savings from extending the cycle into modernization of NAEP's methodology and more regular testing of civics. Both are worthy. Yet just as compelling, at least to this author, is to rectify NAEP's failure to supply state-specific twelfth-grade achievement data, even in reading and math. When Congress mandated biennial data in those subjects for every state and selected urban districts, it specified only grades 4 and 8. Since then, NAEP has been unable to furnish regular twelfth-grade results at the state level (or for TUDA districts), never mind that the end of high school is such a crucial transition point in American education.

This data vacuum, however, is not just a budget issue. It seems that state leaders aren't exactly falling over each other in pursuit of twelfth-grade

NAEP results. Or so one may infer from this episode: helped by a boost in its budget, some congressional encouragement, and apparently some high-level interest within the Bush (43) administration, NAGB moved in 2008 to invite states to take part in a pilot program of twelfth-grade reading and math assessment, which was repeated in 2013. But just eleven states volunteered for the first round and thirteen for the second. Then nothing. No more state-level reporting for twelfth graders, save for windful opportunities (as in 2019) when the national sample incorporated enough schools and students in a handful of big states to generate reasonably accurate data for those states without them having to request it.

It's not entirely clear why there's been scant demand for twelfth-grade state-level results. Do state leaders not trust data derived from the test scores of weary high school seniors? Has NAGB's disinclination to declare that "NAEP proficient" in twelfth grade means "prepared for college" limited the value of this metric for state officials? Do they see no need for additional testing at the end of high school, considering how many students already take college entrance exams, Advanced Placement tests, and sometimes a state's own end-of-course exams or graduation tests? Or do they not want this sort of external "audit" and thereby risk exposing their weak results? That's certainly possible, considering that, in 2013, even high-scoring Massachusetts tabulated just 34 percent of its twelfth graders at or above NAEP's "proficient" bar in math, compared with 55 percent of its eighth graders. (In reading that year, Connecticut showed the reverse pattern, with half its seniors proficient on the NAEP metric—the most of any participating state—versus 45 percent in eighth grade.)[7]

When queried about their understanding of states' seeming apathy, NCES staff added these possible explanations: too much overall testing burden, plus it's hard to motivate twelfth graders at that time of year to participate in a voluntary assessment, especially when it's sample based, does them no good, and doesn't even supply them with feedback. Besides, it's too late to change anything in their lives or schools by the time they're assessed and the results reported. They'll already have graduated!

Still, this issue needs revisiting, given today's lively interest in young peoples' career and college readiness at the end of twelfth grade, the urgency of reforming their high schools, the evidence (from national and LTT NAEP as well as other measures) that actual learning isn't keeping up with rising graduation rates, and the fact that no other end-of-high-school metric is uniform across the county and samples all seniors, not just the college-bound. Indeed, as more colleges go test-optional or even test-averse, participation in such familiar measures as the SAT and ACT is certain to decline, making twelfth-grade NAEP data even more valuable.

How sacred are NAEP's trend lines? Some (including this author) contend that tracking change over time in the achievement of US students and the performance of their schools, however gradual or abrupt it may be, is NAEP's single most valuable function and solemn responsibility. But sticking with a trend line means keeping what's on the test more or less constant over the years, which is certain to raise concern as curricular emphases, education-reform priorities, and testing technologies evolve over time. How informative are assessment results in 2025, say, if they're based on what was being taught in American schools at the turn of the century? Even the three Rs slowly change as the decades pass, while subjects such as science, art, and civics tend to change faster.

On the other hand, how valuable are 2025 results on a measure like NAEP if they cannot be compared with previous results? Is achievement improving or not—and for which kids? That's what state and national leaders—and innumerable analysts, reformers, philanthropists, and pundits—most want to know. There's no way to know if previous years' scores are not comparable. But how long must "previous" last? Do the tests ever get so long in the tooth as not to measure what's important for young Americans to be learning today? Or should the skills and knowledge probed by NAEP be treated as the one stable boulder on an otherwise shifting hillside of curricular and pedagogical fads?

There's no totally satisfactory answer, meaning we're back to the trade-offs and tough choices that NAEP's custodians and constituents have wrestled with for half a century, seeking ways to be current and relevant while clinging to the obligation to monitor gains and losses over time.

One response to that dual challenge is to do both, that is, to retain NAEP's LTT assessment in stable form alongside periodic changes in "main NAEP" and the periodic interruption of its trend lines.

LTT boasts a consistent trend line back to the early 1970s. Keeping it going maintains the historical picture while allowing "main NAEP" to reboot from time to time. Yet there's a rollicking controversy over whether LTT is worth retaining at all, especially considering that it employs an aging testing format based on yesterday's curricular and pedagogical practices.

LTT has been contentious for as long as I can remember. On the plus side, it's by far the most robust measure of the academic achievement of young Americans over the past half century in the core subjects of reading and math—and it has attested to actual gains in both subjects for nine- and thirteen-year-olds from the early 1970s through 2012, as well as a startling decline among thirteen-year-olds between 2012 and 2020 in both reading and math, while also documenting essentially flat scores among seventeen-year-olds nationwide, even as almost every subpopulation has seen improvement.[8] No other data source can compare.

On the negative side, however, what LTT tests is what was deemed important for students to know and be able to do back in the Nixon-Ford era, which in many respects does not correspond to education emphases in the twenty-first century. Because it reports on age groups rather than grade levels (as "main NAEP" does), in addition to probing somewhat different knowledge and skills, results of the two assessments are not directly comparable. The very existence of two forms of NAEP is confusing. And because LTT inevitably gets lower priority in budget and scheduling decisions, it's administered less and less often. Intervals were generally four years through 2012, but then NCES skipped eight years—and because of the pandemic in 2020, that year's LTT administration for seventeen-year-olds proved impossible. At this writing, they're supposed to take it in 2022—a full decade after the last time—but whether that actually happens will depend on budget and much else.

NAGB undertook a comprehensive review of LTT in 2016, launching it with a long, careful paper by Stanford psychometrician (and erstwhile NAGB member) Edward Haertel. He concluded that

> LTT is a critical component of NAEP, adding substantial value not only historically but right up to the present . . . [T]here is an abiding interest on the part of some policymakers, educators, and segments of the public in students' performance on content and skills viewed as simpler and more traditional than those espoused in current curriculum reforms. This is the kind of material tested by LTT.[9]

Haertel did, however, flag—and commentators on his paper underscored—the need to modernize LTT in various ways in order to retain its value and viability, such as navigating a careful shift in test administration from paper and pencil to digital testing—as has been done to "main NAEP"—without disrupting the trends themselves.

Although its timing has been muddled—and extended—along with everything else due to the Covid-19 pandemic, that shift is presently in the works.

How does "main NAEP" get updated from time to time? It starts with revising or replacing an assessment framework. But that's an enormous undertaking and one fraught with plentiful disputes in its own right.

Though individual test questions change from one administration to the next, and some are released for public viewing and cannot be reused in a secure test, repeated testing cycles ordinarily employ the same framework for that subject, a document that spells out in great detail what are the knowledge and skills being evaluated and which elements of a subject should consume how much of the test instrument itself, an allocation that differs by grade level as school curricula and expectations for students move from relatively rudimentary content and skills to the more sophisticated kind. Table 7.2 shows an example from the 2019 math framework.[10]

TABLE 7.2   Item distribution: 2019 NAEP mathematics assessment

Item distribution. The distribution of items among the various mathematical content areas is a critical feature of the assessment design because it reflects the relative importance and value given to each. As has been the case with past NAEP assessments, the categories receive differential emphasis at each grade. The table provides the recommended balance of items in the assessment by content area for each grade (4, 8, and 12). The recommended item distribution is identical to the percentages found in the 2005 NAEP Mathematics Framework. Note that the percentages refer to numbers of items, not the amount of testing time.

Percentage distribution of items by grade and content area	Grade 4	Grade 8	Grade 12
Number properties and operations	40	20	10
Measurement	20	15	30
Geometry	15	20	
Data analysis, statistics, and probability	10	15	25
Algebra	15	30	35

Source: *Mathematics Framework* (Washington, DC: National Assessment Governing Board, 2017), 6, https://www.nagb.gov/naep-frameworks/mathematics.html.

Each assessment framework is developed by NAGB through a multi-year process that includes wide-ranging consultation with experts in the field, practitioners, public officials, and interested members of the general public. Changing or replacing a framework is costly, protracted, and labor-intensive, and most of the time it leads to substantial changes in what's being assessed. Those changes may cause a broken trend line, which is a considerable price to pay and thus a deterrent from doing it very often.

For example, NAGB's current framework for science, adopted for the 2015 assessment cycle, was based on a 2009 framework, which replaced one from the early 1990s and which launched a completely new trend line. In other words, student achievement in science in 2009 and thereafter cannot be compared with prior results. The board provided an extensive and generally convincing rationale for the change, but the trade-off is evident.[11]

As this book was being written, something similar was underway in reading, as NAGB struggled over a proposed new framework that, if adopted, would kick in in 2026, replacing the reading framework in use since 2009, which in turn replaced one dating to 1992. The revision was contentious for many reasons, including the risk that the substantial changes its "visioners" contemplated for reading assessment would likely force a new trend line to commence.[12]

That's no easy choice. Neither is the trend-line restart that may follow a big shift—such as DeVos urged and IES director Schneider seeks—to "NAEP in the cloud," which includes test items generated with the help of artificial intelligence, technology-assisted scoring of assessments, and possibly computer-adaptive individual testing.[13] Intricate "bridging studies" sometimes make it possible to impute previous NAEP results to a new trend line (or vice versa), but the more profound the framework change, the less likely these bridges are to hold strong against the torrent of innovation and replacement.

Messing with the trend line, however, is not the sole difficulty associated with changing a NAEP framework and ensuing tests. Indeed, the challenge of doing this in a way that doesn't produce more headache than benefit calls to mind a quip attributed to Admiral Hyman Rickover, an influential education reformer of the 1980s (as well as legendary "father of the nuclear Navy"), who declared that "changing schools is like moving a graveyard."[14]

When NAGB undertakes to create, update, or replace a framework, dual quandaries swiftly arise: how to frame a national assessment of a particular subject at stated grade levels in a country where decisions about what to teach and how and when to teach it are highly decentralized, where—for example—what eighth graders are supposed to learn about science or writing or civics or the arts in Portland, Maine, may be quite different from lessons taught to their peers in Portland, Oregon; Portland, Georgia; and Portland, Kansas? And, along with curricular decentralization, is it possible to resolve disagreements—sometimes verging on bitter culture wars—among experts in a subject regarding what's most important for kids to learn in school, how it should be learned, how it should be taught, and how it should be assessed?

Given NAEP's role in American K-12 education, its assessment frameworks must straddle or compromise many such divides. Ideally, they represent a wide consensus among experts and practitioners about what's most important for students to know and be able to do in that subject at that grade level, no matter where they live, which means their framers seek to be agnostic about specific curricula. As NAGB explains its try-to-satisfy-multiple-imperatives process:

> For each framework, the Governing Board works with a committee of subject matter experts, practitioners, and members of the general public—including researchers, educators, business leaders, and policymakers—to develop a rich and rigorous set of standards that define what students should know and be able to do in a particular subject.
>
> In order to measure trends in student performance, NAEP frameworks are designed to remain stable for as long as possible. At the same time, all frameworks are responsive to changes in national and international standards and curricula. Without advocating any particular approach to instruction, NAEP frameworks provide a starting point for constructive conversations about high-quality educational standards and assessments.[15]

In practice, NAGB's frameworks do a lot more than "start conversations." Slowly, subtly, indirectly but inexorably, they influence many elements of American K-12 education: other tests and assessments, state academic standards, textbooks, teacher preparation, and more. Because they determine what will be tested at the national—and sometimes state—levels, they inevitably affect what gets taught.

In developing or revising a framework, the board generally appoints several committees to shape and advise on various aspects of it. It hires expert consultants, often orchestrated by an outside contractor engaged to manage the process. Multiple drafts are reviewed and commented on by myriad groups as well as NAGB's own committees, leading to rounds of revisions and refinements. In time, the full board signs off—and another labor-intensive sequence kicks in, as the framework's contents and associated "assessment specifications" get turned into test items that are field tested, checked for possible bias, assembled—jigsaw-puzzle-like—into assessment blocks, then fitted out with all the bells and whistles and operational arrangements that make them possible to administer to carefully chosen samples of American school kids.[16]

For example, creating the ninety-two-page NAEP writing framework, which was developed via a contract with ACT for the 2007 assessment (and reused with slight updating in 2017), involved a twenty-four-member "steering committee," a twenty-eight-member "planning committee," three consultants, one NAGB staffer, and six ACT employees. Their drafts were reviewed and commented on by some fifty organizations ranging from the National School Boards Association and the National Writing Project to the Coca-Cola Company and the South Dakota State Department of Education.[17]

Issues arise every time something like this is undertaken. Developers of that writing framework, for instance, had to contend with whether student responses on the new assessment should be written by hand, as in the past, or typed on a computer keyboard. For some of the flavor of that dispute, see this quote from an article in *Education Week*, published weeks before NAGB's final vote on the framework:

> [A] number of states have incorporated computer-based testing into their writing assessments. Other states are piloting ways of using technology to gauge writing . . . Testing students' writing ability via computer makes sense, some assessment officials from around the country say, not only because of students' widespread familiarity with

computers, but also because of the demands of college and the work-place, where word-processing skills are a must.

"You want a connection between what's going on in the outside world and what's going on in the classroom," said Kathleen Blake Yancey, the vice president of the National Council of Teachers of English . . . "It's a way of saying to schools, 'The 21st century has arrived,'" she said.[18]

That kind of updating is easier said than done, however, and introduces complications that perplex testing officials. For example, should students also be allowed to use the spell-check features that are built into many computerized writing programs? How to deal with school-to-school and home-to-home disparities—more acute in 2007 than today but hardly vanished—in computer access and children's comfort in operating them, disparities that can advantage some students and undermine others?

Automating the assessment would "not make the gap between white and minority students go away. In fact, it may make it larger," contended Edward D. Roeber, then executive director of assessment and accountability for the Michigan education department, which had piloted its own computerized writing test but at the time had not decided whether to use it statewide.[19]

Every subject brings its own arguments. Whether to rebuild NAEP's math assessment around the "new math" (more conceptual, more statistics and data analysis, less measurement and just "getting right answers") consumed NAGB for a time in the late 1990s, as it did the standards-setters of many states.[20] World history turned out to be such a glue trap—what exactly does the subject consist of, and when if ever do states and districts actually teach it?—that NAEP has never been able to assess it. As University of Michigan professor Robert B. Bain wrote of this challenge in 2004, "Given the diversity in curricular approaches, NAGB faces an unusually difficult challenge in creating an exam that will assess students' knowledge of world history . . . [T]he variations in the scope and sequence of what people call world history education challenges the creation of a common assessment."[21]

As for reading, the most basic of subjects, it's universally taught but endlessly fought over by experts, researchers, and advocacy groups. The "reading wars" never seem to end, and the recent effort to develop a new

NAEP framework to guide its assessment was, as noted above and discussed further in later chapters, fraught with controversy and dissension, this time reaching deep into the governing board itself.[22]

Such battles within the obscure realm of National Assessment frameworks are both source and consequence of changes underway in US education policy and practice, as well as in our culture, our politics, even our demographics. The contemporary fracas over reading, for example, included a heated dispute over what additional "supports," if any, should be provided youngsters—often poor and minority—who may lack the vocabulary and experiences that bear on their success in understanding and demonstrating that they understand what's contained in the reading passages that form much of the assessment. Proponents of such supports fly the flag of equity. Opponents say such assistance will mask students' actual reading prowess and lead to falsely positive conclusions about it, thus possibly even blocking educators' efforts to equip those very students with more of what they need to read successfully.

As has happened in other subjects, the new reading framework that NAGB finally agreed to in summer 2021 will not just affect NAEP tests. As noted above, it will echo across American education, gradually influencing state standards, assessments and school accountability regimes, teacher preparation, textbook publishing, and, in time, what's emphasized in classrooms by teachers and their supervisors. NAEP's framework decisions may not make it onto many news broadcasts or twitter storms, but their reverberations underscore the old education maxim that what gets tested is what gets taught. NAEP tests don't "count" for those who take them, yet they count big time for the K–12 system as a whole. Hence the frameworks that drive the tests also matter greatly.

NAEP's custodians understandably want it to be useful and responsive to multiple audiences, constituencies, and interests, both because they're responsible, motivated people who seek better educated Americans and because they're keen to build awareness and support for the assessment. But how far should they extend their work beyond issuing neutrally phrased reports on student achievement? At what point does the push to be responsive and relevant lead to blowback that they're better off avoiding? And what else can they do to make NAEP data accessible and usable without plunging into hot water and possibly placing the assessment at risk?

Neutral reports are NAEP's bread and butter, its best-known products, and producing them is its foremost responsibility. Yet—like most statistical bulletins, whether from the Education Department, the Census Bureau, or the Bureau of Labor Statistics—what's in a NAEP "Report Card" is fundamentally inert: just data. It's what's done with that information that matters in the real world. What problems does it illuminate? What questions does it help answer? To what additional uses can it be put? How can it be made more widely known—and valued?

Over the years, NCES, the governing board, and myriad outside analysts and contractors have undertaken many extra studies utilizing NAEP data. These sometimes involve special samples, nonstandard data collections, or esoteric analyses. Some are needed for NAEP's own housekeeping, such as probing the feasibility—later implemented at scale—of testing student achievement digitally rather than via paper and pencil, as well as multiple efforts to monitor the inclusion (or not) of children with disabilities.

Other special studies range further afield. Examples include examining the transcripts of participating high school students, seeking possible relationships between the courses they've taken and the grades received—and their overall GPA—and their NAEP scores.[23] On another front, at least four projects have been mounted to examine the education and academic achievement of Native Americans.[24] We've seen two appraisals of fourth graders' oral reading prowess and a look at math education in Puerto Rico. And as American education took stock of the damage done by the Covid-19 pandemic, in early 2021 the Institute of Education Sciences (responding to an executive order from President Biden on his second day in office) made imaginative use of schools already in the NAEP sample to initiate a periodic survey of elementary and middle schools on such urgent questions as online versus hybrid versus in-person learning and how many hours a day children were actually engaged with teachers and schools.[25]

Both done in-house and undertaken by outside analysts, multiple forays have been made to link NAEP results to data from other sources, including imaginative efforts to connect scores to TIMSS results such that individual states could see how they would rank internationally, as well as studies of states' own proficiency standards and performance compared with "NAEP proficient."[26]

NAEP's gold mine of data naturally holds keen interest for analysts across the US and beyond, interest that has intensified in an era of school reform and amid a flowering of education research and policy analysis. NCES and NAGB have striven to make those data better known and more accessible, both as a public service and to widen awareness of and stakeholder support for NAEP itself.

Toward that end, they developed the "NAEP Data Explorer" to foster wide use of NAEP results for secondary analyses of many kinds. Accessible there are not just test results but also data from the student, teacher, and school questionnaires that are administered in conjunction with the assessments. Using this web tool, analysts can build their own tables, examine multiple years of assessment results—from 1990 in most cases—for various subjects, grades, and jurisdictions, and view information about factors that may be related to student learning.

NCES also assists researchers to analyze these data and understand how to exploit NAEP's huge information base. Analysts willing to pursue a "restricted use" license and obey the privacy rules can even dig into raw NAEP data, right down to respondent-level information.[27] They may also apply for modest funding from the Institute of Education Sciences to support their analysis of these data.[28]

All this is generally positive, serving to deepen our understanding of American education, make NAEP more transparent, and foster support for it, but such efforts occasionally backfire, most notably when analysts, whether inside or outside the government, employ NAEP data to support findings and recommendations that go beyond what can legitimately be done with those data, or when they apply those data to political hot potatoes.

In 2013, Stephen Sawchuck, an astute journalist at *Education Week*, popularized the term "misnaepery"—borrowed from an analyst at Mathematica Policy Research—to describe ill-conceived efforts to deploy NAEP data to explain things that lie beyond the explanatory power of such data. He wrote:

> [W]hen it comes to many of the ways the exam's data are used, researchers have gotten used to gritting their teeth. Results from the venerable exam are frequently pressed into service to bolster claims about the effect that policies . . . have had on student achievement. While those assertions are compelling, provocative, and possibly even correct, they are also mostly speculative, researchers say. That's because

the exam's technical properties make it difficult to use NAEP data to prove cause-and-effect claims about specific policies or instructional interventions.[29]

He cited multiple examples of elected officials, education leaders, and advocacy groups citing NAEP data to "document" their claims about what was or wasn't working, how many students were or weren't on "grade level" (which NAEP does not estimate or report), and more. He also pointed out instances of the same NAEP results being cited in support of opposite claims!

It's surely tempting. Data look as if they exist to be deployed, and people do this sort of thing all the time. Consider, for instance, how often unemployment rates are invoked as evidence that some federal economic policy has succeeded or failed. As I write, the (truly horrendous) data about Covid-19 infection and death rates are cited dozens of times every day in support of or rebuttal to some assertion about public health practices, statewide shutdowns, vaccination requirements, mask mandates, and much more. Yet data about what is or isn't, what's changed or hasn't, cannot legitimately explain the *cause* of things unless they emerge from a proper experiment that controls for other factors that may affect what's being reported.

Tempting, indeed, yet risky to the data themselves if they seem to be serving as ammunition in policy battles and political contests. This risk mounts when the government agency that collects the data also engages directly in such arguments, as happened (for example) in 2005 when NCES issued a pair of reports that compared pupil achievement in private schools, charter schools, and regular public schools. The initial analyses (based on 2003 NAEP results) suggested that private school pupils were ahead of their public school counterparts but also that "traditional" (i.e., district-operated) public schools were academically superior to charters.[30]

This produced a huge ruckus: commentaries in the *New York Times*, crowing by teacher unions about the shortcomings of the still relatively new charter phenomenon, full-page ads by charter partisans, multiple reanalyses by both disinterested scholars and advocacy groups, and ultimately, admission by the NCES commissioner that his agency ought not to have embarked on this in the first place.

"This is not what we should be doing," Mark Schneider said in an interview with *Education Week*. "It's one thing for [an academic researcher] to put out a study. That's a totally different story than if NCES, as a statistical agency, is weighing in on that front." He also made clear that they weren't going to do it again.[31]

Yet misnaepery continues to rear its head, notwithstanding critics of the practice, although today it arises more often among policy makers and advocates seeking to score points than among scrupulous analysts—and now almost never within NCES itself.[32]

How much and how fast should NAEP embrace technology, modernize its methods, perhaps even submit to a wholesale overhaul? Secretary DeVos's November 2020 letter to Congress may have focused on Covid-induced delays, but in fact she went considerably further, recommending that lawmakers consider a thoroughgoing reboot:

> It is time for Congress to rethink the entire NAEP program and improve its efficiency, efficacy, and budget . . . Other changes that I encourage Congress to explore in concert with IES, NAGB, and the assessment community include moving test administration to the cloud—to eliminate the logistical complexity and cost of sending thousands of test administrators to thousands of schools—and restructuring NAEP assessments on a foundation of technology-enabled adaptive testing.[33]

Nor did DeVos stop there. While swearing in new NAGB members at the board's November 2020 meeting, she also suggested that the governing board replace its tripartite achievement-level reporting schema with an A to F system, much as schools handle kids' report cards and some states rate schools under their ESSA accountability systems.

How vigorously the Biden administration and Secretary Miguel Cardona will pursue (and budget for) such changes is unknowable at this writing but doing so could transform NAEP in fundamental ways. Moving it "to the cloud" and going further than NAEP previously has toward "technology-enabled adaptive testing" would bring benefits on several fronts but must be done with great care to avoid restarting trend lines. Replacing achievement levels with a different reporting system, besides being an awkward fit with the rigor built into NAEP's scoring scales, would clatter disruptively through the country's entire proficiency-centric approach to school reform and accountability. But recouping a portion of the NAEP budget to redeploy for other high-priority assessment needs holds many possibilities.

Money obviously matters, but—as usual in Washington—debates about how best to spend available dollars aren't just about the dollars. They're about priorities, which do change. They're about established practices and interests, which resist change. They're about politics, which are both a constant present and an ever-present source of conflict and gamesmanship. And they're about government programs, large and small, sometimes having to adapt in order to better meet the needs of an ever-changing society. How these decisions get made for NAEP is the rock face we chip at in the next chapter.

CHAPTER 8

Stakeholders and Semi-independence

A S THE NATIONAL ASSESSMENT has enlarged in size, budget, complexity, and influence, its governance has also grown more elaborate and sometimes more conflicted. Though rarely afflicted by partisanship per se, it is tugged in many directions, obliged to accommodate multiple masters, and pressed to juggle competing demands from a lengthening list of interested parties. Increasingly, like so much of contemporary America, it's also showing signs of ideological division. In this chapter, we look more closely at the arenas in which that juggling occurs.

As outlined in chapter 1, the complexities begin with Congress's intentional but clumsy division of authority between NAEP's twenty-six-member governing board (consisting of a meticulously delineated Noah's Ark of roles and categories, appointed by the education secretary) and the National Center for Education Statistics, which is headed by a quasi-independent commissioner but also part of the US Education Department. Within that sprawling cabinet agency, NCES fits within the Institute of Education Sciences (IES), which has its own director (serving a six-year term meant to span presidential administrations) and its own policy board.[1] Looming over IES is the rest of the departmental hierarchy with its many staff offices and political appointees. Loftier still in the pecking order are the White House, Office of Management and Budget, plus the remainder of the executive branch apparatus such as Office of Personnel Management and General Services Administration. Then there's Congress. And then there's all the rest. (See box 8.1.)

BOX 8.1   Statute authorizing the National Assessment Governing Board

SEC. 302. NATIONAL ASSESSMENT GOVERNING BOARD.

1. ESTABLISHMENT—There is established the National Assessment Governing Board (hereafter in this title referred to as the 'Assessment Board'), which shall formulate policy guidelines for the National Assessment (carried out under section 303).

2. MEMBERSHIP

    1. APPOINTMENT AND COMPOSITION—The Assessment Board shall be appointed by the Secretary and be composed as follows:

        1. Two Governors, or former Governors, who shall not be members of the same political party.

        2. Two State legislators, who shall not be members of the same political party.

        3. Two chief State school officers.

        4. One superintendent of a local educational agency.

        5. One member of a State board of education.

        6. One member of a local board of education.

        7. Three classroom teachers representing the grade levels at which the National Assessment is conducted.

        8. One representative of business or industry.

        9. Two curriculum specialists.

        10. Three testing and measurement experts, who shall have training and experience in the field of testing and measurement.

        11. One nonpublic school administrator or policymaker.

        12. Two school principals, of whom one shall be an elementary school principal and one shall be a secondary school principal.

        13. Two parents who are not employed by a local, State or Federal educational agency.

        14. Two additional members who are representatives of the general public, and who may be parents, but who are not employed by a local, State, or Federal educational agency.

    2. DIRECTOR OF THE INSTITUTE OF EDUCATION SCIENCES— The Director of the Institute of Education Sciences shall serve as an ex officio, nonvoting member of the Assessment Board.

BOX 8.1   *(Continued)*

3. BALANCE AND DIVERSITY—The Secretary and the Assessment Board shall ensure at all times that the membership of the Assessment Board reflects regional, racial, gender, and cultural balance and diversity and that the Assessment Board exercises its independent judgment, free from inappropriate influences and special interests.

3. TERMS

1. IN GENERAL—Terms of service of members of the Assessment Board shall be staggered and may not exceed a period of 4 years, as determined by the Secretary.

2. SERVICE LIMITATION—Members of the Assessment Board may serve not more than two terms.

Source: This is a portion of the National Assessment of Educational Progress statute as amended in 2002, which differs slightly from the 1988 law and earlier versions, "The NAEP Law," National Assessment Governing Board, https://www.nagb.gov/about-naep/the-naep-law.html.

That NAEP should have a policy-setting board was neither a novel idea nor an entirely new practice in 1988 when Congress formalized the present structure. The Education Commission of the States had created a small body of this kind before 1970, Congress had spelled out some parameters for such a group in 1978, and ETS had recruited a blue-ribbon cast for the Assessment Policy Committee that functioned in this way after 1983.[2] Yet all those earlier bodies, eminent as their members may have been and seriously as their policy guidance was usually taken, were creatures of the primary NAEP contractor, which was itself answerable to NCES and thus ultimately to the education (or HEW) secretary. They were never truly independent.

Going forward, as we saw in chapter 3, the Alexander-James study group wanted NAEP's governance to be as autonomous as possible, and the National Academy of Education stressed that feature in its review of the panel's report: "[T]he enabling legislation for the new NAEP should clearly assure its independence."

In most respects, Congress took that admonition seriously, mandating a *governing board*—not just a "policy committee"—and stipulating that "[i]n the exercise of its functions, powers, and duties, the Board shall hire its own staff and shall be independent of the Secretary and the other offices and officers of the Department of Education."

Under the 1988 legislation, board appointments were also structured in a way that enhanced the group's autonomy. At the outset, existing members of ETS's policy committee were grandfathered in for the duration of their terms. To fill other slots on the board, plus every future opening, the secretary of education would make appointments for four-year terms with the possibility of one reappointment. Once the first board was assembled (by Bill Bennett and myself), the board—and only the board—was charged with nominating suitable candidates for the secretary's consideration.[3] NAGB would, in that sense, be self-perpetuating, but not without constraints, for in making nominations, it was ordered to consult with relevant constituency organizations, and for each opening it was required to send the secretary at least three candidates who "by reason of experience or training, are qualified in [*sic*] that particular Board vacancy." Moreover, the secretary and board were admonished to ensure that NAGB as a whole "reflects regional, racial, gender and cultural balance and diversity and that it exercises its independent judgment, free from inappropriate influence and special interests." In those two clauses, we can see Congress's slightly schizophrenic dual objective: both to make NAEP's governing body representative of all manner of perspectives, constituencies, and interests *and* to ensure its freedom from the influence of "special interests."

Considering the care taken by lawmakers to ensure a bipartisan and constituency-representative board, NAGB could easily have come to resemble the United Nations or any other turf-obsessed body whose members bicker endlessly over their mostly divergent loyalties and priorities. Remarkably, however, little of that happened. Pretty much from day one, board members worked well together and generally managed to submerge parochial interests beneath an earnest pursuit of the public good. (Perhaps it helped that they often felt that they—we—were combating common foes on matters like achievement levels and state testing.) It's a little awkward for me to cite the flattering recollections of longtime (1989–2002) NAGB executive director Roy Truby, but his take on the board's culture during its early years is important to share:

After I was appointed the first Executive Director of NAGB, I read the minutes of the Board's first and—thus far—only meeting. Which led me to wonder, what had I gotten myself into? I understood that NAGB was structured to be independent and bipartisan (two governors, two state legislators, one of each from each party, plus more than a dozen representatives of various education constituencies). But what would it take to forge such a group into a functioning policy body? I assumed that it would be a huge challenge. Happily, I turned out to be wrong.

It developed very quickly and exceeded my expectations. Members almost immediately looked to the public interest and to what they had in common. Instead of bipartisan, it turned out to be *non*partisan. I like to think that I and my new staff colleagues helped with that but, as I look back, much of the credit goes to Chester Finn, our first Chairman, fresh from the Reagan administration. The first two vice chairs were strong, smart, independent-minded women, both senior state legislators, both Democrats: Pat Frank from Florida and Wilhelmina Delco from Texas. Checker[4] embraced them as full partners and the Board followed his example for the thirteen years that I had the honor of serving as its Executive Director.

I saw a Board that looked after the interests of the country and the education community writ large, putting teachers, students and parents at the forefront. Checker led by working tirelessly to develop consensus and always supported the democratic process even when he had a different opinion. So did the distinguished educators who succeeded him as chair, including Richard Boyd, Mark Musick and William Randall.

A board like that hardly seems possible today. But it appears that this foundation of nonpartisan independence has lasted for over three decades.[5]

In addition to Truby—whose prior career included stints as state superintendent in both Idaho and West Virginia—NAGB benefited from an extraordinary core staff of talented individuals who joined at the outset and remained for a decade or two. They brought to the job imagination, courage, a variety of different experiences and expertise, a penchant for hard work, and remarkable loyalty to the board, to NAEP, and (usually) to each other. Included in that initial honor roll were Mary Lyn Bourque, Mary Crovo, Lawrence Feinberg, Ray Fields, Dan Taylor, and Mary Ann Wilmer. They worked smoothly—but, when necessary, forcefully—with their NCES counterparts, notably including Emerson Elliott, Gary Phillips, and Peggy Carr, as well as with a host of outside contractors, hovering interest groups, and innumerable commentators and critics.[6]

Serving on the board took dedication and entailed real work for little tangible reward. Terms lasted four years, with four full-board meetings per annum, each generally two days long and held in various locations around the country—usually cities where a member wanted to play host—plus honest-to-god committee work in between. Myriad government ethics and conflict-of-interest rules apply to members, yet the compensation is minimal—$100 a day when engaged in board work, plus expenses reimbursed at government rates.[7] Only the governors were allowed to send stand-ins to NAGB meetings. Yet attendance was robust, morale was high, and as Truby's note suggests, relations were generally cordial. People strove for consensus, even when their preferences differed or loyalties conflicted. Many NAGB alums keep in touch with each other and with NAEP goings-on. Many look back on their board terms as challenging but gratifying public service that they're exceptionally proud of. Many also recall their NAGB experience as valuable professional development for themselves and their careers.

Entrusting NAEP's governance to the new board also symbolized—and contributed to—a subtle but fundamental change in the sense of "ownership" of what by the late 1980s was being referred to (per Lamar Alexander's savvy wordsmithing) as "the nation's report card." The assessment had begun as an elite Washington venture, catalyzed by a top federal official wanting more information about US education results, incubated by wealthy private foundations, and designed by senior academics bent on creating a new source of data for analysis and research. A quarter century later, although paid for and operated by the federal government, NAEP was coming to "belong" to America's educators, state and local leaders, even ordinary citizens—all now represented on its governing body. Obscure no longer, the information that it generated was beginning to appear in the morning papers and occasionally on the nightly news, not just in scholarly journals and papers presented at research conferences. And its newly formed board swiftly tackled two big projects that were not only responsive to the Charlottesville summit but that would also amplify NAEP's role. Which is to say, NAEP and those responsible for it were becoming fully engaged—even deeply enmeshed—in the accelerating reform efforts that characterized American public education in the wake of *A Nation At Risk*. It had become part of the real world.

At first blush, NAEP's authorizing law seems to place NAGB in charge of everything that matters. The statute provides, among other things, that the board shall:

> formulate policy guidelines for the National Assessment . . . In carrying out its functions . . . the Assessment Board shall—select the subject areas to be assessed . . . ; develop appropriate student achievement levels . . . ; develop assessment objectives . . . and test specifications that produce an assessment that is valid and reliable, and are based on relevant widely accepted professional standards; . . . develop a process for review of the assessment . . . ; design the methodology of the assessment to ensure that assessment items are valid and reliable . . . ; measure student academic achievement in grades 4, 8, and 12 in the authorized academic subjects; develop guidelines for reporting and disseminating results; develop standards and procedures for regional and national comparisons; take appropriate actions needed to improve the form, content, use, and reporting of results of any assessment . . . ; plan and execute the initial public release of National Assessment of Educational Progress reports . . . The Assessment Board shall have final authority on the appropriateness of all assessment items.[8]

Such sweeping authority and autonomy for a board of this sort is highly unusual in Washington, certainly for constituent parts of large cabinet departments.[9] Though such agencies are typically awash in "advisory committees"—the Education Department has a dozen of them—those rarely wield real power. In fact, the department's listing of "Boards and Commissions" identifies NAGB (and only NAGB) as an "independent organization affiliated with ED."[10]

In reality, however, it's not quite so clear who's in charge of what when it comes to NAEP. For the same statute that created NAGB also empowered the NCES commissioner, "with the *advice* of the Assessment Board" (emphasis added), to "carry out, through grants, contracts, or cooperative agreements with one or more qualified organizations, or consortia thereof, a National Assessment of Educational Progress." Language repeated multiple times in that law authorizes the commissioner not only to "conduct" the assessment but also to "report" on its results. Other provisions admonish that individual to employ "widely accepted professional testing standards" in the design and operation of NAEP. And while several provisions refer to "consultation" between board and commissioner, such arrangements only work smoothly when the parties are in general agreement and on cordial terms, which over the years has often but not always been the case.

It's never been open warfare, but neither has this been a frictionless relationship. The potential for conflict is present in any sort of shared command, and in this case that command is shared between a board comprised primarily of practitioners, public officials, and ordinary citizens, almost all of them nonstatisticians keen to catalyze changes in American K–12 education, and a commissioner (and NCES team) enculturated in the norms and procedures of statistical accuracy, integrity, and caution. In practice, this means their priorities, goals, and sense of urgency are destined to differ. Yet they need each other, too. NAEP since 1988 has been a joint venture, originally a compromise between a Senate that favored the governing board and a House of Representatives that wasn't paying much attention to NAEP but was well acquainted with NCES and its commissioner.[11] That has evolved into a functional but sometimes stressful team effort between an independent governing board and a rather traditional arm of the executive branch, in this case one that's also burdened by its own autonomy anxieties and imbued with the precepts, laws, and regulations that bear on all of the government's dozen or so statistical agencies as well as the norms and ethical standards of the statistics profession.[12]

Codependent as they are, NAGB and NCES have been somewhat jealous of each other's powers and prerogatives, and have engaged in a bit of an arms race. The board has gradually expanded its own staff, assembled its own cadres of experts, consultants, and contractors, sought its own means of circumventing the departmental bureaucracy in (for example) communicating with Congress and the public, and made regular use of its growing network of former board members with their contacts and networks.

On its side, besides using the IES and department staff units to its advantage, especially in budget-making and congressional relations, NCES has edged toward policy analysis and policy making in the NAEP realm, as well as conducting its own external studies and analyses and buttressing the expertise of its career team by naming a long-running "National Validity Studies" panel, comprised of eighteen heavyweight experts, NCES alumni or alumnae, and representatives from key organizations. It focuses primarily on technical matters but has sometimes resembled the agency staff's own counterweight to NAGB.[13]

Nor is NCES the only relevant part of the executive branch. The IES director, particularly when that post is occupied by an energetic activist, is not just an ex officio member of NAGB but also a force in their own right in shaping NAEP policies and programs. Besides IES, the Education Department's budget office, the secretary's office, and OMB and the White House have final authority on budget requests. The department's procurement office has heavy influence over the multifarious contracts that result in (and pay for) NAEP's actual implementation, as well as the many other contractors whose work bears on it. And there are occasional tensions—and sometimes personality conflicts—within the agency. For example, Secretary DeVos's proposed fiscal 2021 budget would have moved NAEP out of NCES altogether and into a completely new "Assessments Center" within IES. The rationale supplied to Congress was to facilitate "more effective administration of IES assessment programs while allowing NCES to focus on its core statistical mission and activities," the reasoning being that the ever-growing NAEP tail had begun to wag the NCES dog. Close IES observers, however, sensed that some interpersonal differences also lay behind the proposed change.[14]

Congress is much involved with NAEP, too, both in periodic authorizations and mandates and through annual appropriations that bring their own priorities. As with most federal programs, NAEP answers to four major committees (authorizing and appropriating, House and Senate) and their cognizant subcommittees, and must deal with staffers (and potentially with members) from both the majority and minority sides of all those bodies.

Within Congress, however, NAEP has had few champions, particularly on the House side. It's fared better in the Senate, notably through the sustained support during their time in that chamber of Senate lions Edward M. Kennedy (D-MA) and Lamar Alexander (R-TN). But Kennedy passed away in 2009 and Alexander retired in January 2021. This leaves NAEP vulnerable and often friendless on Capitol Hill. What it does is complicated and not terribly visible most of the time. There's little built-in constituent interest and no pork-barrel value for members of Congress. Mere data-gathering seldom draws much enthusiasm on Capitol Hill, yet NAEP is periodically dragged into contentious, high-profile issues such as student privacy and Covid-era school reopenings, into macro education questions like whether US schools are getting better or worse (and on whose watch?), into curricular controversies and culture wars, and into the effectiveness—or not—of high-profile national programs such as No Child Left Behind, Race to the Top, and the Every Student Succeeds Act (ESSA).

Because it hasn't excited much interest or understanding, let alone specialized knowledge, among actual members of Congress, NAEP is mostly attended to on Capitol Hill by staff members, some of whom have been extremely influential over the years.[15] Among them are veteran congressional aides who are apt to have strong views and loyalties, who may feel free to insert their own ideas, and who may have built close relationships over time with outside organizations and lobbyists. Others are newcomers to their jobs, often quite young, and unlikely to possess any relevant background knowledge or deep understanding of what NAEP is and does.

On top of all that, the core IES/NAEP legislation is almost two decades old and overdue for the kind of updating that DeVos urged upon Congress, even as NAEP aficionados are wary of subjecting this complicated fifty-year-old program to the political divisions that now roil Capitol Hill and animate many current members. There's no way of knowing what might happen.

Fortunately, NAEP has almost no sworn enemies save for a few died-in-the-wool foes of every sort of testing. Though it prompts endless wrangling and grumping, mostly among social scientists, about specific elements of the assessment, such as achievement levels, framework changes, and the disputed value of LTT tests, NAEP as a whole is widely respected, even among most thoughtful critics of other tests and testing.[16]

NAEP benefits, of course, from its nominally low-stakes nature. It's a sample-based assessment with no immediate impact—not even feedback!—for students, teachers, or schools, or for 99 percent of local school systems. So it's not a direct player in the endless controversies and political furor that surround standards, testing, and test-based accountability in American K–12 schooling. Yet this does not entirely immunize it from the partisanship and occasional fury that have attached to testing in general. For NAEP does function as ultimate auditor and, one might say, arbiter of the K–12 system's effectiveness. That its integrity is widely respected does not mean its results are always welcome, for they bring potential consequences for education leaders and elected officials, as well as reverberations throughout the entire system. That's why the ways that assessment results are presented—"spun," if you will—also matter greatly.

While NAEP has largely sidestepped the sorts of attacks that beset such prominent tests as the SAT and annual state assessments as well as contentious efforts at standard-setting such as the Common Core, it nevertheless triggers all manner of test-linked anxieties: "Why do my school—and my students—need to participate in a testing program from which we get nothing of value?" "How can I be sure that what NAEP tests is what we're teaching—and aligns with the grades in which we teach it?" "Do its standards match our state's standards, which is what I'm responsible for covering in my classroom?" "Doesn't NAEP rely on old-fashioned multiple-choice questions?" "Does NAEP expect way too much, especially from poor and minority pupils?" "Are NAEP tests culturally biased?" "Many of my students have special needs. How can I be sure that they'll be fairly treated by NAEP?" "My eighth-grade math pupils are studying algebra. Is that what NAEP's eighth-grade math assessment is testing?" "Our district serves a highly mobile population, many of them poor or recent immigrants, even homeless, and many of our fourth graders weren't here in third grade. How can this test possibly be fair to our community?"

Such concerns make their way not just to NAGB, NCES, NAEP contractors, and state and local officials doing their best to cooperate with NAEP, but also via unions, professional organizations, paid lobbyists, and others to members of Congress and their staffers.

Those worthies also hear from an army of interest groups, watchdogs, policy wonks, contractors, expert panels, and sundry advisory bodies, all with some sort of stake in NAEP and all of which monitor it closely, sending observers and lobbyists to NAGB meetings, hassling Education Department officials about budgets and regulations, and conveying their strong, self-interested views to congressional staffers when it's time for appropriations.

Try searching for "NAEP" within the website of the American Educational Research Association, for instance, and you get hundreds of hits, ranging from simple announcements of data releases to lengthy organizational submissions to NAGB on a host of issues of concern to education researchers, plus periodic testimony before Congress on matters such as the NAEP (and NCES and IES) budgets. Hundreds of similar hits emerge within the websites of the Council of the Great City Schools (which has a keen interest in TUDA), the National School Boards Association, the National PTA, and the National Education Association. Even the US Chamber of Commerce has dozens, and the AFL-CIO has seventeen. The American Institutes of Research (which contracts for much NCES work, including the NAEP-watching Validity Studies Panel) had as many as forty-seven NAEP-related items in a single year. In short, while NAEP has few enemies, its work—and therefore the decisions that NAGB and NCES make and that others make about NAEP—is entangled with a huge number of interests and agendas. Hence it is scrutinized under many microscopes, and any changes proposed for it will be appraised by how they may affect those interests.

Trying to respond to and, when possible, accommodate all these interested parties and close observers naturally heightens the trade-offs and complicates the choices facing those who make decisions about NAEP. This was on vivid display in late 2020 as NAGB, its staff, NCES, IES, and the full Education Department, including Secretary DeVos herself, agonized amid the Covid-19 pandemic and school shutdowns over whether to try to proceed with the mandated fourth- and eighth-grade assessments of reading and math that were scheduled for spring 2021. Advice, pleas, concerns, and even ultimatums rained in from many directions. No possible decision would please—or even appease—all affected constituencies. NAGB itself was sorely divided. And the technical challenges were real, as NAEP data are only valid if its tests are given to a representative sample of students, its technology at present is workable only on school premises, and there was scant chance that enough students would be physically present in their classrooms during the testing window for this to yield defensible results.

In the end, advised by NCES that it would be very expensive to proceed, might endanger the health of test managers, and probably would not yield sound data, a split NAGB voted to postpone the 2021 assessment for a year. DeVos reluctantly sought Congress's assent for the delay, which was granted. At this writing, we can reasonably expect NAEP to be given to the required grades in 2022. It's slightly awkward, though, even embarrassing, because in February 2021 the new Biden team notified states that *they* must administer the annual spring assessments (of reading and math, grades 3 through 8) in 2021 as required by ESSA.[17] Those are the very same assessments that DeVos waived a year earlier due to school closures resulting from the pandemic.

Insiders understand that NAEP requires a valid sample, while census-style state assessments can simply yield achievement data on whatever students happen to be in school on testing day—or can perhaps participate from home. Those data will aid teachers, principals, and policy leaders as they try to tailor schools' response to the pandemic and rectify the many learning losses that it caused. So there's a sound rationale for persisting with state tests even while deferring NAEP. But that doesn't entirely take the sting out of the charge that "the feds are making us do this but they can't even do it themselves."

Meanwhile, the split that this episode surfaced in NAGB emerged around the same time that board members' disagreements over the new reading framework were deepening. We'll revisit that issue in the following chapters, as it may signal the onset of ideological dissension in a board whose capacity for consensus has—as Roy Truby noted—been among its major strengths and NAEP's chief assets.

CHAPTER 9

Mounting Challenges

W E'VE SEEN THE NATIONAL ASSESSMENT grow more complicated—technically, operationally, and politically. We've also seen it become costlier, struggle to accommodate a lengthening array of interests, and get buffeted by developments and disputes in its environment. As those intensify, new demands get placed on NAEP, which itself is showing some of the strains of middle age.

NAEP dwells within the tetchy world of testing, which is straining these days: embattled and declining in college admissions; in entry to gifted programs, magnet, and "exam schools"; in the erosion of state end-of-course and graduation tests, and elsewhere.[1]

Much of the pushback against testing comes from equity concerns. Though a key role for assessments like NAEP is to document, monitor, and remind us of achievement gaps among student groups, not everyone welcomes that information, at least not unless it's accompanied by causal explanations and—more important—remedies for the situation.

But equity angst is just part of the story, for the very idea of assessing what students "know and can do" is more contentious today, and people are more mindful of its limitations. Not even the best standardized tests can tell the entire story. They can probe knowledge and skills that a student or (in the case of sample-based tests like NAEP) group of students possesses within a particular subject or discipline. But they're not good at gauging creativity, motivation, grit, research prowess, or one's ability to work with others. They can't delve very far or very well into other important schooling outcomes such as citizenship, sportsmanship, and leadership. They can tell us little about students' social and emotional well-being or their physical and mental health. They can't distinguish clearly between the skills and knowledge acquired from schooling and those that students pick up else-where. Nor can they reveal much about the extent to which a child's—or group's—learning is enhanced or retarded by family, home environment, peer group, neighborhood, and so forth.

Some people just plain don't like testing, whether because of the dam-age they think it does to quality instruction and teacher professionalism, the shackles they think it places on curricular breadth and school calendars, the threat they think it poses to student egos, or their aversion toward some uses to which test data may be put: evaluating teachers, labeling schools, keeping children from being promoted, and more.

NAEP gets roiled to some extent by all of that, plus the fact that (unlike almost every other test) it's a federal project, thus introducing anxieties about "big government" and data privacy. Because it yields no useful or informative results for students, parents, teachers, principals, or the great majority of local officials, NAEP bears the added burden of being seen as irrelevant and superfluous. Thus a singular paradox: at one level, NAEP's audience is as big as the entire United States, maybe even beyond, but at another level, that audience is tiny, rather specialized, somewhat self-absorbed, and often disputatious.

When NAEP quietly chugs along doing its assigned work on a pre-dictable schedule, whatever waves it makes arise mainly when assessment results are released. Though subject to countless critical studies and analy-ses by expert panels and individual analysts, it's not the stuff of scandal, only occasionally does it play into partisan politics, and the many studies of it—and the many more studies that employ its data—are chiefly of interest to academics and those who already reside within the smallish fraternity of NAEPsters. But when anyone proposes changing it in any way, interest levels rise—and "interests" rouse themselves. This is compounded—and confounded—by the delicacy of the NAEP instrument itself. Although its data seldom reveal abrupt shifts in student achievement—mostly they show pretty much the same pattern, usually a worrying one, round after round, year after year—the NAEP instrument itself is highly sensitive to alterations, variations, and discrepancies in design and administration. Add sensitivi-ties about race and fairness, and the scrutiny intensifies.

As this book was written, NAEP's technical and ideological vulnerabilities were on vivid display as two significant changes were being weighed.

Modernizing the assessment's creaky relationship to technology turns out to be more than routine maintenance. Getting to the point that students participating in NAEP could do so on digital equipment rather than paper and pencil was a major undertaking, not just because of the technology per se but also because of uncertainty as to the effects that this shift would have on test results and trend lines. In fact, the transition took almost two full decades to pull off.[2]

It's well known that different kids in different schools in different parts of the country have widely differing levels of access, experience, and proficiency with laptops, tablets, and such. Moving to digital NAEP meant trying to equalize that to the maximum extent, while also piloting the shift to gauge what it might to do to scores and trends. Myriad studies were done before universalizing the practice, which finally happened in 2017 and brought its own shelf of evaluations.[3] (Even today, it's not quite universal, as the LTT assessment has not yet completed the digital shift.)

Yet digitizing NAEP did not unfold as one might expect, with schools administering the assessment on their own devices and shooting students' answers into the cloud for storage and analysis. Some states do that (or close to it) with their own tests, but NAEP as yet does not. Instead, federal contractors physically transport their own tablets to every school in which students are participating in the National Assessment that day and NAEP's on-site administrators are responsible for test security, retrieving the devices, harvesting students' responses, and supplying them in orderly fashion to distant analysts.

Here's how NCES describes the process:

> Assessments are set up and administered by a team of approximately three to four NAEP representatives. The National Center for Education Statistics (NCES) provides all necessary equipment, including student tablets with an attached keyboard, stylus, earbuds, administrator tablet, and a router that provides a closed wireless network for the devices to communicate. Schools are asked to provide space, desks or tables, and access to electrical outlets. Schools do not need to provide internet access.[4]

It's almost as if your cable company had to send a technician to your home every time you plan to watch television, had to bring an HD TV set along, set it up for you, make sure it works, then take it away when you're finished. (The analogy is limited, since you probably watch television more often than students in any given school participate in NAEP.) Yes, NAEP uses technology, but in an old-fashioned way, albeit one that enables NCES to keep things uniform, equitable, and secure. It's also expensive, with those multiperson teams having to trek from school to school, hardware in hand, with travel costs added on. It's labor-intensive, inefficient, and slow, as are many other elements of NAEP, such as the development of thousands of test items by hand rather than via "automated item generation" with the help of artificial intelligence (AI), and human scoring of open-response and extended-response questions even as NAEP's own contractors employ AI for scoring similar tests.[5]

Nor has NAEP developed "adaptive" tests, the kind that spare students from wasting time on questions that are far too easy or difficult for them and that instead throw more items at them that are within their present capability range, which permits both faster testing and more precise identification of their strengths and weaknesses. Importantly, adaptive testing also yields more accurate information on what has and hasn't been learned by low and high achievers—because when designing a single time-constrained test for everyone, even with the benefit of bib-spiraling, most items end up clustered around the middle, leaving relatively few to fill in the picture of academic performance among, say, pupils in the tenth and ninetieth deciles. Adaptive testing, however, requires both tons of items—which are costly to develop the old-fashioned way—and nimble devices, probably connected to an online platform. Internet connectivity would certainly be needed to harvest student responses efficiently and with minimum human error.

Leaders at NCES and IES are well aware that these inefficiencies and timeworn practices make NAEP sluggish and expensive. At a NAGB meeting in March 2021, IES director Mark Schneider estimated that its present cost is about $270 per participating student—and that doesn't count sundry overhead costs borne by schools and by the federal agencies themselves, this at a time when the College Board charges about one-third of that for each of its three-hour AP exams, having presumably built into that $95 fee all of its overheads (though not those of participating schools).[6]

The National Assessment Governing Board is also painfully aware that today's high unit cost of NAEP assessments, particularly when combined with its statutory mandate to test reading and math every two years, puts huge pressure on the budget and keeps NAEP from doing other things that the board would like it to do and that various constituencies would also like. At that same March 2021 meeting, for example, the head of the Council of the Great City Schools stated that many more districts would like to join the TUDA program but NAEP's strapped budget prevents them from doing so.

Efficiency and budget are serious considerations, but another factor isn't far below the surface. Over the decades, NAEP and those associated with it have taken considerable pride in being cutting edge, innovating, even pioneering new and improved approaches to large-scale student assessment—and there's no denying that many state testing programs and the international PISA program owe a debt to NAEP for leading the way. That makes it especially uncomfortable, even embarrassing, for NAEPsters to preside over an aging assessment system that's now eclipsed by innovations undertaken elsewhere.

So there are many reasons to modernize NAEP. Schneider sometimes refers to moving it much closer to what he's dubbed "e-NAEP," and he got IES to contract with the National Academies of Sciences, Engineering, and Medicine (NASEM) to make recommendations for doing this. As he characterized its charge:

> The technology underlying NAEP is aging and needs a refresh. NASEM is charged with identifying new technologies, such as automated scoring and auto item generation, that could reduce the ever-escalating costs of NAEP; identifying how to use more modern technologies to reduce the incredible expense of in-person test administration, which is how NAEP is currently administered; and identifying more efficient ways to generate accurate measures of what students know and can do.[7]

Schneider and his team may well need the additional gravitas and legitimacy that the academies will provide on this issue, as well as their specific recommendations, because modernizing NAEP will bring headaches and resistance.

Trend-line issues are the most obvious concern, as any of these changes, let alone an entire suite of them, will replace large parts of the delicate NAEP mechanism and could yield results that cannot easily be compared with the past. Steps can and doubtless will be taken to minimize the damage, but

NAEP veterans still remember the "reading anomaly" (see chapter 3) and are mindful that even small changes in assessment operations can wreak havoc with those precious trends.

That's not all. NAEP's multitude of contractors, although they collectively possess the requisite know-how and technology to do the up-to-date things that Schneider contemplates, didn't sign contracts to do their NAEP work in these new ways, so a fresh competition will likely be needed, and that carries its own hassles as well as much self-interest. What's cheaper and more efficient for NAEP, after all, is bound to mean less revenue and probably fewer jobs for some longtime contractors. It's apt also to create fresh opportunities for glitches to arise.

One again recalls Admiral Rickover likening education reform to "moving a graveyard." Modernizing NAEP also means that the federal government's multiple stubborn bureaucracies will have to adjust to doing things differently, as will states and districts accustomed to working with NAEP under the old rules. There may be complaints to Congress, which will probably have to get involved, perhaps changing NAEP's aging authorizing law plus adding new appropriations language. If operating the traditional core of NAEP will cost less in the future, it's reasonable to expect budget hawks on Capitol Hill to ask why so much money is still needed even as sundry interest groups try to seize the "surplus" for purposes of their own. (For example: more TUDA districts, more frequent civics assessments, or that long-delayed foreign-language assessment?)

It's not impossible. NAEP has a long history of incremental changes such as the gradual, meticulous shift to digital administration, and such evolutionary changes seem manageable within the assessment's regular governance structures. It also has a history of occasional big shifts, as in the reboot that accompanied its move from ECS to ETS in 1983, the 1988 overhaul by Congress that followed the Alexander-James report, and the statutory renewal and organizational relocation that accompanied No Child Left Behind and creation of the Institute of Education Sciences in 2002. Those big shifts, however, weren't internally generated. They followed upon high-profile outside reviews or fundamental changes in the federal role in education. They also required forceful leadership on the part of influential people. Such developments brought the visibility, energy, clout, and ultimately the oomph that triumphed over established ways of doing things and established interests. I suspect that the kind of NAEP overhaul envisioned by Schneider and his allies will require something similar.

NAGB's protracted wrestling match with a new reading framework further displays the graveyard-relocation challenges associated with changing the National Assessment as well as some new stresses that have entered our public life.

NAEP's reading assessments from 2009 through 2019 relied on the same framework. It had emerged from a lengthy development process to replace a framework in use since 1992, and was expected to require the launch of a new trend line for main-NAEP reading scores.[8] After elaborate "bridging" studies, however, that proved unnecessary: so long as some adjustments were made in the course of data analysis, the reading trend could be maintained.[9] That means NAEP's "reading report cards" now show a continuous trend from 1992 through 2019, save for the "dotted line" prior to 1999 when accommodations kicked in for children with disabilities.

Late in 2017, NAGB's Assessment Development Committee began a review of the reading framework, including a quest for expert input, research, and advice. A year later, the board awarded a contract to WestEd to "conduct an update of the NAEP Mathematics and Reading Assessment Frameworks" and to develop specifications for the tests themselves.[10] That led to the assembling by 2019 of an elaborate set of consultants, committees, and staff: a thirty-two-member "visioning panel," a seventeen-person "development panel," an eight-member "technical advisory committee," and ten WestEd employees.

They were ambitious, to put it mildly, and some of their ambitions were bound for controversy. The "visioning" group, in particular, wanted future reading assessments to incorporate various media, not just words on paper; to emphasize the "deep reading" and "disciplinary reading" that are stressed in some new state academic standards (and the Common Core) and in new reading tests used elsewhere; to recognize that "texts inevitably are cultural and political in nature"; to take account of differences among test-takers not only in cultural and racial contexts but also in levels of motivation and interest; and to compensate for differences in students' background knowledge and vocabulary.

The goal was to develop a new reading framework that the board would adopt in time for the painstaking work necessary to translate it into actual assessments to be given for the first time in 2025.[11] But when a draft was put out for public comment in mid-2020, it soon became clear that reaching agreement would not be easy.

More than 2,600 comments flooded in from individuals and organizations. Most welcomed the developers' expanded "vision" of reading and its assessment. But there was also pushback on a host of issues, including two that proved volatile. The drafters had set out to reframe reading and its assessment in "sociocultural" terms, seemingly in opposition to the "cognitive" terms that had long undergirded the assessment process. And in the name of "equity," the drafters proposed a variety of changes in test design, administration, scoring, and analysis, as well as the provision of various "scaffolds" for test-takers, such as supplying background knowledge to help them understand the content or meaning of terms they encounter in the course of the assessment.

Almost nobody doubted the drafters' good intentions, but concern arose—including from this author—regarding several of these changes. Perhaps the hardest-hitting critique came from Johns Hopkins education professor (and former New York State education commissioner) David Steiner and Emory English professor Mark Bauerlein. The new framing, they wrote in *City Journal*,

> relativizes reading across cultures . . . It's a given that students should be examined on their ability to read passages that reflect the diversity of a complex society. But the new NAEP definition asserts that the reading skill *itself* is sociocultural, . . . leaving some students in potentially "unfair" starting points, depending on the relationship between their backgrounds and the texts in question . . . Hence, the designers of the new framework call for testing procedures that will "optimize the performance of the widest possible population of students in the NAEP Reading Assessment." [Toward that end], NAEP will "develop scaffolds that optimize comprehension performance for every reader."[12]

"At first blush," Steiner and Bauerlein acknowledged, "one might see a hopeful progressivism here. Why penalize youths because their background isn't in tune with particular textual passages, even if they are taken from books that have been read for generations?"

The problem, they asserted (and in separate comments I said much the same thing), is that adding such "scaffolds" would divorce "NAEP reading" from "real-world" reading that provides no such assists. "Yet the whole point of the NAEP reading assessment," they explained, "is to tell educators how well states and school districts are teaching students to read the language they will encounter in the real world." Hence adopting the "socio-cultural" model of reading plus scaffold assistance for those getting tested would result in scores that might look better for various student groups but that "will lack any predictive value." And "Rather than allowing poor performance to serve as a signal that large knowledge gaps should be fixed through better education, we will simply lower the impact of background knowledge on the reported test performance."

"If NAEP follows this route," Steiner and Bauerlein concluded, "its assessment will no longer be a reading test that we can trust to demonstrate where students need more help—and where teachers should focus their efforts."

Behind these and other issues lurked the trend-line challenge. Though it's impossible to be certain before an assessment is actually administered, the proposed framework was so profound a departure from the past that it appeared likely to force a fresh start in the trend line. That would make 2023 (now 2024) the final NAEP reading assessment with unbroken trends back to 1992. For many observers, again including myself, that prospect was worrying indeed. The Covid pandemic was upon us, with widespread concerns about learning losses that might take years to recover. The 2020 election was upon us, with the possibility (which materialized) of political changes at the federal level that might result in shifts in national education policies, the effects of which NAEP should be in a position to document. It just did not look like a propitious time to risk loss of trend in the most fundamental of all subjects.

Such pushbacks did not just come from outsiders, and therein lie the seeds of a worrying and possibly widening rift in the assessment's long-running governance structure. NAGB itself split over the major changes and risks associated with the new draft reading framework and with the underlying research base and rationale for making those changes.

As disquiet surfaced within the ranks, the board's Assessment Development Committee and its various panels and staffers undertook—with evident reluctance—to make revisions, and these were shared with the full board in March and again in May 2021. Some of the changes that they proposed seemed cosmetic—as in altering the terminology of help for test-takers in the realm of background knowledge from "scaffolding" to "universal design elements"—while other revisions were more substantive. NCES staffers suggested that the trend line could probably be preserved, though they couldn't be certain in advance. Many board members seemed receptive to the 2021 revisions, but others continued to voice concern, in some cases major concern.

There were several sticking points, both scientific and ideological, including a stark difference of opinion regarding the role of background knowledge and vocabulary in reading assessments. Should the test strive to minimize and suppress that role in various ways—this was the clear preference of several key figures in the development panels—or should it accept the fact that one's comprehension of what one is reading is unavoidably affected by the extent of one's previous knowledge of the topic being read about?[13]

This was not just a difference of opinion. It mattered what body of research one trusted to inform one's views as well as one's sense of whether equity and fairness are best served in the assessment of reading by revealing gaps and differences in students' fluency and comprehension or by attempting to mask, compensate for, and rationalize them. In a reflection of larger developments in the American polity and culture in the early 2020s, NAGB members sometimes seemed to inhabit different worlds, honor different values, and rely on different sources of expertise as well as their own experiences and reference groups.

This led, in one particularly ugly episode, to a (virtual) meeting of the Assessment Development Committee in May 2021 where NAGB member Grover (Russ) Whitehurst, himself the former (founding) director of IES and a major figure in education research, was all but "canceled" by committee members who vociferously objected not only to editorial changes he had drafted to simplify their lengthy document and make it less controversial (without actually altering its substance!) but also to his motives in mooting those suggestions.[14]

The board was on the verge of major discord and, as these disputes leaked into public view, representatives of several large states let it be known that if these radical changes were forced upon NAEP's reading assessment, they would be loath to participate in future rounds of testing. Whereupon NAGB chair Haley Barbour, a former GOP governor of Mississippi who had been leaving the framework updates to the board's standing committees, moved to appoint a special working group comprised of half a dozen of the board's ablest members, all of them mindful of the huge downside of a badly divided governing board and a split vote on the central issue of how to assess reading in US schools. Ably chaired by Alice Peisch, an astute Massachusetts legislator (and Democrat), that subgroup finally forged a consensus version of the new reading framework that all board members could assent to, however grudgingly, thus averting for the time being a major credibility challenge for NAEP and the possibility of state protests and other external pushbacks.

Crisis avoided for now, yes. But this protracted contretemps produced more dissension within the board than characterized most major policy choices that its members have faced over the past three decades. Which may preview a serious governance (and credibility) challenge for NAEP going forward. After all, considering how hard it was to unite around reading, what will happen when they turn to the framework for US history?

When using data for comparisons, what's fair and what isn't? NAEP results are endlessly employed in the making of comparisons. Indeed, that's probably how they're most used. We compare trends over time from place to place, group to group, and subject to subject. We compare states (and some districts). We compare groups of students. We compare gains and losses by high and low achievers. We do "cross-tabs" in which all of the aforementioned comparisons are recombined and recompared in every imaginable way.

But what's "fair"? This is an issue throughout statistics, throughout social science research, certainly throughout the monitoring and evaluating of education reforms and other changes. Fairness was front of mind for the initial architects of the new reading framework discussed above. Fairness draws even keener interest and concern in an era of intense soul-searching over equity in education and society.

Education analysts generally pursue fairness when they try to control for exogenous factors that might affect the results they're examining. But fairness is more than a methodological consideration. Especially in a high-profile national program like NAEP, operated by the federal government, paid for by taxpayers, and closely watched by myriad interest groups, fairness becomes a policy challenge and part of the political environment. What makes it especially hard to wrestle with is that judgments about fairness are also subjective, influenced by one's values and the perspective from which one approaches the issue at hand.

How, for example, can state-to-state comparisons of student achievement be deemed fair when state demographics and economics vary so? Almost as varied are their education policies and practices, most notably those affecting students with special needs. For example, more than 19 percent of Pennsylvania K–12 students participate in special education, while in Idaho it's 11 percent.[15] California counts more than 19 percent of its public school pupils as "English language learners" compared with less than 4 percent in Alabama.[16] Compulsory attendance laws also differ from place to place, as do dropout and high school completion rates, making twelfth-grade data especially squirrely. Even when one pulls out a particular subgroup of students, they may have dramatically different characteristics from one state (or district) to the next. The Latino population of Florida, for example, is famously different from that of Texas and New Mexico. And there are other potentially important differences that the standard NAEP reporting categories may not capture.[17]

NAEP's responsibility is to present the data it gathers as accurately as possible, and it has learned to manage its data-gathering in ways that limit the ability of state and local policy makers to manipulate it (as we saw in chapter 6 with special-ed participation rates). Yet factors beyond its control affect those data in ways that help us understand why some critics aver that comparisons based on NAEP results are not always fair.

Reporting on the 2017 TUDA reading results, for example, and clearly unhappy about his city's low ranking among participating districts as well as mindful of its high poverty rate, Patrick O'Donnell of the *Cleveland Plain Dealer* noted that "even though all the TUDA districts are cities, their demographics are so different that some are barely the same category of community as Cleveland and other post-industrial cities."[18]

Michael Casserly, head of the Council of the Great City Schools, which is TUDA's lead advocacy group, more or less concurred: "Comparing Cleveland to other cities on NAEP is more helpful than comparing the city to national or state averages," he commented. "But it is most helpful to compare Cleveland to specific cities whose demographics look more like Cleveland."

Such differences have led savvy analysts at the Urban Institute, Stanford, and Harvard (among other places) to adjust NAEP results for socio-economics and other demographic differences.[19] This is sophisticated social science, although it gives rise to hearty—and often equally sophisticated—disputes over the policy significance of the differences that it yields.[20] It shows how careful analysts armed with additional data from other sources can employ NAEP results in ways that policy makers—and journalists—find insightful and informative. The paradox for NAEP itself, and for its minders in NAGB and NCES, is that they yearn for their data to be policy relevant. Yet they understand that it's one thing to create more cross-tabs by presenting their data in novel ways but quite another thing to adjust it, much less to venture policy explanations or conclusions based on it. Absent such adjustments, however, they are destined to be hit from time to time with allegations of unfairness as well as inutility.

Aside from race and sometimes gender, the biggest adjustment that researchers and policy makers seek is socioeconomic. This is important because of the well-documented correlation between children's SES status and their academic achievement. Yet such analyses are becoming harder to conduct due to the waning accuracy of the proxy for poverty that NAEP and most other sources of education data have long relied on, namely, students' eligibility (or not) for the federal program of subsidized school breakfasts and lunches.[21] Historically, such eligibility was individually determined according to a child's family income. Beginning in 2010, however, and nationally implemented by 2015, the "community eligibility" feature enables high-poverty schools to supply free meals to *all* their pupils regardless of individual poverty status.[22]

That practice is now widespread, which is a fine thing for juvenile nutrition and school administrators yet which loosens the link between poverty and participation in the subsidized meals program.[23] NAEP does not yet have a better metric, though there's much discussion among governing board members, NCES staffers, and outside experts about possible alternatives. The optimal solution probably entails linking Census Bureau data to NAEP results, but that's a heavy lift with many complications, including likely threats to trend lines.

NAEP's extensive student questionnaires do ask a number of SES-related questions, such as how many books are in the child's home and how much schooling one's mother completed. Researchers using the NAEP Data Explorer can access response patterns on such questions and analyze NAEP results in relation to them. But official NAEP reports don't do that—and there's reason to doubt the accuracy of children's answers to such questions. (Does an eighth grader really know how far in school each of her parents went? What if dad isn't around? How candid is a twelfth grader apt to be about which adults live in his home? What if he isn't sure who exactly is a "female legal guardian"?) Meanwhile, the fine print in NAEP reports now cautions readers to "interpret with caution" trend data based on eligibility for the federal school lunch program.[24]

Fairness, it's clear, is going to continue to challenge NAEP as well as those who use its data for their own purposes. And as if that weren't problem enough, accuracy is also a chronic challenge due to differences—and changing eligibility standards—far beyond NAEP's ability to control or control for.

Have NAGB's achievement levels outlived their usefulness? As we saw in chapter 4, they've been contentious since day one, though that has not stopped them from functioning as de facto national standards for K–12 education. But how useful and informative are they today?

They've long been slightly baffling to non-NAEPsters, in part because "proficient" on NAEP is generally a much higher standard than states have set for "proficiency" on their own federally required assessments, and in part because the word "basic" signals to many Americans a level of educational adequacy that NAGB never intended it to represent. ("He's learned the basics." "She's mastered basic skills.") We've also seen that the wide swath of student performance in the "below basic" range leaves observers without much to go by regarding which populations in which places may be on the cusp of possessing basic skills and which may be truly illiterate.[25]

Former education secretary DeVos suggested to NAGB that it replace the tripartite achievement levels with something akin to the A to F grading system that many states use for their schools as part of the federally mandated ESSA accountability regime. Most Americans, she explained, intuitively understand those letter grades.

DeVos was surely right about that, yet her alternative would be difficult to implement given the structure and rigor of NAEP assessments. An NCES veteran explains that "the typical A-F interpretation of percent correct will not align well with the . . . challenging NAEP test. For example, for 8th grade math, the average percent correct is in the 55 percent range. It would be a hard sale to convince anyone that it's okay to call the average score on NAEP 'C' when it translates into only about 55 percent correct."[26] Which is to say that applying such letter grades to NAEP scores would not turn out in practice to be intuitive. The assessments are intentionally difficult, meant to determine what students can and cannot do in relation to a well-formulated body of knowledge and skills that they ought to possess by the grade levels in which they're tested. Cut scores and achievement levels on those tests are not designed to coexist with "grade inflation."

NAEP's governing board recently set out—yet again—to clarify the definitions of its achievement levels and revise their alignment with actual items and scores on the tests themselves. This is a periodic refresh, here also a response to a 2017 recommendation from the National Academies:

> Alignment among the frameworks, the item pools, the achievement-level descriptors, and the cut scores is fundamental to the validity of inferences about student achievement. In 2009, alignment was evaluated for all grades in reading and for grade 12 in mathematics, and changes were made to the achievement-level descriptors, as needed. Similar research is needed to evaluate alignment for the grade 4 and grade 8 mathematics assessments and to revise them as needed to ensure that they represent the knowledge and skills of students at each achievement level. Moreover, additional work to verify alignment for grade 4 reading and grade 12 mathematics is needed.[27]

The board entered into a contract with the Pearson testing and curriculum firm in late 2020 to conduct a sizable project of this sort. It's worth underscoring, however, that this work is intended to update and improve the achievement levels, their descriptors, and how the actual assessments align with them, not to replace them with something different.

I confess to having helped create NAEP's now-familiar trinity of achievement levels and believe that they've added considerable value to American education and its reform over the past several decades. I wouldn't want to see them replaced (and don't see any imminent risk of that happening.) But they obviously require regular maintenance.

After half a century, challenges seem to arise faster and from more directions than ever before. NAGB's greatest accomplishment over the years—and the rationale for an independent, multi-constituent governing body of this kind—has been its capacity to forge compromise on complicated matters and then stick to its guns regardless of pushback from outside. Adapting and modernizing, of course, but not surrendering.

That's getting harder, as NAGB's very representativeness means it can't avoid, to some extent, mirroring the fraught and fractious environment surrounding American education generally. Some of the issues that rush at NAEP today boil down to dilemmas or disagreements that have no right answer, that inflame passions far beyond assessment, even beyond the K–12 realm entirely, yet still require resolution. That requires a continuing capacity for compromise, but now we live in a time when compromise—much less consensus—has practically gone extinct in so much of our environment.

I want to believe that NAEP's organizational and governance structure, plus the deep roots it has sunk and the widespread acceptance of its work, creates as promising a set of circumstances as any in American education for weathering storms, dealing with complex issues, and forging ahead. But it's definitely getting harder. In the next chapter, we face into more storms as we turn toward the future.

CHAPTER 10

Limitations and Opportunities

I S IT POSSIBLE that NAEP has had its day—half a century, actually—in the education sun, thriving so long as major national policies were substantially based on data and inferences derived from its scores, but now shadowed by hostility to testing and results-based accountability, unrest over too tight a focus on academics alone, and upset arising from comparisons that feel unfair in an equality-driven era? Will it—and measures like it—be eclipsed, even marginalized, by today's preoccupation with children's social and emotional well-being, with multiple indicators of school quality, and with outcomes such as equity, diversity, and citizenship rather than literacy and numeracy? Will it be undone by mixed feelings and hot politics regarding the federal role in education combined with frustration over the limits of NAEP data for sophisticated analysis, evaluation, and research? Will it be left behind by fast-moving developments in testing technology? Might it—should it—be replaced by different kinds of metrics or a different approach to assessment? Or is it possible that NAEP is becoming more important than ever as the twenty-first century unfolds? But if it's still valuable today, how ought it adapt to changing needs and opportunities so as to remain relevant tomorrow?

The foremost value of the national assessment at this time, as when Frank Keppel visualized its creation back in the 1960s, is measuring and tracking what American students "know and can do" in core subjects of the school curriculum at key stages of their progress through the K–12 system: the end of the elementary grades, the finish of middle school, and the conclusion of high school. Its stock in trade is academic achievement for the country as a whole and (in fewer subjects) for individual states and a handful of large cities. Insofar as a familiar and widely respected gauge of such achievement and its changes over time is sought by America's education and policy leaders, NAEP plays a necessary role, perhaps an indispensable one.

But will contemporary changes in the education zeitgeist—and in American society and polity—erode that value, possibly even threatening the existence of assessments like this one? The question deserves pondering. Just because NAEP has been around for ages doesn't justify its continuation in its present form, let alone its ever-rising budget. Unlike the census, it's not enshrined in the Constitution. At day's end, it could be dismissed as just another federal education program, albeit longer in the tooth than most. As former Maryland State Board of Education president Andy Smarick poses the question, "It's had a heck of a run, and it's been indispensable, but do people care about it like they once did?"[1]

As noted in earlier chapters, NAEP has plenty of critics but few true enemies. It has lots of friendly acquaintances—including many who would like it to do more than it presently can—yet almost no bona fide champions in positions of power, particularly on Capitol Hill. Tests seldom attract influential cheerleaders and, considering the anti-testing and "opt-out" movements that have gained traction around the country, plus mounting resistance to school accountability regimes driven by test scores, it's not surprising that political leaders are loath to clasp NAEP to their bosoms.

Indeed, some of the worrying changes we see in contemporary politics in Washington and beyond could portend a fate for NAEP that's worse than mere indifference. Recent arguments over census data, unemployment data, and Covid data are illustrative of an era when data themselves can prove contentious, when their manipulation and denial seem thinkable, and when more people gravitate to "facts" that they like or that support their predilections and shun information, no matter how scrupulously gathered and objectively presented, that disputes or refutes their preferences.

A major federal data initiative such as NAEP is going to need more friends and allies tomorrow than it needed yesterday.

Meanwhile, NAEP is quite good at what it does, if arthritic in how it goes about that. But what NAEP *doesn't* do is also coming to matter more in many quarters, and those lacunae matter even more in the absence of strong partisans and staunch defenders. Paradoxically, NAEP could turn out to be both valuable and marginal at the same time.

Five of the gaps or shortcomings that seem to matter more nowadays deserve attention:

- As noted several times in earlier chapters, even as NAEP reveals much about education outcomes in three key grade levels in core subjects, it has never been able to say *why* those scores are high or low, rising or falling. Because it carefully samples everybody in its assigned grades and subjects, it has nothing akin to a control group, which means it doesn't lend itself to much-sought evaluations of various education reforms and interventions. Hence one cannot legitimately make causal claims on the basis of NAEP data or devise changes in policy or practice whose justification rests entirely on those data. This limit helps keep NAEP out of some political and policy wars, but it also frustrates policy makers, even as NAGB and its minders urgently want it to be relevant and informative and as they often try—via special analyses, separate reports, symposia, and so on—to develop interesting comparisons and possible explanations.

  Yes, NAEP reports frequently flag suggestive correlates that may assist analysts seeking explanations, and its surveys of principals and teachers provide some information about school resources and practices. Occasional transcript studies connect twelfth-grade results with courses taken by high school students. Deep dives into the data can also be illuminating. In April 2021, for example, NCES published a close look at the oral reading fluency of fourth graders (based on a special 2018 NAEP study, akin to one done in 2002) that helped explain why so many youngsters score at the "below basic" level in reading: a key finding indicates that they hadn't mastered phonics and phonemic awareness sufficiently to read the test passages fluently, which limited their comprehension of those passages and reduced their scores accordingly.[2]

  Such analyses can help educators and policy makers understand what they should do differently in the future. But they cannot actually explain what *caused* the weak fluency, nor what curricular and pedagogical practices were (or weren't) deployed in those children's classrooms, much less what was and wasn't happening in the rest of their lives that may contribute to the weakness that many displayed during the study. That's an inherent characteristic of NAEP: accurate as its data may be, the reasons for what those data show are influenced by many factors that no such assessment can detect.

- As also noted previously, NAEP lacks relevance at the classroom and school levels, and its district-level data are available for just a few cities. As Angelika Schroeder, chair of the Colorado State Board of Education, wrote in 2021, "NAEP doesn't serve all the functions that good assessments should. The results don't give teachers and parents an objective report of an individual student's achievement and they don't measure the academic growth that student makes from year to year which is important to parents and families, and equally important to schools and educators who seek to identify where changes may be needed. Actionable information is critical for schools, districts, and policy makers."[3]

Over the years, many have suggested expanding NAEP to yield finer-grained data for more units, levels, and jurisdictions within the K–12 realm, even to deploy it in place of states' own assessments. That could be done—we'll get to one possible pathway a few pages hence—and doing so would assuredly make NAEP more vivid and immediate for more people, likely motivating them to greater efforts to alter their practices so as to boost scores, narrow gaps, and more. Yet doing this would bring huge budgetary and technical issues and would eventually convert NAEP from trusted auditor into a high-stakes test in its own right, which would bring many troubling consequences, almost inevitably leading to corruption of the data. Without such a change, however, NAEP results will probably continue to draw attention from top policy makers and high-level education leaders but will hold scant interest for practicing educators, parents—or voters facing another local levy on the November ballot. All of which contributes to NAEP's thin support.

- Due to its single-minded focus on traditional academic achievement, NAEP conveys a relatively narrow view of what matters in education. Although the gradual incorporation of more subjects has brought some broadening, we're still looking at a familiar "core curriculum." NAEP doesn't begin to address the "whole child" or, for that matter, the "whole school" in any useful fashion. And even within its limits, today it doesn't do a great job on much of the curricular core, because it so infrequently assesses subjects other than reading and math. When it does, it often confines the resulting information to one or two grades and to the national level, that is, not even to the state level. Neither does NAEP provide any information below fourth grade, which is awfully late to find out whether kids are learning to read in the primary grades and unhelpful in gauging the benefits (or not) of their preschool experiences.

- There's lingering vagueness about what exactly NAEP is measuring, how and by whom that gets decided, and whether what it measures is what matters most today. Do we care more about the overall effectiveness of the nation's education system, about students' readiness for college and the labor market, about how states compare with each other, about the content of what's being taught, or about closing equity gaps? Are we more interested in the K–12 system's effectiveness in delivering today's curriculum or in the ups and downs of achievement trends over the long haul? Or something else entirely? Seeming to do some of everything—and staying vague as to its exact mission—may be a tactical plus for NAEP, which can thereby appear to cater to many appetites, albeit without fully satisfying any, but once again it doesn't serve to recruit ardent champions and committed advocates for the long haul.

- NAEP's tendency to generate depressing news about the sorry performance of American education and to document continuing gaps among student groups is both uncomfortable for educators and political leaders and increasingly discordant in an era of "smiley faces" and "good job" comments on whatever kids do, an era that's also increasingly focused on their social-emotional well-being. When NAEP results come out, no matter how cheerily they're spun, seldom do the hard facts reveal much that's getting better for many kids or states. We can understand why the bad news persists—basically the combined effect of lofty standards and paltry real-world gains—but that doesn't make the news any better. Hence NAEP may be seen as a purveyor of failure, inequality, and stasis even as it is also viewed as a vital rapporteur of troubling evidence about continuing gaps and shortfalls in American education. It's hard to resist the temptation to shoot—or at least mute—messengers that regularly bear discouraging messages.

Besides those gaps and uncertainties, most of which are built into NAEP's basic architecture, hairline cracks are emerging on the governance front. Also a feature of NAEP's long-standing design, on the whole that structure has worked well for decades. Indeed, a great strength of NAEP since the early 1990s has been not only the insulation and buffering conferred by its independent governing board but also that diverse body's impressive record of reaching consensus, even unanimity, on just about every big issue facing the assessment. That's a hugely valuable asset, but it's fragile, too, and of late it's showing signs of erosion. Along with continuing tension and ambiguity in the structural relationship between NAGB and NCES, the polarization, schismatic tendencies, and culture wars that we now see across most of US society and its culture are creeping into decision-making about NAEP.

As discussed in the previous chapter, this was visible in 2020 as the board split over whether to push ahead with the scheduled 2021 assessment in the face of a raging pandemic. It was even more visible in 2020 and 2021 as NAGB members (and their many expert advisers, contractors, and constituencies) grappled with—and argued over—how to assess reading in the future. It's certain to return with a vengeance when the time comes to update assessments in other fraught fields such as history and civics, perhaps also geography and science. The culture wars that have seeped from the university campus into the K–12 system, the equity and race-related challenges that roil the country, and the partisan differences that pervade the polity—no buffering system can keep them from affecting NAEP, too. As Harvard education professor and former NAGB member Andrew Ho put it in May 2021, according to journalist Linda Jacobson, "'NAEP has always been above the fray, relative to everything else,'" he said in an interview, adding that if issues before the board are becoming more controversial, that's because "'everything else is, too.'"[4]

Contemplating NAEP's future has a "Goldilocks" quality. As you no doubt recall from the children's fairy tale, one bowl of porridge was too hot, another too cold to be palatable. The heroine had to sample the third bowl (Baby Bear's) before she found some that was "just right."[5] Should NAEP's future be viewed as a continuation of what it's already doing, just doing it a little better, or is that too cold? As a radical replacement by something very different, or is that too hot? Or with some adjustments, additions, and updating that might turn out to be "just right"?

NAEP veteran Ina Mullis took a close look at the assessment's past, present, and future in 2019 on behalf of NCES's Validity Studies Panel.[6] She offered a meticulous and knowing review of NAEP's evolution over time and accomplishments to date—and did so in positive, even celebratory terms:

> NAEP does work vital to maintaining the educational health of our nation and keeping the United States on a course of educational improvement. In its 50 years of operation, NAEP has met a wide range of national needs by greatly expanding the network of constituents to which it is relevant as well as by increasing its relevance to states and districts. NAEP data are well positioned to be in the forefront of education policy discussions about how the United States is faring educationally in a global context as well as the differential impact of individual states on the national standing.
>
> NAEP is to be highly commended for the substantial effort it has invested in improving the validity and accuracy of assessment procedures and data over its history, especially more recently. Finally, the monumental amount of NAEP data and tools to support data use available on the NCES, Governing Board, ETS, AIR, and other websites represents a true national treasure that needs to be more thoughtfully and thoroughly mined.

Mullis also summarized major issues that NAEP has repeatedly faced over the years, mostly having to do with data quality, timeliness, relevance, and cost. When turning to the future, she focused on both the opportunities and limitations afforded by technology as well as the continuing challenge of disseminating NAEP results:

> [T]echnology provides an avenue for improving NAEP's capacity to support in-depth understanding of student achievement by assessing an increased variety of subject areas and more challenging educational goals . . . Now that NAEP has transitioned to digital-based assessments, it will likely require considerable NAEP exploration and research to maximize the measurement potential of this innovation. That is, NAEP needs to systematically move toward assessing a widely

expanded view of achievement that will meet the needs of our 21st century society. The move to digital-based assessments also has considerable potential to develop more efficient data collection and measurement methods.

In contrast to the promise that technology provides for improving assessment content and form, technology is not a panacea for addressing the challenge, which has persisted across NAEP's entire history, of making NAEP more useful and well known . . . *Technology may facilitate dissemination of information, but the fact that this persists as a goal provides evidence that making NAEP more useful and well known remains extremely challenging.* [Emphasis added]

Perceptive and sage as Mullis always is, she seemed to take for granted that NAEP would continue slowly to evolve, not change in fundamental ways. Her porridge, in my view, is too cold, though many will say it's simply realistic.

NAGB also served up a chilly bowlful in its latest "strategic vision," released in 2020. Much like Mullis, but with less concision and grace, the board basically set out to do better in the future at what it was already trying to do. (See box 10.1.)

Both NAGB and Mullis were prudent, predictable, and unexceptionable as they charted a future course for NAEP that resembles the present

---

BOX 10.1   NAGB strategic vision, circa 2020
INFORM

The National Assessment Governing Board will disseminate NAEP resources to inform the work of numerous education stakeholders and to promote high-quality uses of The Nation's Report Card that support improvements in policy and practice. NAEP resources include results; focused studies; assessment questions and tasks; assessment innovations; and contextual variables about the educational experiences of students, teachers, and schools. The Governing Board will:

Identify the needs of stakeholders and refine resources to promote sustained use of NAEP data, enabling educators, researchers, advocates, and policymakers to understand and improve student achievement.

BOX 10.1   *(Continued)*

Elevate high-quality uses of NAEP resources to demonstrate NAEP's utility and to highlight the unique value of the Nation's Report Card to inform education policy and practice.

Link NAEP resources with external data sources and disseminate what is learned from these sources so that NAEP can inform policy and practice in understandable and actionable ways.

INNOVATE

The National Assessment Governing Board will ensure The Nation's Report Card remains at the forefront of assessment design and technology by refining design, content, and reporting, increasing relevancy for NAEP users and inspiring action to improve achievement for all. The Governing Board will:

Optimize the utility, relevance, and timing of NAEP subject-area frameworks and assessment updates to measure expectations valued by the public.

Monitor and make decisions about the NAEP assessment schedule based on the Board's policy priorities of utility, frequency, and efficiency to ensure NAEP results are policy-relevant.

Develop a body of evidence to improve the interpretation and communication of NAEP achievement levels to ensure that they are reasonable, valid, and informative to the public.

ENGAGE

The National Assessment Governing Board will strengthen partnerships and communications with stakeholder organizations, building capacity to understand and harness the resources of The Nation's Report Card to advance policy and practice. The Governing Board will:

Develop, sustain, and deepen strategic partnerships to ensure that NAEP remains a trusted, relevant, and useful resource.

Help stakeholders understand how the Governing Board and NAEP can illuminate important skills for postsecondary education pathways.

Source: *Strategic Vision 2025* (Washington, DC: National Assessment Governing Board, 2020), 2, https://www.nagb.gov/governing-board/strategic-vision.html.

and recent past but does it better. That's probably the right stance for those deeply invested in NAEP as it has evolved. But we should at least consider what a hot version might look like by imagining that what the country needs in the years to come is a fundamental makeover of NAEP, perhaps even a disruptive innovation in the assessment realm.[7]

One can conjure a very different sort of twenty-first-century education-monitoring regime, one that tracks individual students so as to be able to do rigorous longitudinal impact studies, and that uses technology to replace background questionnaires with something more powerful, such as audio or video recordings of the classrooms of kids who are tested, collecting specimens of instructional materials, assignments, and student work, perhaps accompanied by interviews or surveys of parents, teachers, and principals. Such an alternative might assess reading and math less often than NAEP now does and would use adaptive testing technology and thereby both shrink testing time and free resources to investigate other key aspects of education. We could picture this alternative evolving into the marquee federal study of teaching and learning and one that also produces periodic updates on national and state progress. In other words, it would delve deeply into what's working and why, not just report from time to time on how we are doing. Its flexible design would allow it to be used for experimental treatments with matched control groups. Doing all this would, of course, depend heavily on expert judgment—how to code and interpret those video recordings, for example, how to design and analyze those experiments and surveys—and would therefore be costly and more subjective.

Such an assessment would hold intense interest for researchers and policy types yet would do little for teachers or parents. To benefit them directly, any national program would have to be enormous, as it would have to yield information pertinent to the parents or guardians of some 55 million schoolchildren as well as some 4 million teachers in 100,000 or so schools.[§] Sampling cannot do that. Yet even in the wilder reaches of my experience and imagination, I can't picture the federal government mounting (or even sponsoring) a giant, census-style testing program that reaches into every classroom in the land. Just too "big brother," too invasive of privacy, too uniform for a diverse country, too centralized for an education system that's run by states and localities—and way too costly.

Nor are the data priorities of parents and teachers well aligned. Parents want most to know how their own children are faring against real-world norms such as being on track for the next grade, for graduation, for college, or for a rewarding career and happy life. Teachers are less interested in end-of-year summative results—by then their pupils have moved on—and skittish about themselves being judged by those results. They're much keener for periodic "formative" information about who in their classrooms is and isn't learning what during the course of the year. This divergence is real enough that even if a massive national program were politically and fiscally possible, no single design would be equally responsive to both teachers and parents.

On balance, it's tantalizing to contemplate such a replacement. Even if a foolproof recipe could be developed, however, the product would almost certainly be "too hot" to actually serve up and consume. That's certainly been the fate of previous efforts to create a national test.

The reader may not be surprised to find that my own judgments and recommendations for NAEP's future fall mostly in the middle category of "just right," neither too cold nor too hot—and the reader may also wonder whether I've been so invested in NAEP for so long that I've lost perspective on the "hotter" changes that it actually needs or the cooler versions that realpolitik may dictate. That's certainly possible.

Before delving deeper into a "just right" version of NAEP's future—which we undertake in the next chapter—we do well to remind ourselves once more that NAEP's continuing value, certainly its prominence and funding, possibly even its very existence, will hinge to a considerable extent on whether the multidecade reform regime of academic standards, assessments, and results-based accountability linked to those assessments remains at the heart of national (and state) education policy. NAEP has been a vital component of that regime, traceable at least to the Charlottesville summit in 1989 and NAGB's moves to assist with the goals enterprise that emerged from the summit, then boosted by the No Child Left Behind act, and enduring through the Every Student Succeeds Act.

Today, however, we face widespread exhaustion and exasperation with that approach to education reform, plus resistance and pushback from adult interests that don't see themselves well served by it. Even as America seems launched upon a meaner and more divisive period in its politics, we could be heading into a kinder and gentler era of K–12 education, one that's less judgmental and punitive, less focused on measurable academic achievement, and more interested in adequacy, equity, school climate, children's social and emotional (and physical and mental) health, and school outcomes such as civic participation and acceptance of diversity.

I'm not recommending such a shift! While the country would definitely benefit from added measures of school quality and more indicators of student learning than the test scores that we over-rely on today, to head toward a fundamental shift in what Americans value in K–12 education would work against many compelling national interests from economic competitiveness to social mobility. It would also prove deceptive to millions of families that may be lulled into thinking that their children attend great schools that are preparing them well to succeed in the real world. Such deception would do the greatest harm to the most disadvantaged families and least fortunate girls and boys, those that depend most heavily on their schools to give them a boost.

Should such a fundamental change in basic strategy occur, however, NAEP as we know it could emerge as an unwelcome presence. That would invite its replacement either by the kind of data system that researchers crave or by the formative assessments that teachers value or—perhaps—by a cloud-based "lockbox" in which parents can keep all sorts of information pertaining to their own child's education but that is of little use to anyone else.

This is not the place to offer a full-throated rationale for retaining standards-based education and results-driven accountability as essential strategies for the kind of reform that American education still needs, perhaps now even more than ever. Suffice to say that, if the country sticks with that course, NAEP will remain indispensable.

This does not, however, mean that it should stand pat. It's old, it's clumsy, it's expensive (for what it does), and it could relatively easily do more than it's doing. Along with the rest of the country, it has also moved into a more precarious and argumentative time when data themselves are often suspect. Going forward, NAEP needs modernization, refreshing, and some refashioning. Much of that can be done within the bounds of current law, although NAEP's basic authorizing statute is long overdue for renewal and updating.[9] We should, however, acknowledge nervousness about opening the NAEP law to the depredations of today's Washington politics until forward-looking folks outside those politics are able to focus in an organized way on the assessment's future.

That's a taller order than any single author can (or really should) try to fill, but I attempt to jump-start the process in the next chapter by suggesting modifications intended to help make NAEP's future neither too cold nor too hot. These come in four categories.

CHAPTER 11

Toward a Just-right Future

THE FUTURE OF THE NATIONAL ASSESSMENT of Educational Progress should not be just a linear extension of its past. That prospect is inadequate both to fulfill NAEP's potential and to meet the mounting informational needs of the country for which it's become the foremost monitor of student learning and the K–12 system's performance. In the previous chapter, I termed such a future "too cold" a bowl of porridge.

But a too-hot future—essentially replacing NAEP with altogether different kinds of education metrics—also has big downsides. My purpose in this concluding chapter is to suggest four realms in which a carefully revamped assessment could turn out to be just right, at least within the realm of American education as we approach the second quarter of the twenty-first century.

- As Ina Mullis and NAGB both recognize, and as IES's Mark Schneider and NCES's Peggy Carr have initiated, NAEP could *modernize* and make far better use of technology. This is most obvious in test administration, which—no-brainer alert!—should be done with schools' own equipment, transmitted electronically, and stored in the cloud rather than schlepped from building to building by NCES contractors. That doesn't mean it's simple, as not all devices are compatible with NAEP test questions and not all schools yet have adequate technology or broadband. There are issues with uniform administration across thousands of schools in very different locations and circumstances. But other testing regimes have figured out how to do this and so could NAEP.

Test administration, however, is just the start when it comes to NAEP's potential uses of technology. For example, there's also the application of artificial intelligence to the construction and scoring of test questions, which can save much time and expense, though how much depends on the type of items employed in the assessment.

The six thousand or so schools and hundreds of thousands of students in the present NAEP sample are a valuable resource that could be used more extensively and not just for gauging achievement. Questions important to educators and policy makers can be included in the background questionnaires that students, teachers, and principals fill out, though careful thought needs to be paid to what's most important—and possible—to learn via background items and survey-style questions without becoming too burdensome or intrusive.

Within reason, the NAEP sample can also be used for special surveys, as IES began to do on a monthly basis in 2021 to obtain data on how schools were handling the challenges of instruction during a pandemic.[1] This use of already-drawn samples of schools and students as a "panel," somewhat akin to the University of Michigan's long-running "panel study of income dynamics" or the National Opinion Research Center's "AmeriSpeak" project, is a way to extend and amplify NAEP's value to American education and to assist policymakers in gathering data on urgent matters in the K–12 realm that go beyond student learning.[2]

Also ripe for reimagining and reconstructing is the entire procurement system by which NAEP's work gets done by contractors. Operating within federal rules and procedures that resemble those of the Defense Department, this has ossified into a costly, semipermanent oligopoly of organizations that team up—the so-called NAEP Alliance—to merge their bids whenever there's a competition. This cozy arrangement deters competition, inflates the price tag, and tends to freeze everything in place, discouraging (for example) the kind of innovation that took place back in 1983 when, in a genuine competition, ETS prevailed over ECS for the primary NAEP contract.

After three decades of widening acceptance across the K–12 universe as the standards by which American education gauges its performance, increasing sophistication in how they're developed, and reasonable certainty that they're here to stay, NAGB's trio of achievement levels—"basic," "proficient," and "advanced"—is overdue to lose the word "trial" in NCES reports. That's not even modernizing! It's accepting a fait accompli.[3]

Also overdue is a faster, leaner, more efficient approach to the revision and replacement of assessment frameworks. Most testing programs—state assessments, professional licensure exams, and so forth—update their frameworks and instruments every three to five years and do so in ways that almost never menace trend lines. That's because the changes are gradual and incremental, not "start from scratch." Most participants in the panels that update those testing programs are bona fide practitioners who work from day to day with the actual knowledge and skills needed to succeed at whatever it is. The mix gets leavened by a handful of participants with other perspectives—employers, for example, some researchers, and some who look ahead to the field's future needs and demands. But NAGB, as longtime member (and eminent psychometrician) Gregory Cizek notes, has "turned this on its head" and instead created giant "visioning panels" comprised overwhelmingly of academics—often with novel but strongly held notions of what NAEP should do—and organizational representatives far distant from the daily work of figuring out what fourth (or eighth or twelfth) graders need to know about reading or math, say, in order to handle the challenges of the real world that they will inhabit, whether that means preparing for the demands of the next grade or the expectations of outside employers. How to teach what they need to learn is even more remote from the ken of many of NAGB's "visioners."[4] Because its panels do so much theorizing and imagining (and scrutinizing international tests that in key respects are very different from NAEP), and because this only happens every fifteen or twenty years, the results often point toward abrupt shifts in what's tested and thus pose serious threats to trend lines. This, then, is a further example of a core NAEP practice that would benefit from modernizing and rationalizing.

As frameworks are updated along with test formats and items, some catching up is also needed in the skills and knowledge that NAEP assesses. For example, contemporary students need to know how to seek and obtain information from many different sources, how to evaluate its veracity, and how to make logical choices based on valid information. Such skills cut across the curriculum—science and history are obvious, but they figure in every subject that NAEP tests— and tomorrow's assessments should do far more than today's to gauge students' mastery of them.[5]

Perhaps the stickiest modernization wicket is whether to halt NAEP's long-standing bib-spiraled testing of composite students using a format that focuses on item blocks, and move instead to computer-adaptive testing of individual pupils.[6] Such a move would have clear benefits: reducing testing time, augmenting information about what low and high achievers can and cannot do, removing some of the mystery of "matrix sampling," and possibly rooting out obscure biases that may lurk in today's complex statistical manipulations. But such a change may be too hot to handle, beginning with its immense technical and logistical challenges; the trend-line threat that it presents; and, above all, the seductive but problematic prospect of shifting to a system that would yield individual results for students in the NAEP sample while continuing to yield valid data for groups of students.[7] Besides the myriad technical challenges that presents, it would open Pandora's box, within which lurks the temptation to stop sampling altogether and expand NAEP into an individual test that generates district, school-level, and perhaps pupil-level data, a test that potentially replaces other assessments and, in so doing, invites the political blowback of "national testing" and the hazards of turning NAEP from impartial auditor into another form of high-stakes assessment.

Expanding NAEP in this way (minus the futuristic "adaptive" feature) was essentially what presidents Bush (41) and Clinton each proposed in the 1990s and what Congress shot down. Today, once again, despite its appeal, I sense that full-fledged adaptive testing at the individual level would kindle fires that are likely to burn out of control. One possible Solomonic solution—a trade-off, really—would be to move to adaptive testing but continue to restrict NAEP to student samples, which means limiting it to jurisdictions large enough to generate such samples. That alone could add many more districts and charter-school networks to NAEP. It would, however, require such a different test design (and so many more test items) as almost certainly to force a fresh start on all trend lines.

Sticking with a sample strategy over time could also prove difficult, as there will be a powerful tug, if NAEP were to start generating student-level results, to extend this further, and we ought not minimize the pushback to follow. One idea for dealing with this, albeit with ample technical and political complexities of its own, is also to develop a "short form" NAEP or NAEP derivative that could be given in smaller units, perhaps by individual schools, perhaps even given online by parents to their own children. The point of the short-form spin-off is not to meet NCES standards of statistical precision. It's more like the SAT practice tests that the College Board makes available (and their ACT counterparts), on which you can check your own scores and see how you did, how you compare, and whether you're getting better at it. This would be done online and limited in the kinds of items that could be deployed that way. But it could give NAEP approximations or rough equivalents to units that cannot qualify for the full NAEP treatment.

- The second major category for nudging NAEP into a "just right" future may be thought of as the *scope* of the assessment. What subjects should be tested how often, in what grade levels, and for what jurisdictions? The rule of thumb going forward should be regularity. Right now, the assessment schedule keeps jumping around, which makes NAGB seems whimsical and unreliable, even though some of the variability is due to budget decisions beyond its control.

  Because NAEP historically (and by law) tests at grades 4, 8, and 12, sticking with four-year testing intervals makes sense, as that arrangement retains the same student cohorts in consecutive test samples. For example, kids in fourth grade in 2021–2022 will be in eighth grade in 2025–2026 and seniors in high school in 2029–2030. Testing on a four-year cycle makes it possible to gauge the achievement growth (or stasis) of the same pupil cohorts, even as different individuals are sampled.

  Four-year intervals are probably also sufficient for tracking trends, considering how glacial are almost all changes in US student achievement, although I respect the view of some NAEP veterans that such infrequent bulletins will foster complacency or obliviousness about achievement among educators and policy leaders and perhaps also tend to marginalize NAEP itself. They would much prefer to stick with the current two-year interval for reading and math, even move to annual testing, despite the budgetary burden that would cause and the snail-like pace of achievement change. It must be noted, though, that getting NAEP's other core subjects—writing, history, civics, geography, science, perhaps the arts—onto a four-year cycle (and getting every subject routinely tested at all three grade levels) would be an enormous value enhancer for NAEP and for American education. It may also be noted—this is written as President Biden is proposing epic increases in federal education spending, including a modest rise in NAEP's budget—that possibly the fiscal trade-offs will grow less stark in years to come, although for that to be more than wishful thinking will require as-yet-undiscovered champions in the executive branch or on Capitol Hill.

As discussed earlier, to assess a subject in just one or two of NAEP's three grade levels is akin to giving someone a partial physical exam, maybe checking chest and/or abdomen but ignoring head and neck. The three grade levels are there for a reason—end of elementary, end of middle, end of high school—and almost every subject worth assessing is worth assessing at least in eighth and twelfth grades. For some subjects, notably the three Rs (and perhaps science), fourth grade is essential, too. It's certainly the most crucial for reading, even as it doesn't seem essential to test fourth graders in history or economics, for example.

Twelfth grade is especially important as it represents the end of formal schooling and the point from which young people proceed into college, career, and adulthood. To neglect the end of high school in *any* subject is utterly irresponsible. Not routinely displaying what they know and can do at that stage in key realms of the curriculum is among NAEP's foremost failings today. Also lost from NAEP over the decades (but present at the outset) is any effort to gauge the achievement of seventeen- and eighteen-year-olds who are *not* in school, that is, who have dropped out. Though some of them reappear in pursuit of "equivalency" diplomas and suchlike, we have almost no information about how far they actually got in acquiring skills and knowledge that will powerfully affect their futures.

Although the costs of test administration would rise, we can picture NAEP assessments adhering to four-year cycles even as some are given—and reported—*every* year. If that sounds confusing, consider—for example—testing reading and math on four-year cycles beginning in 2021–2022; testing science on quadrennial cycles beginning in 2022–2023; history, civics, and geography on cycles beginning in 2023–2024; and art and technology on cycles beginning in 2024–2025.[8] In other words, some students in some schools would participate in NAEP every year, and every year there would be a NAEP report on how they did. This would help keep NAEP in the public eye and keep the public regularly informed about the progress (or lack thereof) of young Americans in key subjects, as well as about such pressing equity concerns as achievement gaps among groups of young Americans.

As important as regular cycles and the inclusion of all three grade levels is NAEP's responsibility to make all that information available not just for the nation but also for states and TUDA districts, at least those that want it. Yes, that makes for a much larger sample and adds further to the cost as well as the testing burden on states. So maybe let them decide how much and how often they want such information. In subjects not mandated by Congress, it would not be crazy for NCES to ask states and districts to sign up in advance for assessments that provide data they want and perhaps to share in the added cost of gathering those data. But in a country where states bear primary responsibility for K–12 education and where most of the educating is done by local authorities, not to afford those authorities at least the opportunity to access this vital third-party information on student achievement is, in my view, totally unacceptable.

As for which jurisdictions participate in NAEP besides the states and territories, more districts would like to but have been stopped by budget constraints. If the fiscal picture brightens, many more could enter the TUDA program, along with charter-school networks and private school groups large enough to yield valid NAEP samples. They should have the option of joining and, if funding stays tight, perhaps joining at their own expense. At least 130 public school systems in the US, plus dozens of charter networks and private school groupings, are larger than Cleveland, which already participates in TUDA and is (obviously) large enough for a valid sample. As suggested above, if federal appropriations are insufficient, districts seeking inclusion might be asked to share in the cost.

- There are both benefits and dysfunction—including plenty of the latter—in the two-headed *governance* arrangement that places both NAGB and NCES in charge of NAEP, with responsibilities and authority that are semi-separate and semi-overlapping. (See figure 11.1.) It's tricky, even

FIGURE 11.1   Two-headed wildebeest
Source: Sammy33/Shutterstock.com.

paradoxical, to operate a government program that must meet federal norms for procurement and statistical integrity even as its important decisions are "governed" by a quasi-independent board that's meant to buffer it from the usual forces that hem in a federal agency. Other agencies, such as the National Science Foundation and National Endowment for the Humanities, seem to have somewhat less difficulty with this, as do quasi-autonomous (but federally funded) entities such as the Smithsonian and the Corporation for Public Broadcasting. On balance, though, a one-headed structure is preferable.

I see some advantage in extricating NAEP entirely from the Education Department and conferring a form of autonomous status on it and its governing board. Doing so would simplify several key processes (such as budget creation, procurement, and congressional relations) where it's especially awkward to run a major assessment venture that's supposed to be independent within a giant cabinet department. But it would also be weird to separate the country's foremost barometer of educational achievement from the principal national agency concerned with education (and in which NAEP has been housed since its creation five decades ago.)[9] A loss of clout within the executive branch is also likely if the education secretary no longer represents NAEP in cabinet meetings, in budget tussles with OMB, and so forth. Assuming, then, that NAEP is destined to remain part of the Education Department, perhaps it should become its own unit inside IES, parallel to NCES rather than a project of NCES. (The last Trump/DeVos budget submission to Congress recommended such a structure.) If it's to continue operating as an NCES project—by far the largest such project, a hefty tail that does tend both to wag the whole dog and to consume its budget—the present awkwardness could be eased by some clarifications in authority and responsibility.

The two most vexed realms—how vexed in a given year depends on the chemistry between NAGB and its staff on the one hand and NCES and IES leaders on the other—are the development of NAEP's budget and the release of its results. Surely these, at least, can be clarified and simplified. Under current law and practice, the board has little to say about the president's annual budget request for NAEP (and the separate line that funds NAGB itself). As a former NAGB staffer explained to me, though the law requires

> "the Commissioner for Education Statistics to report to the [Governing] Board on the Department's actions to implement the decisions of the [Governing] Board," this has not occurred with respect to the annual request for the NAEP budget until after the President's annual budget request is delivered to Congress and made public . . . The lack of a role in the development of the annual NAEP budget request is counter to the Board's responsibility under law for setting the schedule of assessments. It is potentially detrimental to the effective operation of the very complex NAEP program. Intimate knowledge of the budget requests and budget outlook for NAEP is essential for informing the Board's decisions about the schedule (as well as other policy matters), and having this information as it is being developed and proposed is consistent with the intent of Congress in assigning this responsibility to the Board.[10]

As for reporting results, there's been recurrent tension over the years regarding whether that's the board's job or the responsibility of the NCES commissioner. In fact, there's a statutory conflict between NAGB's duty to "plan and execute the initial public release of [NAEP] . . . reports" and "develop guidelines for reporting and disseminating results" and the separate authority given to the NCES commissioner to "collect and report assessment data . . . in a valid and reliable manner."

Untangling this will require involvement by Congress, which is both an unsettling prospect at a time of dysfunction, gridlock, and heavy partisanship in Washington, and yet another example of overdue work that Washington's decision-makers must face if they intend to keep the nuts and bolts of federal machinery from further rusting.

- The final domain in which NAEP invites modernization is the *dissemination and utilization* of its assessment results. Board members and NCES and IES officials have long been frustrated by what they regard as the low visibility and limited impact of those results. They're understandably keen that the data they work so hard to produce and verify should get more widely disseminated, discussed, and applied to the solution of sundry education problems facing the nation.

That eagerness stands out in Ina Mullis's stocktaking and even more so in NAGB's strategic plan, both cited in the previous chapter. Mullis acknowledged that "making NAEP more useful and well known remains extremely challenging," while almost every item in the board's multifaceted plan focuses in some way on dissemination, utilization, and recognition. Board members and NAGB staff also take great pains to plan the release of NAEP data in ways designed to maximize their visibility and impact. At a March 2021 meeting of the board's reporting and dissemination committee, for example, a play-by-play plan for the forthcoming release of 2019 science results was worked over in detail.[11] One small piece of that plan reads this way: "In the weeks before the release event, the Governing Board will launch a social media campaign to build interest in the release, with special focus on stakeholders involved in science, tagging influencers in this field and former Board members prominent in science education. The Board's website will dedicate a webpage to release events."

The board's frustration is easily understood. Its members preside over what they view as an immensely valuable resource for educators and policy makers—and parents and citizens—yet they see that resource vanishing from public view after an initial newspaper article or brief squib on the *PBS NewsHour*. Sure, it lingers in the "trade press," with more extended coverage in *Education Week*, *Education Next*, *The 74*, and sundry blogs and websites that focus on K-12 goings-on, and its data will continue for years to draw analysts and scholars. Yet that doesn't suffice for board members and others who want NAEP to raise alarms and drive informed change in what happens in schools and what's learned by young Americans. They're naturally disheartened when the results they've worked so hard to produce appear to be little more than a flash in the pan, perhaps an object of interest but not a force for change.

The good news is that their dismay, understandable though it may be, is not entirely warranted. NAGB members and other NAEP aficionados tend to focus overmuch on the short and medium term, yet the changes that assessment results help to force are glacial and the causal link—as always with NAEP—is impossible to prove. That, however, doesn't mean nothing changes—sometimes even for the better—with the help of data provided by NAEP.

It's not crazy to view NAEP as education's counterpart to the National Weather Service. Go to the latter's home page and you find several major categories of information with NAEP analogues. The most obvious parallel is "past weather," which the Weather Service splits among "climate monitoring," "past weather," "monthly temps," "records," "astronomical data," and "certified weather data."

No, NAEP doesn't do forecasting, which the Weather Service is best known for, and NAEP's "current" data aren't exactly up to the minute. (Some other NCES data series come closer to real time.) So the analogy is limited, yet in many respects it works. The Weather Service tabulates, measures, tracks, and compares weather in many places, analyzing and organizing those data in dozens of ways and making them available to every sort of user. NAEP does all those things with education achievement data and thereby equips thousands of people and organizations with information they need to do better at what they do, most of which involves educating American children. They can analyze, compare, diagnose, and potentially improve it with the help of NAEP data, much as a continuous flow of Weather Service data enables users to build more accurate models and algorithms, generate sounder predictions, meld it with information from other sources, monitor trends over time, and assist people to make suitable preparations and accommodations as storms brew, the climate changes, and strategies for adapting to it multiply. Moreover, because of its unparalleled and widely trusted "audit" function, NAEP serves as an impartial outside check on achievement results as tabulated and reported by others. Thanks to NAEP, it's far harder today to get away with "Lake Wobegon"-style fake good news about student achievement than in the days before we had state-level data arrayed on stable national scales onto which are fixed three ambitious achievement levels.

None of this means that NAEP or its data loom large in the eyes of the general public, nor in the gaze of many parents, teachers, or principals. That's going to remain a fact of life—and a frustration for NAGB members and other NAEP promoters—so long as the assessment remains distant from individual students, classrooms, schools, and the great majority of districts. So remote a body of data cannot ever get much traction with people who care chiefly about only their own children, pupils, and schools. We know that national unemployment data have little meaning for people focused on their own job situations, and national pandemic data don't seem terribly relevant to those focused on their own family's health. Today's NAEP is, at day's end, a premier source of national (and state) data on educational achievement but not very relevant to those on the ground. NAEP does wholesale, not retail. That simple truth places a big limit on its visibility and direct impact. And that fact should—though it probably won't—encourage ardent board members to take a deep breath and perhaps settle for the assessment's real value to American education, which is long term and indirect.

Yet more could be done to raise NAEP's profile a bit. For instance, the "short-form" version suggested above could add a retail element to the assessment, giving people a way to estimate how their district, school, or child is faring against NAEP standards and compared with national and state achievement data.

Once again, though, there are trade-offs. Just as the imputation of a state's NAEP results into TIMSS scores is less accurate than the state participating directly in TIMSS, any short form of NAEP that's designed for retail use won't be as accurate as "main NAEP," won't compare precisely, and won't meet NCES standards of statistical integrity and test validity. Thus, it could even serve to diminish NAEP. The choice is painful: between something revered but remote and something close to home but perhaps devalued.

Other steps to make NAEP better known are worth doing although not very exciting. They include conducting additional analyses that apply the data to topics of importance; maximizing access to this immense trove of data for further analyses by others; making skillful use of the NAEP school sample for further surveys; adding and subtracting background questions asked of students, teachers, and principals so as to keep them current without becoming too burdensome or intrusive. And then bending every effort to inform NAEP's many audiences that such information exists, help them gain entry to it, and understand how to manage it. Increasingly, this will depend on the internet and social media more than on traditional communications and dissemination arrangements.[12]

That porridge feels tepid—and doesn't differ greatly from what NCES and NAGB are already trying to do. It won't transform NAEP into a rival for *Monday Night Football* or *Saturday Night Live*. In combination with more regular testing of more subjects in more grades in more places, however, plus competent dissemination of those test results, it will make the National Assessment a more frequent presence in more media markets, on more computer screens, and in more people's minds, which will make it a more versatile and valued tool for more education leaders and policy makers, albeit still not at the retail level.

Recent years have witnessed the rise of an entire industry devoted to getting people to notice things: advertising and marketing, of course, but also publicizing through all sorts of media and mechanisms, working to optimize visibility on search engines, booking slots on talk shows, blogging and podcasting, and much more. The space has grown cluttered and noisy, making it even harder for any one voice to get heard, yet those who really want to get themselves or their products and achievements noticed are active in this space and often engage expert help to amplify and augment their own actions.

Government agencies, especially statistical agencies, aren't great at this sort of amplification, and it's possible that Americans don't really want them to be, as efforts to rub the public's nose in the latest data can readily take on the political coloration of its current masters and smack of federal propaganda. Nevertheless, the directors of both the Bureau of Labor Statistics and the Census Bureau, for example, have blogs, although these are not terribly active. They don't yet have podcasts. The NCES commissioner and IES director have their own blogs, but NAGB doesn't, though it has a Twitter account (@GovBoard) with a few thousand "followers" and an occasional presence on Facebook and LinkedIn. In recent years, it's gotten much more adept at multimedia presentations as well as targeting emails to its extensive list, and from time to time the board has engaged communications consultants to advise and assist with such things.[13]

That's all good, as far as it goes, and would likely get better if NAEP and its governing board acquired a clearer institutional identity— roughly akin (if not equivalent) to the Council of Economic Advisers or Federal Reserve Board, rather than continuing as the dog-wagging tail of NCES. Which speaks, once again, to structural and governance arrangements that need attention in the years ahead.

With long-established federal programs, the past is usually prologue, and gradual evolution is far more common than abrupt change. Just warming this chilly porridge to the palatable stage would be an accomplishment. And as our lightning tour of NAEP's half-century history has shown, gradual evolution has generally characterized the National Assessment. The half-dozen notable exceptions—times when NAEP has been altered in fundamental ways—have all been triggered by compelling external events, pressures, or leaders: the move from NAEP's academic origins to an organization of state education leaders; a scathing critique of NAEP's performance followed by a new federal competition that led to the project's relocation to ETS and a fresh design; the rebirth of NAEP by Congress in the aftermath of the Alexander-James report; the launch of state-level reporting and NAGB's achievement levels in the wake of the Charlottesville summit; the mandating of NAEP for every state as part of NCLB; and with it the assessment's emergence as auditor and benchmark for academic standards and achievement.

In the two decades since NCLB, NAEP has returned to gradualism, generally getting better at what it does, dealing with issues as they've arisen, and launching a number of updates and partial modernizations. That there's been no fundamental change is underscored by congressional inattention to the basic NAEP statute since 2002.

Absent another strong push from outside, gradualism is apt to continue, and congressional inaction will persist. Fortunately, much of the "just right" future for NAEP that's outlined above could be managed without legislative action. Much of what needs to be done to modernize NAEP and make its data more accessible, relevant, and usable to more people in more ways and places can be accomplished via competent leadership, smart planning, plausible trade-offs, and reasonable budget choices. That doesn't mean modernization is easy—it never is for a complicated and rather creaky government program that's encumbered by many interests and power centers—but it is not all doomed by contemporary politics.

Nor can we ignore the fact that some of the cracks that are beginning to emerge in NAEP have more to do with cultural and ideological rifts and tensions in the education field and the larger polity and thus would not even lend themselves to statutory repairs. Deft board leadership can help, of course, but we're at a time when, for example, disputes over reading assessments are driven by latter-day concerns about equity, even by strong—and perhaps politically motivated—affinities for different bodies of research, and when arguments about a civics or history assessment arise from divergent views of modern citizenship or of the nation's past. We ought not be surprised that the quest for comity and consensus grows exceedingly difficult. This difficulty extends far beyond the twenty-six members of NAEP's governing board, to be sure, but insofar as it reverberates in key decisions about the assessment, a vital asset will be diminished. If civility and compromise become things of the past for NAEP, too, then a worrisome cloud will hover over the assessment's future.

The uncertainties and opportunities surrounding that future need attention, not just by the usual NAEPsters but by everyone concerned with the future of American education—and, arguably, the future of American society. The National Assessment of Educational Progress has been a remarkable accomplishment not only in the narrow world of testing but also in the broader quest for a better country, powered in part by schools in which children learn more, standards are high, excellence is prized, yet gaps and failings also get exposed as the unacceptable obstacles they pose to excellence and equity alike. NAEP's been part of a half-century-long push to strengthen K–12 education in the United States, and along the way it has carved out a distinctive and valuable role. But America has arrived at a vexed time when honest data are sometimes suspect, when some doubt the credibility of information that emanates from the government (possibly depending on who's in charge of that government), when some prefer their own facts (and certainly their own spin on the facts), and when consensus about key measures of progress and performance is far harder to attain.

It's an open question how these weighty challenges can best be managed within the NAEP context and a viable future course can be charted and followed for the assessment. Perhaps it's time for another thoroughgoing outside review, akin to the Wirtz-LaPointe analysis and the Alexander-James study group. IES director Mark Schneider's recent move to enlist the National Academies in modernizing a number of NAEP operations moves part way in that direction. But I sense that something bolder is required, something prompted, organized, led, and paid for entirely outside the government, something with a much grander mandate, and something that engages a wider swath of interests and perspectives than the academies' experts. It may be time for leading philanthropists to re-engage and apply their mounting interest in the future of assessment in general to pull together a blue-ribbon panel or commission on national assessment in particular.

The goal is not to replace NAEP, and certainly not to terminate it. But getting it in shape for the next fifty years is an undertaking as ambitious and demanding as it is vital.

NOTES

CHAPTER 1

1. As discussed later, the congressional mandate does *not* extend to state-level reporting of twelfth-grade NAEP results. It does, however, include the District of Columbia and Puerto Rico (math only) as well as the fifty states. Some twenty-seven urban school districts also participate voluntarily in the biennial assessment of reading and math as part of the "Trial Urban District Assessment" program known as TUDA.
2. "Focus on NAEP: Sampling for NAEP Assessments," Nation's Report Card, https://www.nationsreportcard.gov/focus_on_naep/#/reports/sampling/; "NAEP State Assessment Sample Design Frequently Asked Questions," Nation's Report Card, https://nces.ed.gov/nationsreportcard/assessment _process/samplesfaq.aspx.
3. When NAEP tests subjects other than reading and math, school participation is voluntary and some must be persuaded by NCES staff, NAEP contractors, or state and local officials to take part.
4. "Poverty" is gauged by student participation in the federal subsidized lunch program that, as we discuss later, is a less and less reliable proxy. A concise report on 2019 math results can be seen at "NAEP Report Card: 2019 NAEP Mathematics Assessment," Nation's Report Card, https://www.nationsreportcard .gov/highlights/mathematics/2019/; Links to more detailed results (for fourth grade) can be found at "NAEP Report Card: Mathematics," Nation's Report Card, https://www.nationsreportcard.gov/mathematics/?grade=4.
5. "NAEP Technical Documentation: Student Booklet Block Design," National Center for Education Statistics, https://nces.ed.gov/nationsreportcard/tdw /instruments/cog_blockdesign.aspx.
6. "NAEP Accommodations Increase Inclusiveness," National Center for Education Statistics, https://nces.ed.gov/nationsreportcard/about/accom_table .aspx.
7. Taslima Rahman et al., *Mapping State Proficiency Standards Onto the NAEP Scales: Results From the 2017 NAEP Reading and Mathematics Assessments* (Washington, DC: US Department of Education, Institute of Education Sciences, National Center for Education Statistics, 2019), https://nces.ed.gov/nationsreportcard /subject/publications/studies/pdf/2021036.pdf.

8. "Score the Assessment," National Center for Education Statistics, https://nces.ed.gov/nationsreportcard/assessment_process/score.aspx.

9. For example, high performers will want to emphasize their level of achievement (even if it's been flat), while low performers generally prefer to emphasize gains they have made over time.

10. "Item Response Theory: Simple Definition," Statistics How To, https://www.statisticshowto.com/item-response-theory/.

11. Nathan Thompson, "How do I conduct a modified-Angoff study?" Assessment Systems, https://assess.com/conduct-a-modified-angoff-study. In recent years, the governing board has sometimes used other methods for setting achievement levels, including the "Bookmark" and "Body of Work" methods. Edward H. Haertel and William A. Lorié, "Validating Standards-Based Test Score Interpretations," *Measurement: Interdisciplinary Research and Perspectives* 2 (2004): 61–103, doi: 10.1207/s15366359mea0202_1/.

12. *How High the Bar: How would other nations perform if their students were judged by Common Core or NAEP Benchmarks?* (Seattle, WA: National Superintendents Roundtable and The Horace Mann League, 2018), http://www.superintendentsforum.org/archives/2019-2/how-high-the-bar-report.

13. As discussed in several chapters to follow, a new draft framework for reading assessments, intended to take effect with the 2025 NAEP testing cycle, was the subject of much controversy in 2020 and 2021. Natalie Wexler, "What We Talk About When We Talk About Reading Comprehension," *Forbes*, July 22, 2020, https://www.forbes.com/sites/nataliewexler/2020/07/22/what-we-talk-about-when-we-talk-about-reading-comprehension/?sh=3f5b6bf624e9.

14. The psychometrics of item review get complicated fast. "NAEP Pre-Tests: Overview of NAEP Pre-Test Administration Types," National Center for Education Statistics, https://nces.ed.gov/nationsreportcard/tdw/overview/naep_pretests_2009.aspx; "Advancements in Assessments," National Center for Education Statistics, https://nces.ed.gov/nationsreportcard/about/advancements.aspx; Jeanne A. Teresi, Marjorie Kleinman, and Katja Ocepek-Welikson, "Modern psychometric methods for detection of differential item functioning: application to cognitive assessment measures," *Statistics in Medicine* 19, no. 11-12 (2000): 1651–1683, doi: 10.1002/(sici)1097-0258(20000615/30)19:11/12<1651::aid-sim453>3.0.co;2-h.

15. "Science Student Questionnaire: 2019, Grade 12," National Center for Education Statistics, https://nces.ed.gov/nationsreportcard/subject/about/pdf/bgq/student/2019_sq_student_s_g12.pdf.

16. "Reading, Mathematics, and Science Teacher Questionnaire: 2019, Grade 8," National Center for Education Statistics, https://nces.ed.gov/nationsreportcard/subject/about/pdf/bgq/teacher/2019_sq_teacher_rms_g08.pdf. The thirty-eight pages included separate sections for each of the three subjects assessed that year, so few teachers would have to complete the entire thing.

17. "Reading, Mathematics, and Science School Questionnaire: 2019, Grade 12," National Center for Education Statistics, https://nces.ed.gov/nationsreportcard/subject/about/pdf/bgq/school-sdlep/2019_sq_school_rms_g12.pdf.

18. In some years when this has proven especially difficult, I've had calls from Education Department officials asking whether I might be able to nudge certain state leaders to persuade more schools to take part in NAEP.

19. In addition to the appropriation figure shown here, NAEP received $28 million as a part of a one-time Covid-19 relief supplemental. The Biden administration's budget request for NAEP for fiscal 2022 is $180 million, a $15 million increase (not including NAGB's $7.8 million, which was level funded.) The per-student cost shown here is crude: simply the total NAEP appropriation divided by the number of students assessed. It may be noted that, when similar calculations are made for international assessments such as PISA and TIMSS, the per-student cost is much larger than NAEP's.

20. Perry Stein, "DeVos calls on Congress to postpone federal standardized exams until 2022," *Washington Post,* November 25, 2020, https://www.washingtonpost.com/local/education/naep-exams-2021-devos/2020/11/25/8f8741a4-2f3c-11eb-860d-f7999599cbc2_story.html.

21. "Livestream Release: Civics, Geography and U.S. History," National Assessment Governing Board, https://www.nagb.gov/naep-results/2018-naep-civics-geography-and-us-history-release.html. NCES staff point out that this delay was not typical for NAEP as it included additional analyses related to the transition from paper-and-pencil to digital testing.

22. "NAEP Report Card: Civics Sample Questions, Grade 8 Sample," Nation's Report Card, https://www.nationsreportcard.gov/civics/sample-questions/.

23. Michael Hansen, Diana Quintero, and Alejandro Vazquez-Martinez, "Latest NAEP results show American students continue to underperform on civics," *Brown Center Chalkboard Blog,* April 27, 2020, https://www.brookings.edu/blog/brown-center-chalkboard/2020/04/27/latest-naep-results-show-american-students-continue-to-underperform-on-civics/.

CHAPTER 2

1. Lyle V. Jones and Ingram Olkin, eds., *The Nation's Report Card: Evolution and Perspectives* (Bloomington, IN: Phi Delta Kappa Educational Foundation, 2004).

2. "Ralph W. Tyler," Education Encyclopedia—StateUniversity.com, https://education.stateuniversity.com/.

3. Eric A. Hanushek, "What Matters for Student Achievement," *Education Next* 21 (Summer 2021), no. 3, https://www.educationnext.org/what-matters-for-student-achievement/; Elizabeth Evitts Dickinson, "Coleman Report Set the Standard for the Study of Public Education," *Johns Hopkins Magazine,* Winter 2016, https://hub.jhu.edu/magazine/2016/winter/coleman-report-public-education/.

4. John Gardner, "Chapter 3: Interviews—An Interview with John Gardner," in *The Nation's Report Card: Evolution and Perspectives,* eds. Jones and Olkin (Bloomington, IN: Phi Delta Kappa Educational Foundation, 2004), 114–115.

5. Francis W. Keppel quoted in James A. Hazlett, "A History of the National

Assessment of Educational Progress, 1963–1973" (PhD diss., University of Kentucky, 1973), 352–353.

6. Frederic A. Mosher, "Chapter 2: The Age of Innocence," in *The Nation's Report Card: Evolution and Perspectives*, eds. Jones and Olkin, 93.

7. Irvin J. Lehmann, "Chapter 1: The Genesis of NAEP," in *The Nation's Report Card: Evolution and Perspectives*, eds. Jones and Olkin, 26–27.

8. In 1966, the US Office of Education made a modest grant to the University of Minnesota to hold a series of conferences related to national assessment.

9. Gardner, "Chapter 3: Interviews," 114.

10. "History," Education Commission of the States, https://www.ecs.org/about -us/history/.

11. Mosher, "Chapter 2: The Age of Innocence," 110.

12. Gardner, "Chapter 3: Interviews," 117.

13. Lehmann, "Chapter 1: The Genesis of NAEP," 60.

14. You can glimpse a specimen Maryland driver's test here: "Maryland DMV Practice Test," DMV Permit Test, https://dmv-permit-test.com/maryland/practice-test-1 .html?gclid=EAIaIQobChMI7YWyh4el6wIVg4nICh1iRAvXEAAYASAAEgIww _D_BwE.

15. *Maryland Driver's Manual* (Glen Burnie, MD: Motor Vehicle Association, n.d.), https://mva.maryland.gov/Documents/DL-002.pdf.

16. Lehmann, "Chapter 1: The Genesis," 61.

17. The unsurprising exception was social studies, a perennially fraught realm of study.

18. Lehmann, "Chapter 1: The Genesis," 65.

19. Ibid., 72.

20. Ibid., 73.

21. The author was able to enter college in 1962 with "sophomore standing" thanks to a quartet of decent AP scores.

22. For a helpful explanation, see "What's the difference? Criterion-referenced tests vs. norm-referenced tests," Renaissance, https://www.renaissance.com/2018/ 07/11/blog-criterion-referenced-tests-norm-referenced-tests/.

23. See a sample report at "Understanding the ISEE Report," Education Records Bureau, https://erblearn.org/sites/default/files/images/parents/ Understanding%20the%20ISEE%20Report_r3.pdf.

24. Mosher, "Chapter 2: The Age of Innocence," 110.

25. Ibid.

26. A list of US Education Commissioners from 1867 to 1980 (when the US Office of Education was transferred out of HEW, the "Education Division" of which morphed into the newly created US Department of Education) can be found at "United States Commissioner of Education," Wikipedia, https://en .wikipedia.org/wiki/United_States_Commissioner_of_Education#List_of _Commissioners_of_Education.

27. Lehmann, "Chapter 1: The Genesis," 86.

28. Dorothy M. Gilford, "Chapter 5: NAEP and the U.S. Office of Education,

1971–1974" in *The Nation's Report Card: Evolution and Perspectives*, eds. Jones and Olkin, 171.

29. Ibid., 182.
30. Ibid.

CHAPTER 3

1. "What does the NAEP Long-Term Trend Reading Assessment Measure?," National Center for Education Statistics, https://nces.ed.gov/nationsreportcard /ltt/what_measure_reading.aspx; "What does the NAEP Long-Term Trend Mathematics Assessment Measure?," National Center for Education Statistics, https://nces.ed.gov/nationsreportcard/ltt/what_measure_mathematics.aspx. The latest Long-Term-Trend results were released in October 2021: "NAEP Assessment Shows Long-Term Improvement in Reading and Math, But Short-Term Declines for 13-Year-Olds," National Assessment Governing Board, October 14, 2021, https://www.nagb.gov/content/dam/nagb/en/documents /newsroom/press-releases/2021/NAGB_NAEP-LTT-Press-Release_508.pdf.

2. William Greenbaum, Michael S. Garet, and Ellen Rachel Solomon, *Measuring Educational Progress: A Study of the National Assessment* (New York: McGraw-Hill, 1977).

3. Some of these recommendations would influence the 1978 legislation that first authorized NAEP. US Government Accountability Office (GAO), *The National Assessment of Educational Progress: Its Results Need to be Made More Useful*, HRD-76-113 (Washington, DC, 1976), https://www.gao.gov/assets/hrd-76 -113.pdf.

4. Ibid., 34.
5. Ibid., 12.

6. This deployment of NAEP methodologies and techniques began early, including annual conferences on large-scale assessment that ECS was holding for state leaders even before 1970, largely led by Frank Womer, who directed ECS's NAEP project in the early days.

7. GAO, *The National Assessment*, 28.

8. Barbara Ward, *Achievement in Mathematics and Science*, Issuegram 6 (Denver: Education Commission of the States, 1983), https://files.eric.ed.gov/fulltext /ED228060.pdf.

9. Lee J. Cronbach, "Chapter 3: Interviews—An Interview with Lee Cronbach," in *The Nation's Report Card: Evolution and Perspectives*, eds. Lyle V. Jones and Ingram Olkin (Bloomington, IN: Phi Delta Kappa Educational Foundation, 2004), 147.

10. Ibid., 153.

11. Archie LaPointe, "Chapter 6: A New Design for a New Era," in *The Nation's Report Card: Evolution and Perspectives*, eds. Jones and Olkin, 185.

12. Ibid., 186.

13. Willard Wirtz and Archie LaPointe, "Measuring the Quality of Education: A Report on Assessing Educational Progress," *Educational Measurement: Issues and Practice* 1, no. 4 (1982): 5–6, doi: 10.1111/j.1745-3992.1982.tb00673.x.

14. Ibid.

15. Anrig was a friend of mine from 1969 when we met until his untimely death in 1993. Greg played a significant role in several phases of NAEP, including serving as a member of the "Council of Seven" that helped shape the Wirtz-LaPointe report.

16. Albert E. Beaton, *Implementing the New Design: The NAEP 1983–84 Technical Report* (Princeton, NJ: Educational Testing Service, 1987), https://eric.ed.gov/?id=ED288887.

17. Ina V. S. Mullis, "White Paper on 50 Years of NAEP Use: Where NAEP Has Been and Where It Should Go Next" (white paper, NAEP Validity Studies Panel, National Center for Education Statistics, American Institutes for Research, Arlington, VA, June 2019), 5, https://www.air.org/sites/default/files/downloads/report/50-Years-of-NAEP-Use-June-2019.pdf. Item response theory in psychometrics isn't easily explained in everyday terms. See, for example, "What is item response theory," Assessment Systems, https://assess.com/what-is-item-response-theory/; and John Rust et al., "Introduction to Item Response Theory" (University of Cambridge: The Psychometrics Centre, n.d.), https://www.psychometrics.cam.ac.uk/system/files/documents/SSRMCIRT2017.pdf.

18. "Federal File: The White House and the 'Wall Chart'; Information, Please," *Education Week*, March 22, 1989, https://www.edweek.org/ew/articles/1989/03/22/08220015.h08.html.

19. *Measuring Student Achievement: Comparable Test Results for Participating Southern States, the South, and the Nation* (Atlanta, GA: Southern Regional Education Board, 1985), https://files.eric.ed.gov/fulltext/ED267101.pdf.

20. *Measuring Student Achievement: Comparable Test Results for Participating SREB States, the Region, and the Nation. A Report of the Southern Regional Education Board/National Assessment of Educational Progress 1986 Program with Arkansas, Florida, Louisiana, North Carolina, South Carolina, Tennessee, Virginia, West Virginia* (Atlanta, GA: Southern Regional Education Board, 1986), https://eric.ed.gov/?id=ED292863.

21. Lamar Alexander, "Governor Alexander's Summary of 'Time for Results,'" *Education Week*, September 10, 1986, https://www.edweek.org/ew/articles/1986/09/10/governor-alexanders-summary-of-time-for-results.html.

22. Lynn Olson, "Bennett Panel Urges Major Expansion of NAEP," *Education Week*, March 25, 1987, https://www.edweek.org/ew/articles/1987/03/25/26naep.h06.html.

23. Robert Rothman, "Normed Tests Skewed to Find Most Pupils 'Above Average,' a Disputed Study Finds," *Education Week*, December 9, 1987, https://www.edweek.org/education/normed-tests-skewed-to-find-most-pupils-above-average-a-disputed-study-finds/1987/12.

24. Robert Rothman, "Physician's Test Study Was 'Clearly Right,' A Federally Sponsored Analysis Has Found," *Education Week*, April 5, 1989, https://www

.edweek.org/education/physicians-test-study-was-clearly-right-a-federally
-sponsored-analysis-has-found/1989/04.

25. Albert E. Beaton et al., *The NAEP 1985–1986 Reading Anomaly: A Technical Report* (Princeton, NJ: Educational Testing Services, 1988).

26. Robert Rothman, "NAEP's 'Anomaly' Blamed on Changes in Test's Design," *Education Week*, June 22, 1988, https://www.edweek.org/ew/articles/1988/06/22/x39ecs.h07.html.

27. We look more closely at the National Assessment Governing Board in chapter 8 and subsequent chapters.

CHAPTER 4

1. Minnesota's Rudy Perpich didn't make it.

2. The "Goals 2000" legislation that followed a few years later added foreign languages, civics and government, economics, and arts to the five subjects specified in Charlottesville.

3. "Text of Statement on Education Goals Adopted by Governors," *Education Week*, March 7, 1990, https://www.edweek.org/education/text-of-statement-on-education-goals-adopted-by-governors/1990/03.

4. *Measuring Progress toward the National Education Goals: Potential Indicators and Measurement Strategies. Discussion Document* (Washington, DC: National Education Goals Panel, 1991), 17–18.

5. Ramsay Selden, "Chapter 7: Making NAEP State-by-State," in Lyle V. Jones and Ingram Olkin, eds., *The Nation's Report Card: Evolution and Perspectives* (Bloomington, IN: Phi Delta Kappa Educational Foundation, 2004), 197.

6. Ibid., 198.

7. Emerson Elliott and Gary Phillips, "Chapter 9: A View from the NCES," in Jones and Olkin, 245–246. This "embedding" continued until Congress enacted No Child Left Behind in 2002, requiring that every state participate in NAEP. NCES then took over test administration, obviating the need for what had amounted to two parallel national samples.

8. Lamar Alexander and H. Thomas James, *The Nation's Report Card: Improving the Assessment of Student Achievement* (Washington, DC: National Academy of Education, 1987), 58.

9. Maris A. Vinovskis, *Overseeing the Nation's Report Card: The Creation and Evolution of the National Assessment Governing Board* (Washington, DC: National Assessment Governing Board, 1998), 43–44.

10. That, of course, turned out to be an issue two decades later when the No Child Left Behind Act required states to designate a single level of "proficiency."

11. Because of the widespread view that a child who has acquired "basic" skills is well on his way to being satisfactorily educated, much confusion would follow from our decision to use the word "basic" to describe a level of achievement that was *not* satisfactory.

12. *The Reading Report Card: Progress Toward Excellence in Our Schools. Trends in Reading*

over Four National Assessments, 1971–1984, Report No. 15-R-01 (Washington, DC: Department of Education, National Institute of Education, 1985).

13. Mary Lyn Bourque, "Chapter 8: A History of the National Assessment Governing Board," in Jones and Olkin, 211.

14. Ibid., 213.

15. Psychometrician Gregory J. Cizek (himself a later NAGB member) was engaged by the board to evaluate the National Academy's review. He found four categories of "errors and inaccuracies" in that review as well as a quartet of legitimate concerns. Gregory J. Cizek, *Reactions to National Academy of Education Report, "Setting Performance Standards for Student Achievement* (Washington, DC: National Assessment Governing Board, 1993).

16. Mary Lyn Bourque, "Chapter 8: A History of the National Assessment Governing Board," in Jones and Olkin, 215.

17. *America 2000: An Education Strategy* (Washington, DC: US Department of Education, 1991).

18. Kevin R. Kosar, "National Council on Education Standards and Testing, Raising Standards for American Education (1992)," Federal Education Policy History, https://federaleducationpolicy.wordpress.com/2013/05/24/national-council-on-education-standards-and-testing-raising-standards-for-american-education-1992/.

19. David Whitman, *The Surprising Roots of the Common Core: How Conservatives Gave Rise to 'Obamacore'* (Washington, DC: Brookings Institution, Brown Center on Education Policy, September 2015).

20. Michael Guerra, "National Assessment Governing Board and Voluntary National Tests: A Tale of Tribulations without Trials" (paper presented at the 20th Anniversary of the National Assessment Governing Board, Washington, DC, March 4, 2009), 5.

21. Because it's national-only (and at the original age levels of 9, 13, and 17 rather than grade levels), LTT requires much smaller samples than "main NAEP," in the range of 26,000 students per subject. Budget pressures would intensify after Congress mandated via NCLB that state and national assessments in reading and math at grades 4 and 8 be administered every two years. But fiscal considerations weren't the entire reason for restricting long-term trend assessments to reading and math, for there were serious technical and substantive challenges with maintaining them in writing and science.

22. "Linking NAEP and TIMSS Study," National Assessment of Education Progress, https://nces.ed.gov/nationsreportcard/studies/naep_timss/. See also Gary W. Phillips, *International Benchmarking: State and National Education Performance Standards* (Washington, DC: American Institutes for Research, September 2014). The IEA also administers a test of fourth graders' "reading literacy" known as PIRLS, which the US has taken part in since 2001. Individual states may also participate directly in TIMSS and PIRLS, and several have done so, most recently in 2015. See "Trends in International Mathematics and Science Study: Participating Countries," National Center for Education Statistics, https://nces.ed.gov/timss/participation.asp.

23. *National and International Educational Assessments*, IF11021 (Washington, DC: Congressional Research Service, November 2, 2018).

24. "Germany's PISA Shock," Organisation for Economic Co-operation and Development (OECD), https://www.oecd.org/about/impact/germanyspisashock .htm.

25. "Program for International Student Assessment (PISA): Participation in PISA by Year," National Center for Education Statistics, https://nces.ed.gov/surveys /pisa/countries.asp. In 2015, both Massachusetts and North Carolina fared quite well among the participating nations. "Program for International Student Assessment (PISA): 'State Results: Massachusetts,'" https://nces.ed.gov /surveys/pisa/pisa2015/pisa2015highlights_7.asp.

CHAPTER 5

1. Ina V. S. Mullis, "White Paper on 50 Years of NAEP Use: Where NAEP Has Been and Where It Should Go Next" (white paper, NAEP Validity Studies Panel, National Center for Education Statistics, American Institutes for Research, Arlington, VA, June 2019), 8, https://www.air.org/resource/50-years-naep-use -where-naep-has-been-and-where-it-should-go-next.

2. *The Trial State Assessment: Prospects and Realities. The Third Report of the National Academy of Education Panel on the Evaluation of the NAEP Trial State Assessment: 1992 Trial State Assessment* (Stanford, CA: National Academy of Education, 1993), https://eric.ed.gov/?q=TSA&pg=4&id=ED367699. This was one of many examples—dating back to 1987's Alexander-James study group and continuing into the present era—when federal or foundation-financed contracts and grants to appraise various aspects of NAEP (and other large-scale assessments) have functioned as something of a bonanza for the Academy.

3. Ibid., XXVII.

4. Several participating states did not, however, manage to recruit enough schools to meet the sampling requirements or otherwise failed to fulfill all the rules, so their data were not reported by NCES or were annotated to explain their limitations. Catherine Shaughnessy, Jennifer Nelson, and Norma Norris, *NAEP 1996 Mathematics Cross-State Data Compendium for Grade 4 and Grade 8 Assessment* (Washington, DC: National Center for Education Statistics, December 1997) https://nces.ed.gov/pubsearch/pubsinfo.asp?pubid=98481.

5. Chad Aldeman, "School Accountability Before, During, and After NCLB," *Education Next* 21, no. 3 (2021), https://www.educationnext.org/school -accountability-before-during-and-after-nclb/.

6. A good explanation of differences between a state's NAEP results and the results of its own assessments can be found here: Krista D. Mattern and Catherine Lacina, *Different Assessments, Different Results: A Cautionary Note When Interpreting State Test Results* (Columbus, IN: ACT Research & Policy, 2015), http://www .act.org/content/dam/act/unsecured/documents/2015-Issue-Brief-Different -Results.pdf.

7. Mark Musick, *Setting Education Standards High Enough* (Atlanta, GA: Southern Regional Education Board, June 16, 1997), https://files.eric.ed.gov/fulltext/ED414309.pdf.

8. Ibid.

9. "Gore hails improved student reading levels," *CNN*, February 10, 1999, http://www.cnn.com/US/9902/10/gore.reading/.

10. David Hoff, "Board Contends Gore's Role Politicized NAEP Release," *Education Week*, March 10, 1999, https://www.edweek.org/teaching-learning/board-contends-gores-role-politicized-naep-release/1999/03.

11. Robert Pear, "Modest Gains Are Reported for Reading In 3 Grades," *New York Times*, February 9, 2012, https://www.nytimes.com/1999/02/11/us/modest-gains-are-reported-for-reading-in-3-grades.html?searchResultPosition=8.

12. Hoff, "Board Contends." Richard Riley was himself a former NAGB member as well as former governor of South Carolina, and a longtime friend of Mark Musick.

13. David Hoff, "Renomination Blocked, Forgione To Depart," *Education Week*, May 26, 1999, https://www.edweek.org/policy-politics/renomination-blocked-forgione-to-depart/1999/05.

14. David Grissmer et al., *Improving Student Achievement: What State NAEP Test Scores Tell Us* (Santa Monica, CA: RAND Corporation, 2000), https://www.rand.org/pubs/monograph_reports/MR924.html.

15. Bob Herbert, "In America; Bush's Education Record," *New York Times*, August 7, 2000, https://www.nytimes.com/2000/08/07/opinion/in-america-bush-s-education-record.html; Debra Viadero, "RAND Report Tracks State NAEP Gains," *Education Week*, August 2, 2000, https://www.edweek.org/ew/articles/2000/08/02/43rand.h19.html.

16. Debra Viadero, "Candidates Spar Over Test Gains in Texas," *Education Week*, November 1, 2000, https://www.edweek.org/ew/articles/2000/11/01/09rand.h20.html; John Mintz, "Study Disputes Bush Claims on Texas Education Record," *Washington Post*, October 25, 2000, https://www.washingtonpost.com/archive/politics/2000/10/25/study-disputes-bush-claims-on-texas-education-record/7bd624fe-6e29-41d4-b8cf-3256a6497f60/.

17. Millicent Lawton, "NAEP To Cut Exams, Test More Disabled Pupils," *Education Week*, September 6, 1995, https://www.edweek.org/education/naep-to-cut-exams-test-more-disabled-pupils/1995/09.

18. National Research Council, *Reporting District-Level NAEP Data: Summary of a Workshop* (Washington, DC: National Academies Press, 2000).

19. "Eligibility Criteria and Procedures for Selecting Districts for Participation in the National Assessment of Educational Progress: Trial Urban District Assessment, Policy Statement," National Assessment Governing Board, August 4, 2012, https://www.nagb.gov/content/nagb/assets/documents/policies/Trial-Urban-District-Assessment-Policy.pdf.

20. See for example the various annotations on this report on how fourth graders in Baltimore fared in science in 2009:"The Nation's Report Card: Science 2009: Trial Urban District Snapshot Report: Baltimore City Public Schools Grade 8

Public Schools," National Center for Education Statistics, 2009, https://nces
.ed.gov/nationsreportcard/pdf/dst2009/2011454XM8.pdf.

21. Personal communication to the author.

22. Personal communication.

23. Ina V. M. Mullis et al., *The State of Mathematics Achievement: NAEP's 1990 Assessment of the Nation and the Trial Assessment of the States* (Princeton, NJ: Educational Testing Service, June 1991), https://files.eric.ed.gov/fulltext/ED330545.pdf.

24. Mary Lyn Bourque, *A History of NAEP Achievement Levels: Issues, Implementation, and Impact 1989–2009*, (Washington, DC: National Assessment Governing Board, March 2009), 7, https://eric.ed.gov/?id=ED509389.

25. Ibid., 14.

26. For an example of how NAEP-like achievement levels were incorporated into Title I requirements, see: *Standards and Assessments Peer Review Guidance: Information and Examples for Meeting Requirements of the No Child Left Behind Act of 2001* (Washington, DC: US Department of Education, Office of Elementary and Secondary Education, January 12, 2009), 16, https://www2.ed.gov/policy/elsec/guid/saaprguidance.pdf?exp=6.

27. Chad Buckendahl et al., *Evaluation of the National Assessment of Educational Progress* (Washington, DC: US Department of Education, September 2009), https://www2.ed.gov/rschstat/eval/other/naep/naep.pdf.

28. Chester E. Finn, Jr., "The Value of NAEP Achievement Levels," *Education Next*, June 20, 2016, https://www.educationnext.org/why-tom-loveless-is-wrong-about-naep-achievement-levels/.

29. *How High the Bar?* (Seattle, WA: National Superintendents Roundtable and Horace Mann League, January 2018), http://www.superintendentsforum.org/archives/2019-2/how-high-the-bar-report.

30. "Scale Scores and NAEP Achievement Levels," National Center for Education Statistics, https://nces.ed.gov/nationsreportcard/guides/scores_achv.aspx.

31. Personal communication.

CHAPTER 6

1. This was highlighted in a video segment on December 1, 2020, featuring Bush and Spellings at the first keynote session of that year's "EdPalooza," sponsored by ExcelinEd. "National Summit on Education," ExcelinEd, https://excelined.org/national-summit/.

2. Edward Haertel et al., *NAEP: Looking Ahead, Leading Assessment into the Future* (white paper, NAEP Summit, National Center for Education Statistics, May 2012), https://nces.ed.gov/nationsreportcard/pdf/future_of_naep_panel_white_paper.pdf.

3. Reported via *Education Week*: "In field tests, conducted last fall, only 42 percent of the representative sample of schools and students selected to take the exam opted to participate. Those numbers would not meet NCES standards for reporting results, and therefore, the data might not be considered valid." Kathleen

Kennedy Manzo, "National Foreign-Language Assessment Delayed Indefinitely," *Education Week*, March 17, 2004, https://www.edweek.org/ew/articles/2004/03/17/27nagb.h23.html.

4. Manzo, "National Foreign-Language"; Sarah Sparks, "'Nation's Report Card' to Get Trimmed, Four Subjects Dropped," *Education Week*, July 24, 2019, https://www.edweek.org/ew/articles/2019/07/24/nations-report-card-to-get-trimmed-four.html.

5. "Assessment Schedule," National Assessment Governing Board, March 5, 2021, https://www.nagb.gov/about-naep/assessment-schedule.html.

6. "About AP Scores," College Board, https://apstudents.collegeboard.org/about-ap-scores; "ACT Scores for Higher Education Professionals," ACT, https://www.act.org/content/act/en/products-and-services/the-act-postsecondary-professionals/scores.html; Jeffrey Wyatt, Mylene Remigio, and Wayne Camara, *SAT Subject Area Readiness Indicators: Reading, Writing, and STEM*, College Board, August 31, 2012, http://files.eric.ed.gov/fulltext/ED562872.pdf.

7. "Criterion Related Validity," Science Direct, *2008*, https://www.sciencedirect.com/topics/nursing-and-health-professions/criterion-related-validity.

8. Ray Fields, *Towards The National Assessment of Educational Progress (NAEP) as an Indicator of Academic Preparedness for College and Job Training* (Washington, DC: National Assessment Governing Board, May 2014), http://files.eric.ed.gov/fulltext/ED582999.pdf; Mark Schneider et al., *Using the National Assessment of Educational Progress as an Indicator for College and Career Preparedness* (Washington, DC: American Institutes for Research, October 2015), https://www.air.org/resource/using-national-assessment-educational-progress-indicator-college-and-career-preparedness.

9. The key difference is that ACT and SAT report on the college preparedness of their test-takers, a college-minded subset of students, not necessarily in twelfth grade, while NAEP's twelfth-grade sample represents all high school seniors. It's also important to note the shift in NAGB terminology from "readiness" to "preparedness," reportedly due to concern that its assessments don't measure the full range of factors that bear on students' "readiness" to engage successfully in postsecondary work.

10. "NAEP Report Card: 2019 NAEP Reading Assessment," The Nation's Report Card, 2019, https://www.nationsreportcard.gov/highlights/reading/2019/g12/; "NAEP Report Card: 2019 NAEP Mathematics Assessment," The Nation's Report Card, 2019, https://www.nationsreportcard.gov/highlights/mathematics/2019/g12/.

11. NCES protocols require a "nonresponse bias analysis" any time the school response rate falls below 85 percent. "Chapter 4-1: Processing and Editing of Data," in *Restricted-Use Data Procedures Manual* (Washington, DC: US Department of Education, National Center for Education Statistics, 2000), https://nces.ed.gov/statprog/2002/std4_4.asp.

12. "Focus on NAEP: Grade 12 Participation and Engagement in NAEP," The Nation's Report Card, August 2017, 8, https://www.nationsreportcard.gov/focus_on_naep/files/g12_companion.pdf.

13. Ibid., 16.
14. "FAQs About Private Schools: NAEP Report Cards," Council for American Private Education, https://www.capenet.org/facts.html#NAEP.
15. Janie Scull and Amber Northern, *Shifting Trends in Special Education* (Washington, DC: Thomas B. Fordham Institute, May 25, 2011), https://fordhaminstitute.org/national/research/shifting-trends-special-education.
16. At this writing, NCES does not routinely report at the state level on the achievement of children with disabilities who participate (often with "accommodations") in NAEP testing, although such data are reported for the country as a whole and can be determined for states (and TUDA districts) via the NAEP "Data Explorer."
17. "NAEP Accommodations Increase Inclusiveness," National Center for Education Statistics, https://nces.ed.gov/nationsreportcard/about/accom_table.aspx.
18. *Measuring the Status and Change of NAEP State Inclusion Rates for Students with Disabilities*, NCES 2009-453, (Washington, DC: National Center for Education Statistics, American Institutes for Research, November 2008), v, https://nces.ed.gov/nationsreportcard/pdf/studies/2009453.pdf.
19. Lyndsey Layton, "Md. exclusion of special ed students affects national scores," *Washington Post*, November 24, 2013, https://www.washingtonpost.com/local/education/md-exclusion-of-special-ed-students-affects-national-scores/2013/11/24/9b390054-53b2-11e3-9fe0-fd2ca728e67c_story.html.
20. "Inclusion of Students with Disabilities and English Learners," National Center for Education Statistics, https://nces.ed.gov/nationsreportcard/about/inclusion.aspx. Similar "flagging"—and non-reporting—is done for student groups and school categories whose data are insufficient to meet NCES standards.
21. See, for example, Secretary DeVos's comment upon release of the 2019 NAEP "report card" on twelfth-grade reading and math, quoted in: "U.S. DOE Releases the 'Nation's Report Card Results for 12th Graders,'" All On Georgia, November 2, 2020, https://allongeorgia.com/georgia-education-k12/u-s-doe-releases-the-nations-report-card-results-for-12th-graders/.
22. Phil Daro et al., *Validity Study of the NAEP Mathematics Assessment: Grades 4 and 8* (Washington, DC: American Institutes for Research, September 2007), 121, https://www.air.org/sites/default/files/downloads/report/Daro_NAEP_Math_Validity_Study_0.pdf.
23. Sheida White et al., *The 2018 NAEP Oral Reading Fluency Study*, NCES 2021-025 (Washington, DC: US Department of Education, National Center for Education Statistics, Institute of Education Sciences, National Assessment of Educational Progress, Washington, DC, April 2021) https://nces.ed.gov/nationsreportcard/subject/studies/pdf/2021025_2018_orf_study.pdf.
24. Mark Schneider, "A Year for Reflection and Continued Transformation," Institute of Education Sciences, https://ies.ed.gov/director/remarks/1-12-2021.asp; "Opportunities for the National Assessment of Educational Progress in an Age of AI and Pervasive Computation: A Pragmatic Vision for 2030 and

Beyond," National Academies of Sciences, Engineering, Medicine, https://www
.nationalacademies.org/our-work/opportunities-for-the-national-assessment
-of-educational-progress-in-an-age-of-ai-and-pervasive-computation-a
-pragmatic-vision-for-2030-and-beyond.

25. Their teachers and principals are also given many background questions, but
these have raised fewer eyebrows over time as they tend not to ask "personal"
questions. Moreover, adults don't enjoy the same privacy protections in education data—and grownups are generally more patient when filling out forms.

26. "Family Educational Rights and Privacy Act (FERPA)," US Department of Education, December 15, 2020, https://www2.ed.gov/policy/gen/guid/fpco/ferpa
/index.html; "Legislative History of Major FERPA Provisions," US Department
of Education, February 11, 2004, https://www2.ed.gov/policy/gen/guid/fpco
/ferpa/leg-history.html.

27. "Chapter 2: Licensing Procedures," National Center for Education Statistics,
https://nces.ed.gov/statprog/rudman/chapter2.asp; "Chapter 4-2: Processing
and Editing of Data," in *Restricted-Use Data Procedures Manual* (Washington, DC:
US Department of Education, National Center for Education Statistics, Institute of Education Sciences, 2000), https://nces.ed.gov/statprog/2002/std4
_2.asp.

28. Mary Lyn Bourque, *Contextual Information Framework for the National Assessment of
Educational Progress* (Washington, DC: National Assessment Governing Board,
December 2013), https://www.nagb.gov/content/nagb/assets/documents
/publications/frameworks/contextual-information/contextual-information
-framework.doc.

29. "NAEP Background Questions: An Underused National Resource," National
Assessment Governing Board, February 22, 2012, https://www.nagb.gov/
content/dam/nagb/en/documents/publications/expert-panel-naep-bq-report
.pdf.

30. Lynn Olson, "NAEP Board Wants to Reduce Background Queries," *Education
Week*, May 14, 2003, https://www.edweek.org/teaching-learning/naep-board
-wants-to-reduce-background-queries/2003/05.

31. Ina V. S. Mullis, "White Paper on 50 Years of NAEP Use: Where NAEP Has Been
and Where It Should Go Next" (white paper, NAEP Validity Studies Panel,
National Center for Education Statistics, American Institutes for Research,
Arlington, VA, June 2019), 14–15, https://www.air.org/sites/default/files
/downloads/report/50-Years-of-NAEP-Use-June-2019.pdf.

32. With the introduction of Item Response Theory in the 1980s, NCES began
reporting scores for all three of its key grade levels on a single 500-point scale.
More recently, however, for reasons of psychometric validity and content
expectations that differ as grade levels rise, NAEP has moved to replace those
multigrade scales with 300-point single-grade scales. At this writing, only reading is reported for all three grades on a 500-point scale, as is math for grades
4 and 8 (but not 12). David Thissen, "Validity Issues Involved in Cross-Grade
Statements About NAEP Results" (white paper, NAEP Validity Studies Panel,
National Center for Education Statistics, American Institutes for Research, San

Mateo, CA, January 2012), https://www.air.org/sites/default/files/downloads
/report/1267_NVS_Cross-Grade_Scaling_formatted_1-9-12_0.pdf.

CHAPTER 7

1. Those are current dollars. The 1991 NAEP appropriation of $18.4 million was approximately equivalent to $35.3 million in 2020 dollars, which translates to a bit less than quintupling in actual purchasing power over the three decades—still pretty remarkable.
2. "1990 NAEP Budget Is Sufficient, Head of E.D. Research Unit Says," *Education Week*, May 15, 1989, https://www.edweek.org/education/1990-naep-budget-is -sufficient-head-of-e-d-research-unit-says/1989/03.
3. Kathleen Kennedy Manzo, "U.S. Testing Poised to Be Scaled Back," *Education Week*, November 19, 2007, https://www.edweek.org/teaching -learning/u-s-testing-poised-to-be-scaled-back/2007/11.
4. "National Assessment of Educational Progress (NAEP) Alliance," GovTribe, https://govtribe.com/opportunity/federal-contract-opportunity/national -assessment-of-educational-progress-naep-alliance-91990018r0018; Institute of Education Sciences, *Fiscal Year 2021 Budget Request* (Washington, DC: US Department of Education, 2021), 39, https://www2.ed.gov/about/overview/ budget/budget21/justifications/w-ies.pdf.
5. Betsy DeVos, "Secretary Letter on NAEP 2021," US House of Representatives, Committee on Education and Labor, November 24, 2020, https://edlabor .house.gov/imo/media/doc/2020-11-24%20-%20Secretary%20Letter% 20on%20NAEP%202021%20-%20Scott:Murray.pdf.
6. Personal communication to the author.
7. "Top Stories in NAEP Mathematics 2013," The Nation's Report Card, https:// www.nationsreportcard.gov/math_2013/.
8. This phenomenon is sometimes termed "Simpson's Paradox": a trend in several groups that disappears when the groups are combined. In the case of NAEP's long-term trend assessment, the country's changing demographics meant that each subgroup's score might be rising but the composition of the national sample changed in ways that masked this. However, the long-term trend results for thirteen-year-olds that were released in October 2021, based on tests given in January 2020, showed stark declines for the first time in both math and reading not only for the full student sample but also for most subgroups: Laura Meckler, "'Nation's Report Card' finds falling test scores, even pre-covid," *Washington Post*, October 14, 2021, https://www.washingtonpost .com/education/2021/10/14/nations-report-card-scores-falling/.
9. Edward Haertel, "Future of NAEP Long-Term Trend Assessments" (white paper prepared for the National Assessment Governing Board, Stanford, CA, December 9, 2016), 34, https://www.nagb.gov/content/nagb/assets/documents /newsroom/naep-releases/naep-long-term-trend-symposium/long-term -trends.pdf.

10. At this writing, the National Assessment Governing Board is in the middle of a framework revision for math.

11. *Science Framework for the 2015 National Assessment of Educational Progress* (Washington, DC: US Department of Education, National Assessment Governing Board, 2014), 1, http://www.nagb.gov/content/nagb/assets/documents/publications /frameworks/science/2015-science-framework.pdf.

12. Rick Hess, "Treat NAEP as a Reality Check, Not an Advocacy Exercise," *Education Week*, November 16, 2020, https://www.edweek.org/teaching-learning /opinion-treat-naep-as-a-reality-check-not-an-advocacy-exercise/2020/11.

13. "Opportunities for the National Assessment of Educational Progress in an Age of AI and Pervasive Computation: A Pragmatic Vision for 2030 and Beyond," National Academies of Science, Engineering, and Medicine, https://www .nationalacademies.org/our-work/opportunities-for-the-national-assessment -of-educational-progress-in-an-age-of-ai-and-pervasive-computation-a -pragmatic-vision-for-2030-and-beyond.

14. Larry Cuban, "School Reform: Foolish Fads or Impossible Dream?," Larry Cuban on School Reform and Classroom Practice, July 8, 2017, https://larrycuban .wordpress.com/2017/07/08/school-reform-foolish-fads-or-impossible -dream/.

15. "Frameworks Overview," National Assessment Governing Board, https://www .nagb.gov/naep-frameworks/frameworks-overview.html.

16. Carol Jago, *A History of NAEP Frameworks* (paper for the 20th Anniversary of NAGB, National Assessment Governing Board, Washington, DC, March 2009), https://www.nagb.gov/focus-areas/reports/history-naep-assessment -frameworks.html.

17. *Writing Framework for the 2017 National Assessment of Educational Progress* (Washington, DC: US Department of Education, National Assessment Governing Board, 2017), https://www.nagb.gov/content/dam/nagb/en/documents/ publications/frameworks/writing/2017-writing-framework.pdf.

18. Sean Cavanagh, "On Writing Tests, Computers Slowly Making Mark," *Education Week*, February 13, 2007, https://www.edweek.org/teaching-learning /on-writing-tests-computers-slowly-making-mark/2007/02.

19. Ibid.

20. "Mathematics Framework Changes," National Center for Educational Statistics, https://nces.ed.gov/nationsreportcard/mathematics/frameworkcomparison .asp; "The 1990–2003 Mathematics Framework," National Center for Educational Statistics, https://nces.ed.gov/nationsreportcard/mathematics /previousframework.aspx.

21. Robert B. Bain, *NAEP 12th Grade World History Assessment: Issues and Options* (Washington, DC: US Department of Education, National Assessment Governing Board, May 2004), 12, https://eric.ed.gov/?id=ED500978.

22. E. D. Hirsch Jr., "An Open Letter to the NAEP Governing Board," *Education Week*, December 1, 2020, https://www.edweek.org/teaching-learning /opinion-an-open-letter-to-the-naep-governing-board/2020/12; David Steiner and Mark Bauerlein, "A Feel-Good Report Card Won't Help Children," *City*

Journal, October 13, 2020, https://www.city-journal.org/naep-proposes -changes-to-reading-tests.

23. "High School Transcript Study," National Center for Education Statistics, https://nces.ed.gov/nationsreportcard/hsts/.

24. "National Indian Education Study: Study Overview," National Center for Education Statistics, https://nces.ed.gov/nationsreportcard/nies/study_overview .aspx.

25. "Monthly School Survey Dashboard," Institute of Education Sciences, https:// ies.ed.gov/schoolsurvey/.

26. TIMSS experts comment privately that these "linking" efforts don't align very well to, and are less accurate than, the actual performance of individual states that have occasionally participated in the international studies.

27. "NAEP Restricted-Use Datasets," National Center for Education Statistics, https://nces.ed.gov/nationsreportcard/researchcenter/variablesrudata.aspx.

28. "Research Grants Focused on NAEP Process Data for Learners with Disabilities," Institute of Education Sciences, https://ies.ed.gov/funding/grantsearch /program.asp?ID=1112.

29. Stephen Sawchuk, "When Bad Things Happen to Good NAEP Data," *Education Week*, July 24, 2013, https://www.edweek.org/teaching-learning /when-bad-things-happen-to-good-naep-data/2013/07.

30. *Comparing Private Schools and Public Schools Using Hierarchical Linear Modeling*, NCES 2006-461 (Washington, DC: US Department of Education, National Assessment of Educational Progress, 2006), http://nces.ed.gov/NAEP/pdf /studies/2006461.pdf; Henry Braun, Frank Jenkins, and Wendy Grigg, *A Closer Look at Charter Schools Using Hierarchical Linear Modeling*, NCES 2006-460 (Washington, DC: US Department of Education, National Center for Education Statistics, 2006), https://nces.ed.gov/pubsearch/pubsinfo.asp?pubid=2006460.

31. Sean Cavanagh and Erik W. Robelen, "NCES Calls for Sticking to the Stats," *Education Week*, August 29, 2006, https://www.edweek.org/policy-politics /nces-calls-for-sticking-to-the-stats/2006/08; Diana Jean Schemo, "The 2004 Campaign: Student Scores; Education Secretary Defends Charter Schools," *New York Times*, August 18, 2004, https://www.nytimes.com/2004/08/18/ us/the-2004-campaign-student-scores-education-secretary-defends-charter -schools.html; Debra Viadero, "AFT Charter School Study Sparks Heated National Debate," *Education Week*, October 2, 2004, https://www.edweek .org/teaching-learning/aft-charter-school-study-sparks-heated-national -debate/2004/10; Christopher Lubienski and Sarah Theule Lubienski, *Charter, Private, Public Schools and Academic Achievement: New Evidence from NAEP Mathematics Data* (New York: Columbia University, National Center for the Study of Privatization in Education, 2006), https://nepc.colorado.edu/sites/default/ files/EPRU-0601-137-OWI[1].pdf; Martin Carnoy et al., *The Charter School Dust-Up*, (Washington, DC: Economic Policy Institute, January 2005), https://www .epi.org/publication/book_charter_school/. Mark Schneider was then NCES Commissioner. He returned to government in 2018 as IES director.

32. "Morgan Polikoff says enough is enough when it comes to misNAEPery,"

Education Post, October 6, 2015, https://educationpost.org/morgan-polikoff
-says-enough-is-enough-when-it-comes-to-misnaepery/; Kevin Mahnken,
"California makes some gains in reading, but NAEP scores remain flat amid
signs of a widening gap between highest and lowest performers," *LA School
Report*, April 10, 2018, http://laschoolreport.com/california-makes-some
-gains-in-reading-but-naep-scores-remain-flat-amid-signs-of-a-widening-gap
-between-highest-and-lowest-performers/.

33. Betsy DeVos, "2020-11-24—Secretary Letter on NAEP 2021," https://edlabor
.house.gov/imo/media/doc/2020-11-24%20-%20Secretary%20Letter%20on%
20NAEP%202021%20-%20Scott:Murray.pdf; Stephen Sawchuk, "It's Official: National Test Is Postponed Due to COVID-19 Concerns," *Education Week*, November 25, 2020, https://www.edweek.org/teaching-learning
/its-official-national-test-is-postponed-due-to-covid-19-concerns/2020/11.

CHAPTER 8

1. Full disclosure: during preparation of this book, I was also appointed to the
National Board for Education Sciences, although it hasn't actually met in a
number of years.

2. As assistant secretary starting in 1985, I attended several of its meetings on the
sprawling ETS campus in Princeton and elsewhere.

3. In time, Congress would conclude that this monopoly on nominations gave
the board too much control and the secretary too few options, which led it
to widen the process to allow other organizations to suggest members, to
require that the secretary receive at least six candidates per opening, and to
empower the secretary, if dissatisfied with those initially presented, to request
additional names. In practice, however, the National Assessment Governing
Board remains the primary seeker, vetter, and supplier of nominees for all
board openings except those to be filled by governors, who are nominated to
the secretary by the National Governors Association.

4. Well-worn, longtime nickname.

5. Personal communication with the author.

6. Their successors have, on the whole, been just as dedicated and capable,
though I've had fewer direct dealings with them.

7. Because the compensation for board service hasn't changed despite inflation,
the daily payment of $100 in 1988 purchases the equivalent of $44 today.

8. "The NAEP Law," National Assessment Governing Board, https://www.nagb
.gov/about-naep/the-naep-law.html.

9. Board-based governance is somewhat more common in independent agencies,
such as the National Science Foundation, https://www.nsf.gov/nsb/about/index
.jsp.

10. "Boards and Commissions," US Department of Education, https://www2.ed
.gov/about/bdscomm/list/index.html.

11. In fact, the historic changes in the National Assessment of Educational Progress—and its governance—that emerged from Congress in 1988 started in the

Senate, the House having already finished its version of a multifaceted bill, and were then hashed out in conference committee.

12. "Statistical Standards and Guidelines," Federal Committee on Statistical Methodology, 2018, https://nces.ed.gov/FCSM/policies.asp; "Ethical Guidelines for Statistical Practice," Committee on Professional Ethics, American Statistical Association, 2018, https://www.amstat.org/ASA/Your-Career/Ethical-Guidelines-for-Statistical-Practice.aspx; *Principles and Practices for a Federal Statistical Agency: Seventh Edition* (forthcoming report, National Academies of Sciences, Engineering, and Medicine, National Academies Press, Washington, DC, 2021), https://nap.edu/catalog/25885/principles-and-practices-for-a-federal-statistical-agency-seventh-edition.

13. "NAEP Validity Studies Panel," American Institutes for Research, https://www.air.org/project/naep-validity-studies-nvs-panel.

14 "Fiscal Year 2021 Budget Request," US Department of Education, Institute of Education Sciences, https://www2.ed.gov/about/overview/budget/budget21/justifications/w-ies.pdf. In any case, the change has not taken place—and probably would need more explicit congressional action than a simple adjustment via the appropriations process.

15. Among the most influential over several decades was Jack Jennings, who served as staff director of the key House education subcommittee, then the full committee, during the formative years of the modern National Assessment, including the drafting and negotiating of several seminal statutes. As recently as 2018, 24 years after retiring from Capitol Hill, Jennings was submitting testimony to the governing board, in this case arguing that the board's achievement levels needed a total rethink, "National Assessment of Educational Progress: Statement Submitted by Jack Jennings," *Jack Jennings in DC Blog*, October 7, 2018, https://www.jackjenningsdc.com/national-assessment-of-educational-progress/.

16. Dan Goldhaber, "A Gloomy Perspective on High-Stakes Testing," *Education Next* 18, no. 2 (Spring 2018), https://www.educationnext.org/gloomy-perspective-on-high-stakes-testing-review-the-testing-charade-daniel-koretz/.

17. States do not, however, have to use the 2021 results for school "accountability," only for information about the status of student achievement.

CHAPTER 9

1. Chester E. Finn, Jr., "The War on Testing," *The Hill*, June 28, 2020, https://thehill.com/opinion/education/504951-the-war-on-testing.

2. "Digitally Based Assessments," National Center for Education Statistics, https://nces.ed.gov/nationsreportcard/dba/.

3. Paul Jewsbury et al., "2017 NAEP Transition to Digitally Based Assessments in Mathematics and Reading at Grades 4 and 8: Mode Evaluation Study" (white paper, US Department of Education, National Assessment of Educational Progress, National Center for Education Statistics, Washington, DC, 2020),

https://nces.ed.gov/nationsreportcard/subject/publications/main2020/pdf/transitional_whitepaper.pdf.

4. "Administer the Assessment," National Center for Education Statistics, https://nces.ed.gov/nationsreportcard/assessment_process/administer.aspx.

5. "Automated Scoring of Written Content," ETS Research, https://www.ets.org/research/topics/as_nlp/written_content/.

6. A careful later analysis by NCES staff placed the per-student cost of NAEP north of $300.

7. Mark Schneider, "A Year for Reflection and Continued Transformation," Institute of Education Sciences, January 12, 2021, https://ies.ed.gov/director/remarks/1-12-2021.asp.

8. *Reading Framework for the 2009 National Assessment of Educational Progress* (Washington, DC: US Department of Education, National Assessment Governing Board, 2008), vii, https://www.nagb.gov/content/dam/nagb/en/documents/publications/frameworks/reading/2009-reading-framework.pdf.

9. "Understanding the Reading Trend Study," National Center for Education Statistics, https://nces.ed.gov/nationsreportcard/reading/trend_study.asp.

10. "About," 2025 NAEP Framework Update, https://www.naepframeworkupdate.org/aboutread.

11. Due to the pandemic-induced need to delay the 2021 assessment cycle by a year, subsequent two-year intervals for reading and math testing moved to even-numbered years so the new reading framework will actually shape the 2026 cycle and those that follow.

12. David Steiner and Mark Bauerlein, "A Feel-Good Report Card Won't Help Children," *City Journal*, October 13, 2020, https://www.city-journal.org/naep-proposes-changes-to-reading-tests.

13. Adam Tyner and Sarah Kabourek, *Social Studies Instruction and Reading Comprehension: Evidence from the Early Childhood Longitudinal Study* (Washington, DC: Thomas B. Fordham Institute, September 24, 2020), https://fordhaminstitute.org/national/resources/social-studies-instruction-and-reading-comprehension; Reid Smith et al., "The Role of Background Knowledge in Reading Comprehension: A Critical Review," *Reading Psychology* 42, no. 3 (2021): 214–240, https://www.tandfonline.com/doi/full/10.1080/02702711.2021.1888348.

14. Chester E. Finn, Jr., "The culture wars come for the Nation's Report Card," Thomas B. Fordham Institute, May 10, 2021, https://fordhaminstitute.org/national/commentary/culture-wars-come-nations-report-card.

15. "Number and percentage of children served under Individuals with Disabilities Education Act (IDEA), Part B, by age group and state or jurisdiction: Selected years, 1990–91 through 2018–19," National Center for Education Statistics, https://nces.ed.gov/programs/digest/d19/tables/dt19_204.70.asp?current=yes.

16. "English language learner (ELL) students enrolled in public elementary and secondary schools, by state: Selected years, fall 2000 through fall 2018," National Center for Education Statistics, https://nces.ed.gov/programs/digest/d20/tables/dt20_204.20.asp?current=yes.

17. The usual reporting categories can be found at: "National Student Group Scores and Score Gaps," The Nation's Report Card, https://www.nationsreportcard .gov/reading/nation/groups/?grade=4.

18. Patrick O'Donnell, "Vast poverty differences create unfair comparisons on Nation's Report Card," Cleveland.com, January 30, 2019, https://www.cleveland .com/metro/2018/04./vast_poverty_differences_create_unfair_comparisons _on_nations_report_cards_make.html.

19. "America's Gradebook: How Does Your State Stack Up?," The Urban Institute, https://apps.urban.org/features/naep/.; Andrew D. Ho, "What Is the Stanford Education Data Archive Teaching Us About National Educational Achievement?," *AERA Open* 6, no. 3 (July 2020), https://doi.org/ 10.1177/2332858420939848.

20. See, for example: Jill Barshay, "Inside the Reardon-Hanushek clash over 50 years of achievement gaps," *The Hechinger Report*, May 27, 2019, https:// hechingerreport.org/inside-the-reardon-hanushek-clash-over-50 years-of-achievement-gaps/.

21. "Child Nutrition Programs: Income Eligibility Guidelines," Food and Nutrition Service: US Department of Agriculture, https://www.fns.usda.gov/cn /income-eligibility-guidelines.

22. "More Than Half of High-Poverty Schools Now Offer Free Meals to all Students," Food and Nutrition Service: US Department of Agriculture, https:// www.fns.usda.gov/pressrelease/2014/fns-001314.

23. There are other issues of accuracy associated with this measure, such as the reluctance of many high school students, especially those from low-income families, to take part in the subsidized meal program. "Measuring Student Poverty: Dishing Up Alternatives to Free and Reduced-Price Lunch," Urban Institute, September 20, 2019, https://www.urban.org/features/measuring -student-poverty-dishing-alternatives-free-and-reduced-price-lunch.

24. "Interpreting NAEP Reading Results," National Center for Education Statistics, https://nces.ed.gov/nationsreportcard/reading/interpret_results.aspx.

25. Considerable work is underway by NCES and NAGB to fill this void. See *Committee on Standards, Design and Methodology* (Washington, DC: US Department of Education, National Assessment Governing Board, 2021), 7–8, https://www.nagb .gov/content/dam/nagb/en/documents/what-we-do/quarterly-board-meet-ing-materials/2020-03/08-committee-on-standards-design-and-methodology .pdf.

26. Personal communication.

27. *Committee on Standards*, 11.

CHAPTER 10

1. Private communication with the author.

2. Sheida White et al., *The 2018 NAEP Oral Reading Fluency Study*, NCES 2021-025 (Washington, DC: US Department of Education, National Center for Education

Statistics, Institute of Education Sciences, National Assessment of Educational Progress, April 2021), https://nces.ed.gov/nationsreportcard/subject /studies/pdf/2021025_2018_orf_study.pdf.

3. Chester E. Finn, Jr., *Testing: Education's Indispensable GPS* (Stanford, CA: Hoover Institution, 2021), 1, https://www.hoover.org/research/testing-educations -indispensable-gps.

4. Linda Jacobson, "Role of Equity in Reading Tests Divides Board Overseeing 'Nation's Report Card'," *The 74 Million*, May 20, 2021, https://www. the74million.org/article/role-of-equity-in-reading-tests-divides-board -overseeing-nations-report-card/.

5. "The Story of Goldilocks and the Three Bears," DLTK Sites for Kids, https:// www.dltk-teach.com/rhymes/goldilocks_story.htm.

6. Ina V. S. Mullis, "White Paper on 50 Years of NAEP Use: Where NAEP Has Been and Where It Should Go Next" (white paper, NAEP Validity Studies Panel, National Center for Education Statistics, American Institutes for Research, Arlington, VA, June 2019), 22, https://www.air.org/sites/default/files/ downloads/report/50-Years-of-NAEP-Use-June-2019.pdf.

7. "Disruptive Innovation," Clayton Christensen Institute, https://www .christenseninstitute.org/disruptive-innovations/.

8. Those big numbers assume every student in every grade, kindergarten through twelfth, in every US school, public and private, plus all their teachers. One could of course test the "universe" of students but only in specified grades, as NAEP now does, though that approach would leave out millions of parents and teachers.

9. *The Education Sciences Reform Act*, R43398 (Washington, DC: Congressional Research Service, 2017), https://crsreports.congress.gov/product/pdf/R /R43398.

CHAPTER 11

1. "Monthly School Survey Dashboard," Institute of Education Sciences, https:// ies.ed.gov/schoolsurvey/.

2. "Panel Study of Income Dynamics (PSID)," University of Michigan Institute for Social Research, https://psidonline.isr.umich.edu. See also "AmeriSpeak: NORC's Breakthrough Panel-Based Research Platform," National Opinion Research Center, https://www.norc.org/Research/Capabilities/Pages/ amerispeak.aspx.

3. The NAEP statute says: "The achievement levels shall be used on a trial basis until the Commissioner for Education Statistics determines, as a result of an evaluation under subsection (f), that such levels are reasonable, valid, and informative to the public." "The NAEP Law," National Assessment Governing Board, https://www.nagb.gov/about-naep/the-naep-law.html.

4. Personal communication.

5. I owe thanks for these suggestions to former NCES commissioner Emerson Elliott.
6. "Create the Assessment," National Assessment of Educational Progress, https://nces.ed.gov/nationsreportcard/assessment_process/create.aspx.
7. As discussed below, it's possible and perhaps desirable to administer adaptive tests to a NAEP-style sample of students and avoid reporting individual scores.
8. Changing the frequency of the reading and math assessments would require a statutory change. The rest, I believe, is within NAGB's purview, budget permitting.
9. Strictly speaking, until the Department of Education was carved out of HEW in 1979, NAEP was housed in antecedent agencies.
10. Personal communication. It should also be noted that a culture of secrecy generally prevails within the executive branch when it comes to budget preparation, with the heads of major units within an agency often kept in the dark regarding OMB presentations and negotiations. "The parts of the Department are vassals" is how a former senior education official put it to me.
11. *Draft Release Plan for the National Assessment of Educational Progress (NAEP); The Nation's Report Card: 2019* (Washington, DC: National Assessment Governing Board, March 1, 2021), https://www.nagb.gov/content/dam/nagb/en/documents/what-we-do/quarterly-board-meeting-materials/2021-03/11-Reporting-and-Dissemination-Committee.pdf.
12. Congress moved in 2018 to encourage such dissemination of data (and potential merging of data sets from multiple sources) across the government when it passed the "Evidence-Based Policy Act," but progress in implementing it has been slow, due in part to data-privacy considerations. "Evidence Act Resource Hub," Results for America, https://results4america.org/evidence-act-resources/.
13. "Showcasing the Nation's Report Card," The Hatcher Group, https://www.thehatchergroup.com/case-studies/t/national-assessment-governing-board/.

ACKNOWLEDGMENTS

THOUGH I AM SOLELY TO BLAME FOR THE INFORMATION, analyses, and conclusions in these pages, they would be far skimpier and less accurate had I not enjoyed the benefit of wonderful advice and assistance from many others. Words on a page cannot do justice to the scores of people whose participation in the NAEP saga over the past half century has informed my understanding and enriched my experience even as they made that saga happen. I'm thinking, for example, of former colleagues at the Education Department, on the National Assessment Governing Board, and in the myriad committees, panels, counsels, and advisory bodies that have also drawn me in. But they're just part of a vast and misty mountain, rivulets from which have trickled into this book, often in roundabout ways.

The seed that they watered, which eventually grew into the volume in your hands, was planted over a casual office lunch with NAGB staffers Lesley Muldoon and Laura LoGerfo. It began as one of our periodic touch-base and catch-up get-togethers, in the course of which I randomly inquired whether anyone, to their knowledge, had written a "biography of NAEP" suited for a general audience and, if not, shouldn't somebody? None of us could think of anything like that in recent years, although fine work of a somewhat specialized nature was done in years past by the likes of Maris Vinovskis, Lyle Jones, and Ingram Olkin. Lesley and Laura semi-seriously suggested that maybe I should try my own hand at it. Within weeks, such a possibility began to sprout between my ears.

Yet little would have come of it had not my Fordham colleague and friend, Mike Petrilli, immediately encouraged me to pursue this possibility. That included asking key current NAEPsters—mostly at NCES and NAGB—whether they'd be game to cooperate; asking some fellow former NAEPsters if they thought it was worth doing (and if anyone had done or was doing it); querying then-chief editor Caroline Chauncey at the Harvard Education Press (HEP) as to whether this was something she might be interested in publishing; and commencing a quest for financial support for the big chunk of my work life that I'd have to commit to it.

Responses were swift, affirmative, and gratifying, including a near-immediate offer of assistance from LaVerne Srinivasan and Elise Hensen at the Carnegie Corporation of New York, which (as you'll see) has been a key benefactor and facilitator of NAEP from the get-go, which means back to the mid-1960s when Frank Keppel was US Commissioner of Education and John W. Gardner headed the foundation, most recently led by my friend, the late Vartan Gregorian.

Mark Steinmeyer and the Smith Richardson Foundation provided additional support and HEP offered a book contract. Along the way, both those named here and their anonymous reviewers supplied superb feedback and wise counsel for strengthening the plan.

As I dug in, I became the grateful beneficiary of all manner of help: documents, memories, data, anecdotes, phone calls, Zoom sessions, emails, and much more. Among the many who lent a hand, let me call out former governing-board staffer (and my onetime colleague at the department) Ray Fields, whose NAGB archive is unmatched; NAGB's longtime public affairs maestro (and former *Washington Post* education reporter) Lawrence Feinberg; NAGB's founding executive director, Roy Truby, and current executive director, Lesley Muldoon; former NAGB members Andrew Ho and (my old friend) Mark Musick; current members Grover (Russ) Whitehurst, Gregory Cizek, Eric Hanushek, and Martin West; NAGB staffer Laura LoGerfo; IES director (and another friend) Mark Schneider; John Whitmer; and veteran NAEP executive (at ECS and ETS) and TIMSS superhero, Ina Mullis.

Words cannot convey my special gratitude to former NCES commissioner Emerson Elliott and current commissioner Peggy G. Carr. They know NAEP inside and out and have lived through most of its history. (They've also known me for longer than they probably care to remember.) Both took extraordinary pains with drafts of chapter upon chapter, correcting my history, amplifying my understanding, introducing important elements I had forgotten (or never knew), gently suggesting alternative ideas or interpretations, and plain old copyediting. Emerson is supposed to be enjoying a well-earned retirement, and Peggy continues to labor valiantly (and almost 24/7) in the NAEP vineyard, but both made the time and took the pains to help me get this right. (Which isn't to say they agree with all of it!)

At the Thomas B. Fordham Institute, in addition to Mike Petrilli, I've had wonderful help with every aspect of book creation and revision from production and staff associate Pedro Enamorado, who has cheerfully and efficiently shifted from esoteric research to mundane find-and-copy-and-send to meticulous annotation and back again. And then again. I also owe great thanks to Olivia Piontek, Victoria McDougald, Gary LaBelle, Rachel Stubber, Tran Le, and former interns Julie Fitz and Melissa Gutwein.

At the Hoover Institution, I benefited throughout from the wisdom, ed-reform energies, and assessment savvy of my colleagues on the Hoover Education Success Initiative—Eric Hanushek, Paul Peterson, Margaret (Macke) Raymond, and Christopher Ruszkowski—as well as director Condoleezza Rice.

Mid-project (and mid-pandemic), Caroline Chauncey retired from HEP, passing the leadership reins to Jayne Fargnoli, who has been wonderfully supportive, helpful, and insightful in her feedback on early drafts and her encouragement to bring it in for a landing. She and her team, including Anne Noonan, Laura Cutone Godwin, Molly Grab, and veteran copy editor Jane Gebhart have helped in so many ways to improve this book and assure its timely completion.

On the home front—and most of the heavy lifting was indeed done at home as a pandemic raged outside—I've had nothing but encouragement (and forbearance) from my wife, Dr. Renu Virmani, who had lived through multiple earlier phases of my entanglement with NAEP but who this time had to live through it about seventy feet away while doing her own work with the help of two computers and a big microscope in what had been our guest room. In truth, it helped immeasurably to have each other close by.

But to end where I began, I'm solely to blame.

ABOUT THE AUTHOR

Chester E. Finn, Jr., is Distinguished Senior Fellow and President Emeritus at the Thomas B. Fordham Institute and a Senior Fellow at Stanford's Hoover Institution.

For five decades, Finn has been in the forefront of the national debate about school reform, including such positions as Staff Assistant to the President of the United States; Special Assistant to the Governor of Massachusetts; Counsel to the US Ambassador to India; Research Associate at the Brookings Institution; and Legislative Director for Senator Daniel P. Moynihan. He's been professor of education and public policy at Vanderbilt, assistant secretary for research and improvement at the US Department of Education, chairman of the National Assessment Governing Board, and senior fellow at both the Manhattan and Hudson Institutes. He also served on the Maryland State Board of Education and on that state's Commission on Innovation and Excellence in Education.

Finn is author or coauthor of hundreds of articles and more than twenty books, most recently *Learning in the Fast Lane: The Past, Present & Future of Advanced Placement* (Princeton, 2019) and *How to Educate an American* (Templeton, 2020). Previous Harvard Education Press books are *Charter Schools at the Crossroads* (2016, with Bruno Manno and Brandon Wright) and *Failing Our Brightest Kids* (2015, with Brandon Wright).

INDEX